DISTANT FIELDS

Distant Fields

Eighteenth-century Fictions of Wales

ଷ

Moira Dearnley

UNIVERSITY OF WALES PRESS
CARDIFF
2001

© Moira Dearnley, 2001

British Library Cataloguing-in-Publication Data.
A catalogue record for this book is available from the British Library.

ISBN 0–7083–1695–6

All rights reserved. No part of this book may be reproduced, stored in a retrieval system, or transmitted, in any form or by any means, electronic, mechanical, photocopying, recording or otherwise, without clearance from the University of Wales Press, 6 Gwennyth Street, Cardiff, CF24 4YD.
www.wales.ac.uk/press

The right of Moira Dearnley to be identified as author of this work has been asserted by her in accordance with the Copyright, Designs and Patents Act 1988.

Published with the financial support of the Arts Council of Wales

THE ASSOCIATION FOR
WELSH WRITING IN ENGLISH
CYMDEITHAS LLÊN SAESNEG CYMRU

Typeset at University of Wales Press
Printed in Great Britain by Dinefwr Press, Llandybïe

To my husband, John

Contents

List of illustrations	ix
Acknowledgements	x
Introduction	xiii

1. 'Ludicrous stratagems and humiliating misadventures': an introductory view of the Welsh in the popular literature of the seventeenth century — 1
2. A place 'rich in Virtue': *The Life of Madam de Beaumount* by Penelope Aubin — 12
3. 'A Genuine Account of the Life': travellers' tales — 26
4. A revenge tragedy: *The True Anti-Pamela* by James Parry — 50
5. 'Ye chaste Abodes of happiest Mortals': *The History of Ophelia* by Sarah Fielding — 68
6. '*O Rus, quando te aspiciam!*': *Humphry Clinker* and other satires of London — 80
7. 'God has called us into Wales': *The Spiritual Quixote* by Richard Graves — 94
8. The first Welsh industrial novel?: *Eugenius* by Richard Graves — 106
9. 'The venerable name of religion': Druidism in *Imogen* by William Godwin — 114
10. Proud Cambrians and mantua makers: *Anna, or, Memoirs of a Welch Heiress* by Anna Maria Bennett — 130
11. 'In the airy Regions of Fancy': *Ellen, Countess of Castle Howel* by Anna Maria Bennett — 145
12. Removing silver buttons: *Elisa Powell* by Edward 'Celtic' Davies — 158

13 Perdita, Wales and the monster: Mary Robinson's
   Welsh novels   172

Notes   190

Appendix: Eighteenth-century fictions of Wales   237

Index   241

List of Illustrations

page

Title-page of *The Pleasant History of Taffy's Progress to London: With the Welshman's Catechism* [1709?]   6

Frontispiece and title-page of *The Life of Madam de Beaumount* by Penelope Aubin, 1721   14–15

Frontispiece and title-page of *The Voyages, Travels and Adventures of William Owen Gwin Vaughan, Esq.*, by W. R. Chetwood, 1736   28–9

Title-page of the *The Journal of Llewellin Penrose, a Seaman*, by William Williams, illustrated by Edward Bird, 1825   36

William Williams wearing the green cloak and red cap of the Merchants' and Sailors' Almshouse, Bristol: self-portrait   39

Memorial to the Revd John Eagles, Bristol Cathedral   43

Frontispiece and title-page of *The True Anti-Pamela, or, Memoirs of Mr. James Parry*, 1741   52–3

Illustration in *The Life and Surprizing Adventures of James Wyatt*, 1748   64

Illustration in Sarah Fielding's *Ophelia*, 1785 edition   73

The Welch Curate, published by Bowles and Carver, c.1770   103

Mary Robinson, c.1782: drawing by Sir Joshua Reynolds   174

Acknowledgements

This book, slight as it may seem, has taken a number of years to research and write. My earliest debt is to Dr Roland Mathias whose encouragement ('It needs to be done'), together with a crucial bibliographical reference to the early fictions of Wales, gave me the confidence I needed to begin work on what was at that time virtually unknown territory. I also owe a considerable debt to Dr Belinda Humfrey whose series of colloquia on Welsh women writers, held at Gregynog, gave me an opportunity to present a series of papers which became the nucleus of the present study. I am particularly grateful to Professor Jane Aaron for her enthusiasm and kindness: her insistence that I 'must' write up my research for publication has helped to keep me going in circumstances which have rarely been conducive to sustained academic work. I also wish to thank Professor M. Wynn Thomas for his support, and Mrs Barbara Prys-Williams and Mr Dewi Roberts for their friendship and generosity in giving me references which I have gladly used in this book. I have greatly appreciated the unfailing courtesy and help I have received from Mr Nicholas Lee and Mr Michael Richardson during the many hours I have spent reading in the Special Collections room at the University Library, Bristol. Dr John Pikoulis has been a kind and patient editor, and I have received a great deal of helpful advice from Ceinwen Jones and the staff of the University of Wales Press during the preparation of this book for publication.

The author and publishers gratefully acknowledge the permission of the following to reproduce material in this volume:

Title-page of *The Pleasant History of Taffy's Progress to London*, 1076.l.22(44); 'Mr Parry shooting at the Author', from *The Life and Surprizing Adventures of James Wyatt*, 1419.a.44; frontispiece and title-page of *The Life of Madam de Beaumount*, 12613.a.5; 'Lord Dorchester meets Ophelia and her aunt', from *Ophelia*, 1207.c.6(1); frontispiece and title-page of *The Voyages, Travels and Adventures of William Owen Gwin Vaughan, Esq.*, N.1878; title-page of *The Journal of Llewellin Penrose*, 837.c.6, by permission of the British Library.

Frontispiece and title-page of *The True Anti-Pamela*, by permission of the Beinecke Rare Book and Manuscript Library, Yale University.

Self-portrait of William Williams, courtesy, Winterthur Museum.

Memorial to the Revd John Eagles, by permission of the Dean of Bristol Cathedral.

The Welch Curate, by permission of the National Library of Wales.

Mary Robinson, by Sir Joshua Reynolds, by courtesy of the National Portrait Gallery, London.

An early version of chapter 12, 'Removing silver buttons: *Elisa Powell* by Edward "Celtic" Davies', first appeared as '*Elisa Powell*: an Anglo-Welsh novel of the eighteenth century', in *New Welsh Review*, 12 (Spring 1991), 14–18.

In the Acknowledgements to my first book, I thanked my husband for sharing with me an unflagging interest in Kit Smart. More than thirty years later, I thank him yet again for his tireless encouragement and support – and at long last I have the pleasure of actually dedicating a book to him.

Moira Dearnley
Llandogo, June 2001

Tho' grief and fondness in my breast rebel,
When injur'd Thales bids the town farewell,
Yet still my calmer thoughts his choice commend,
I praise the hermit, but regret the friend,
Who now resolves, from vice and London far,
To breathe in distant fields a purer air,
And fix'd on Cambria's solitary shore,
Give to St. David one true Briton more.

Samuel Johnson

Introduction

On 13 June 1790, the fourteen-year-old Jane Austen finished *Love and Freindship*, a novel comprising all of fifteen letters exchanged between Isabel, Laura and Marianne. The Austen family were 'great Novel-readers and not ashamed of being so'[1] and, as a recent editor of the Juvenilia points out, it is evident from Jane's surviving writings that by the end of the 1780s she was deeply familiar with most of the English fiction of the eighteenth century.[2] Since she was 'entirely aware of thematic patterns and plot structures, or paradigms that could be familiar only to a reader of a multitude of books',[3] perhaps it is not entirely surprising that the young author should make merry over the early Welsh novel. Thus it is that after receiving a convent education in France, the heroine of *Love and Freindship* returns to the paternal roof in Wales: 'Our mansion was situated in one of the most romantic parts of the Vale of Uske.'[4] Laura's fourth letter, written to Marianne, duly makes fun of several motifs characteristic of 'Welsh' fictions of the time – the retreat into Wales as a measure of economy, its extreme seclusion from 'civilization', and the contrast between the simple rustic life and the dissipated, luxurious life of the city, especially London and Bath:

> Our neighbourhood was small, for it consisted only of your Mother. She may have already told you that being left by her Parents in indigent Circumstances she had retired into Wales on oeconomical motives. There it was, our freindship first commenced. Isabel was then one and twenty – Tho' pleasing both in her Person and Manners (between ourselves) she never possessed the hundredth part of my Beauty or Accomplishments, Isabel had seen the World. She had passed 2 Years at one of the first Boarding schools in London; had spent a fortnight in Bath and had stopped one night in Southampton.
>
> 'Beware my Laura' (she would often say) 'Beware of the insipid Vanities and idle Dissipations of the Metropolis of England; Beware of

the unmeaning Luxuries of Bath and of the Stinking fish of Southampton.'

'Alas!' (exclaimed I) 'how am I to avoid those evils I shall never be exposed to? What probability is there of my ever tasting the Dissipation of London, the Luxuries of Bath or the stinking fish of Southampton? I who am doomed to waste my Days of Youth and Beauty in an humble Cottage in the Vale of Uske.'

Ah! Little did I then think I was ordained so soon to quit that humble Cottage for the Deceitfull Pleasures of the World.[5]

Like Sarah Fielding's Ophelia, Jane Austen's Laura is swept off her feet by the arrival of a 'beauteous and amiable' young Englishman who finds his way to her 'rustic Cot' after being hopelessly lost: 'My Father's house is situated in Bedfordshire, my Aunt's in Middlesex, and tho' I flatter myself with being a tolerable proficient in Geography, I know not how it happened, but I found myself entering this beautifull Vale which I find is in South Wales, when I had expected to have reached my Aunt's.'[6] The young people fall in love at first sight, are united on the spot and a few days after their marriage leave for the Aunt's in Middlesex.

The absurdities of *Love and Freindship*, together with *A Tour through Wales – in a Letter from a Young Lady*[7] and *A Tale* ('A Gentleman whose family name I shall conceal, bought a small Cottage in Pembrokeshire about two Years ago . . .'),[8] demonstrate the young writer's acquaintance with the romances, epistolary novels and 'tours' of the day. They also suggest that specifically Welsh material was familiar enough to be laughed at even before the spate of such publications flowed on to the market in the 1790s, and some years before the famous statement in *Northanger Abbey* (written in 1798–9) about the proper location of Gothic horror in Italy, Switzerland and the south of France: 'Catherine dared not doubt beyond her own country, and even of that, if hard pressed, would have yielded the northern and western extremities.'[9] Thereafter, Austen confined her attention to 'the midland counties of England', though Katie Trumpener argues persuasively that in *Mansfield Park* (1814) 'she invokes a nationalist rhetoric of cultural difference and authenticity in order to establish her own localist agenda'. Thus when Mary Crawford sends for her harp and finds it impossible to find a farmer to transport it during the hay harvest, the bardic instrument – cherished vehicle of Irish, Welsh and Scottish nationalism and emblem of the organic relationship between a people, their land and their culture – is deployed for purely picturesque effect: 'The episode at once illustrates the transportability of nationalist tropes into the English novel and problematizes the act of transport itself.'[10]

The present study focuses on some of the eighteenth-century novels that may have provoked Jane Austen's satire of the 'principality contiguous to England'.[11] As there is as yet no complete bibliography available, my own list of titles was initially based on W. J. Hughes's *Wales and the Welsh in English from Shakespeare to Scott* (indispensable, though containing a number of inaccuracies),[12] with additional items from Dorothy Blakey's study of the Minerva Press,[13] and essays by James Henderson and E. Loomis in pursuit of the Gothic novel in Wales,[14] supplemented over a period of time with titles gleaned from other sources.[15] As I worked through this list, I was soon forced to consider the hoary question of authorship which has so often been discussed in relation to Welsh writing in English. The trickle of blood in Gwyn Jones's definition of what used to be called Anglo-Welsh writers makes the modern reader more than a trifle queasy ('those authors of Welsh blood or connexion who for a variety of reasons write their creative work in English').[16] Yet one can scarcely ignore the fact that, as far as writers of eighteenth-century fictions of Wales were concerned, 'Welsh blood' (where it existed at all) was very thin – while any 'connexions' the authors might have had with Wales were mostly problematic. To date, only two writers on my list are known to have been born in Wales: James Parry, born in Carmarthen, whose autobiography, *The True Anti-Pamela* (1741), may or may not include large dollops of libellous fantasy, and Edward 'Celtic' Davies, born in Llanfaredd, creator of *Elisa Powell* (1795). Similarly, although I hoped to challenge Gwyn Jones's pronouncements at the first W. D. Thomas Memorial Lecture, *The First Forty Years,* delivered at the University College of Swansea in February 1957, which in principle established the canon of Anglo-Welsh fiction for the next forty years ('I came hither not to measure fragments of temples, or trace choked aqueducts, but to look upon the various scenes of the present world'),[17] I soon had to acknowledge that among eighteenth-century fictions of Wales even fragmented temples were rare indeed – most of the artefacts I unearthed during my own archaeological dig were imported and rarely of great intrinsic value. Nevertheless, the 'artefacts' survive and as such require cataloguing and describing.

Since eighteenth-century fictions are riddled with stereotypical representations of Wales and the Welsh, I have introduced my study, in Chapter 1, with a note on a range of popular literature published in the previous century — pamphlets, chapbooks and song-sheets — in which the common beliefs and prejudices about 'Taffy' are visible in all their crudity. The lampooning of the people of Wales was by no means a new phenomenon in English literature, but, exacerbated by Taffy's execrable performance in the Royalist cause in the Civil War (or so Parliamentary propaganda would have it), satires of the Welsh began to pour off the popular presses in the 1640s and continued to do so for several decades afterwards. The Welsh were ridiculed for being dishonest and stupid, credulous and superstitious. They were depicted as abjectly poor but comically insistent on their gentle birth, their long names linked with *ap* and their massive pedigrees. They were constitutionally hot-tempered and quarrelsome. They lived on mountains and had peculiar ways of computing time and distance. They were a cowardly, conquered people but nevertheless proudly resentful of their loss of national liberty. They were addicted to cheese, ale and astrology. They were overrun by goats and cousins. They wore leeks in their hats and got drunk on St David's Day. They spoke gobbledegook. All these seventeenth-century prejudices about the Welsh can be readily traced in eighteenth-century fictions, sometimes crudely expressed, as in the portrait of a poverty-stricken Welsh 'gentleman' in the opening and closing sequences of *A Genuine Account of the Life and Transactions of Howell ap David Price, Gentleman of Wales* (1752), sometimes more subtly adapted, as in Anna Maria Bennett's study of the Welsh obsession with genealogy in *Anna, or, Memoirs of a Welch Heiress* (1785).

In complete contrast to the 'chapbook' view of the Welsh, there is another major strand in eighteenth-century fiction which idealizes Wales as 'a place of virtue'. Linked with prevalent ideas of Nature and the noble savage, the country was often depicted as the locus of innocence, uncorrupted by the iniquities of low life in the city or the fashionable vices of high society. In pursuit of this 'idea' of Wales, the novels of the day describe a two-way traffic between the metropolis and the remote mountainous interior of 'the Principality': in one direction, city-dwellers retreat westwards in search of peace and quiet in which to nurse a broken heart or mend a broken fortune, while in the other direction the constant exodus of the Welsh along the road to London provides a constant supply of innocents abroad. In the epigraph to the present study, taken from Johnson's *London* (1738), the situation of Thales is archetypal — a 'true Briton' (but not, it seems, an

Ancient Briton) who is about to leave the sinful city for a hermit's life on 'Cambria's solitary shore', but who may well return at some point in the future to collaborate with the Great Cham in his self-imposed task of satirizing contemporary society. Both Penelope Aubin and Sarah Fielding adopt what Johnson refers to as the 'distant fields' of Wales as a suitable geographical location for working out the moral schema of their fictions. In Chapter 2 I argue that Aubin's bizarre tale, in which Madam de Beaumount, fleeing from religious persecution in France, takes up residence in a cave near 'Swansey' after being shipwrecked on the coast of south Wales, while her Jacobite uncle maintains a band of brigands in the mountainous interior of the country, can be shown to be a symbolic representation of religious toleration, predicated on the idea of Wales as 'a place of virtue'. Similarly, I argue that Fielding describes in *Ophelia* a symbolic landscape which is Wales and Nowhere, a place where the heroine can be reared not only in total ignorance of evil but imbued with ideas dangerously smacking of deism; the removal of the heroine to London allows the author not only to include the usual satire of high society seen through the eyes of an innocent abroad but also to subvert (perhaps) both orthodox Christianity and prevalent ideas about marriage. In another essay specifically devoted to satires of London through the eyes of Welsh visitors to the metropolis, I aim to show that although the anonymous 'parasite', Dick Swallow, Jenner's Altamont and Lawrence's Crab family may give a rather sketchy idea of Wales as 'a place of virtue', Smollett's Matthew Bramble, acerbic commentator on the iniquities of Bath and London, magnificently establishes Brambleton-hall, near Crickhowell, as an organic vision of a benevolent, patriarchal, overflowingly productive estate, to be set against 'the folly and the fraud' of city life.

In an essay on 'travellers' tales', in Chapter 3, I consider briefly a number of novels which transport their Welsh heroes a great deal further than Bath or London: Chetwood's William Owen Gwin Vaughan, the anonymous Howell ap David Price and those intrepid travellers through the heart of Africa, Messieurs Thomas Jenkins and David Lowellin, are involved in a succession of hair-raising adventures, almost certainly pure fantasy. This essay is mainly concerned with authorship. The researches of D. H. Dickason have established, probably beyond reasonable doubt, that *The Journal of Llewellin Penrose, a Seaman* was indeed the work of William Williams, as claimed by its first editor, John Eagles. Almost certainly Dickason must be allowed to hail the work as 'the first American novel' (though he acknowledges that Williams's family 'was of immediate Welsh extraction'). In view of the unreliability of some of the evidence, however, and with an eye to the recent discoveries of Mike Parker Pearson in establishing through his archaeological researches in Madagascar the authenticity of Robert Drury's journal (long attributed to Defoe), I feel that it is at least permissible to ask whether *The Journal of Llewellin Penrose* might be exactly what it appears to be – a diary of a Welshman, born near Caerffili and stranded on the South American coast, where he lived and died in a small community of Rama Indians.

Since 'the imagined nation'[18] to be discovered in eighteenth-century fictions of Wales is rarely brought into being by the Welsh themselves, I have felt it important to include, in Chapter 4, an essay on the memoirs of James Parry, which end at the point where he is about to set sail for the Canaries as master-at-arms on board the privateer *The Revenge* in 1741 (five years before Llewellin Penrose is said to have set sail for Jamaica on board the privateer *The Harrington*). Hughes lists *The True Anti-Pamela, or Memoirs of Mr James Parry* as a novel though quite clearly it should be read as an autobiography. It is indeed possible to read the text as a 'window' on eighteenth-century Wales, as Parry's comings and goings between Ross-on-Wye, Monmouth and Llantilio Crossenny allow glimpses of the everyday life of the times, including Monmouth races (in 1733 he was part of a group of musicians, including Valentine Snow on trumpet, 'some French horns' and Mr Harry Parry 'the famous harp', who entertained the racegoers), billiards at the King's Head (still standing today), and the conditions inside Monmouth gaol where he was incarcerated for several months in 1736. My main objective, however, is to show how the significance of Parry's text lies beyond the historical accuracy (or otherwise) of his testimony, arguing that it should be read as a literary artefact in which it is possible to identify, in Gusdorf's terms, a 'parable of consciousness in quest of its own truth'. *The True Anti-Pamela* can thus be read as a revenge tragedy perpetrated by one who was suffering a castration complex (traceable not only through his own memoir but in that of the trumpeter on *The Revenge*, the witness who eventually saw him drown in the Canaries). *The True Anti-Pamela* is also, in effect, the parable of a Welshman referred to by one commentator as 'a cad'. Parry is thus inscribed in his autobiographical text as the embodiment of one of the most persistent stereotypes of contemporary fiction – a Welsh rogue of chapbook proportions.

Introduction

In contrast to James Parry's private history, two of Richard Graves's novels deal with momentous happenings in eighteenth-century Wales – the Methodist Revival and the beginnings of the Industrial Revolution. While giving Graves's sense of humour its due, in Chapter 7 I examine whether his account of Wildgoose's missionary activities in the Welsh scenes of *The Spiritual Quixote* (1773) provides in any sense an authentic view of the early days of Welsh Methodism. In *Eugenius, or, Anecdotes of the Golden Vale* (1785), the subject of Chapter 8, Graves offers an Enlightenment account of the Industrial Revolution in which he specifically rejects an early Romantic view of the Welsh landscape and welcomes the woollen manufactories of the Golden Valley as a modern enterprise with social and economic benefits for the local people. *Eugenius* may well be the first Welsh industrial novel but it can safely be said that few others written since have taken a similar line on the 'rape of the fair country'.

Both William Godwin's *Imogen: A Pastoral Romance* (1784), set in north Wales at the time of the Druids, and Edward 'Celtic' Davies's *Elisa Powell, or Trials of Sensibility* (1795), which features a Welsh antiquarian and a local bard, might seem to be diametrically opposed to Graves's agenda in *Eugenius* and fully in accord with 'bardic nationalism', defined by Katie Trumpener as a response to 'Enlightenment programs for economic improvement, read as a form of political and cultural imperialism'[19] and in particular to Enlightenment dismissals of Gaelic oral traditions:

> Irish and Scottish antiquaries reconceive national history and literary history under the sign of the bard. According to their theories, bardic performance binds the nation together across time and across social divides; it reanimates a national landscape made desolate first by conquest and then by modernization, infusing it with historical memory. A figure both of the traditional aristocratic culture that preceded English occupation and of continued national resistance to that occupation, the bard symbolizes the central role of literature in defining national identity.[20]

Trumpener herself comments that, in *Imogen*, Godwin 'tries to re-imagine a new kind of literary history in which Ossian, not Homer, is the foundational figure' and she argues that the antiquarian framing of the novel 'prepares the reader to enter its Ossianic world, to visualize the natural and social landscape of ancient Britain, to absorb at first hand its bardic strains'.[21] In Chapter 9, however, I analyse *Imogen* in the light of Godwin's own accounts of his early religious experience; I show that the novel may be read as a critique of Druidism and that far from inviting his readers to admire or 'absorb' its bardic strains, the three hymns should be read as an angry rejection of organized religion and its priesthood. Similarly, one might have expected that a novel by Edward 'Celtic' Davies, collector and translator of Welsh poetry and author of several mighty tomes on the culture of the Celtic peoples, would have contributed to the 'invented Wales, a Wales of the imagination' associated with Iolo Morganwg's 'Druido-Bardism'.[22] In fact, as I argue in my essay on *Elisa Powell* in Chapter 12, while the traces of Davies's enthusiasm for the 'Renaissance' of Welsh culture in the eighteenth century are evident (to the extent of unwittingly including in the text of his novel one of Iolo's forgeries of Dafydd ap Gwilym), he merely succeeds in ridiculing what he himself undoubtedly cherished in his native culture. Davies's *Elisa Powell* – a poor attempt at a novel of sensibility – thus offers only a kind of photographic negative of 'bardic nationalism'.

Although biographical evidence about Anna Maria Bennett's family background and place of birth is as yet inconclusive, it seems likely that she had Welsh 'connexions'. Mary Robinson certainly did. In my essay on *Anna, or, Memoirs of a Welch Heiress* in Chapter 10, I relate the heroine's experience of work to recent feminist studies of 'needlework narratives' and argue that Anna's ambivalent attitude to her trade, together with Lady Cecilia Edwin's peculiarly Welsh obsession with genealogy, may be pointers to emergent radical ideas about social class in the novel. In a second essay on Bennett, in Chapter 11, I focus on her preoccupation in *Ellen, Countess of Castle Howel* with her heroine as a Welsh innocent subjected to the temptations of the metropolis. I suggest that the novel is possibly affected by the author's own anxieties about her daughter, Harriet Esten (recently 'elevated' to the position of mistress to the Duke of Hamilton), and argue that in this novel too there may be some indicators of a radical view of social class. My chapter on Mary Robinson is mainly concerned with a comparison between *Walsingham, or, The Pupil of Nature* (1797) and William Godwin's *Fleetwood, or, The New Man of Feeling* (1805): I argue that while both novels appear to offer a critique of the Romantic doctrine of Nature as an educative moral force in human development, the literary 'influence' apparently at work here was not necessarily working in the expected direction.

It is not the purpose of the present study to provide a taxonomy of eighteenth-century fictions of Wales. The bibliography printed as an Appendix to the essays included here sufficiently demonstrates that I have made no attempt, for instance, to write on the Gothic novel in Wales – nor have I attempted to trace through the 'domestic' novels published in the 1790s the growing awareness of cultural 'difference' and the new interest in local customs that would eventually develop into the national tales of the next century. My intention is a strictly limited one – to shed a little more light on a selection of eighteenth-century texts which on the whole have received little critical attention in Wales, even though they record in their own way a small part of the history of the Welsh people, viewed from afar as the romantic or ridiculous inhabitants of those 'distant fields'.

1
'Ludicrous stratagems and humiliating misadventures'

AN INTRODUCTORY VIEW OF THE WELSH IN THE POPULAR LITERATURE OF THE SEVENTEENTH CENTURY

The view of the Welsh conveyed in the crudely written chapbooks and other popular literature of the seventeenth century is clearly recognizable in a number of fictions written in the following century. Along the road out of Wales, on a route which almost always leads to London in eighteenth-century novels, there occasionally walks an identifiable descendant of the chapbook Taffy, poor, naïve and cunning. More generally, the poverty-stricken 'Welch shentleman' is a recognizable figure in the novels of the period, to be lampooned as insensitively, if not as brutally, as the much maligned protagonists of the chapbooks. Similarly, other features of the national temperament pilloried in seventeenth-century popular literature – the Welshman's obsession with genealogy, his peculiar language, hot temper and quarrelsome nature, his patriotism and peculiar way of calculating time and distance – are regularly featured in later fictions, in the clear expectation that the reader will smile, perhaps with an affectionate recognition of a national type, but always with some degree of contempt.

Since the chapbooks almost certainly appealed to an unsophisticated readership, they offer, as Roger Thompson suggests, 'a rare window on the minds of ordinary people'.[1] These small booklets, made of octavo sheets folded to make sixteen pages, or duodecimo folded to make twenty-four, were part of the stock-in-trade of the men (and some women) who carried household goods, knick-knacks and pamphlets up and down the roads of England and Wales, sometimes on horseback but more usually on foot. Generally working a circuit of about twenty miles, with occasional journeys further afield, the chapmen visited towns and villages, farms and remote homesteads with their goods.[2] It is not known whether customers in Wales were offered chapbook tales about their fellow countrymen, but if so they would have certainly needed a robust sense of humour and very thick skins in order to enjoy them.[3] The chapbooks dealt with a great variety of subject matter, including religion, the supernatural, superstition, romance, humour, legend, history, biography and crime, and they were frequently reprinted until the beginning of the nineteenth century when their popularity declined rapidly, giving way to the *Penny Magazine* and Chambers's penny Tracts and Miscellanies.[4] The tales dealing with the Welsh were exclusively humorous, satirizing without mercy Taffy's stupidity and dishonesty. It is no accident that, in his anthology of extracts from Pepys's collection of 115 chapbooks known as the *Penny Merriments*,[5] Thompson places several 'Welsh' texts in the section devoted to 'ROGUES AND FOOLS', commenting:

> Some fools had much of the rogue in them . . . Other fools, like Boord's Gothamites or despised Welsh braggarts, have an almost surreal appeal, and their ludicrous stratagems and humiliating misadventures would boost the egos of the most exploited or unfortunate reader, provided he did not hale from Wales or Gotham.[6]

The 'ludicrous stratagems and humiliating misadventures' of Wales's answer to the Gothamites are described in a group of four chapbooks, *The Welch Traveller* and *The Distressed Welshman* (in verse) and *The Life and Death of Sheffery Morgan* and *The Wonderful Adventures, and Happy Successes of Shon ap Morgan* (in prose). But Taffy, Sheffery and Shon, heroes of these sorry tales, did not leap fully armed from the popular press, with toasted cheese already impaled on a dagger.[7] The comic Welshman had already put in an appearance in Andrew Boorde's *Fyrst Boke of the Introduction of Knowledge* (1548),[8] in the Tudor jest-books[9] and on the stage, notably in the character of Fluellen in Shakespeare's *Henry V*.[10] But in order to appreciate the historical and literary significance of the chapbook tales of the Welsh, it is essential to place them in the immediate context of the tracts and pamphlets, frequently targeting the Welsh as objects of ridicule, that began to pour from the popular press during the years of the Civil War. As W. J. Hughes notes, a large proportion of the collection of nearly three hundred Civil War tracts at the National Library of Wales 'are violently satirical and aim solely at holding up the Welshman to scorn and ridicule'.[11] It is also illuminating to make some reference to the single-sheet folios published later in the seventeenth century, usually printed in black letter typography and featuring verses to be sung to well-known tunes. A brief account of these tracts and song-sheets may serve to demonstrate how the chapbook tales of the Welsh echo the stereotypes and prejudices current in other popular literature of the time.

The virulence of the satire directed against the Welsh during the Civil War itself was prompted by the fact that by and large, despite reservations and local misgivings and with some conspicuous exceptions, the Welsh initially gave their support to the Royalist cause. As Gwyn A. Williams puts it, 'In the Civil War, Poor Taffy was certainly Charles the Martyr's most loyal unknown soldier.'[12] In his account of Royalist recruitment in Wales, Peter Gaunt describes the efforts made by Sir Thomas Salusbury to raise a regiment in north Wales: 'by October [1642] his regiment was at full strength and had marched off to join the king. It was referred to later as "1,200 poor Welsh vermin, the offscourings of the nation".'[13] In order to rendezvous with his Welsh forces, the King had set up his headquarters at Shrewsbury in September. Several Welsh regiments and their commanders had joined the main royal army when it clashed with Parliamentary forces on 23 October: 'The Welsh troops did not perform conspicuously well, allegedly breaking quickly under attack and turning tail, though parliamentary prejudice may lay behind many of the subsequent comments, including a scurrilous ditty on the woeful performance of "poor Taffy".'[14] The Battle of Edgehill, referred to in the popular press as Kenton or Kynton after a village in the locality, became proverbial for Welsh cowardice in the satires of the day. The slaughter went on, though the reports of 2,500 Welshmen slain at Tewkesbury in November, with 1,200 more captured and the rest put to shameful flight, are not confirmed by any surviving documentation 'and were probably complete inventions or wildly inflated descriptions of unsuccessful raids, published in London for propaganda purposes'.[15]

It is thus as Parliamentarian propaganda that the Civil War satires of the Welsh probably have to be read. The writer of *The Welsh-Mans Postures* (1642) claims he has lost his arm at Kenton but is still able to give good advice to his countrymen. They must be sober and keep close rank providing the smell is not too strong; they must run away if the enemy comes on too fast; they must continue to brag, as if they were still in Wales, about their pedigrees, of being great Shentlemen, of being as valiant as Pendragon and of their loyalty to one another;

they are given what Gaunt refers to as pornographic instructions for handling their guns and pikes,[16] while other advice includes tips on getting rid of fleas.[17] In other words, the Welshman of 1642 is depicted as drunken, dirty and boastful and the humour deployed at his expense is invariably unpleasant and often indecent. *The Welch-Mans Warning Piece* (1642) purports to be the text of a sermon in which the humour is based on an extreme dislocation of the English language, with gobbledegook substituted for Welsh (*'vishilata torata'*), the use of 'her' for 'he' and 'his', and the identification of the harp-playing and adulterous King David with his namesake, Taffy, while the alteration of the Biblical 'watch and pray' refers once again to the Welsh as the great unwashed:

> *Taffie, Taffie,* her nown Country-man was porn in *Monmouth shire,* neer to Creek of te well, was first man plaid Welsh Harp was prave King, and *Saul* was a mighty King, but *Taffie* was wise King; yet *Taffie* was fell too, and where was *Taffie* fell *Taffie* was fell upon *Pershepa*: O how was *Taffie* fell upon *Pershepa,* for lack of coot take heed; terfore take heed *vishilata torata, wash and pray,* I warrant her keep her text still. [3][18]

The Welch Doctor (1643) promises to set all bones broken at Kenton and, more picturesquely, professes to restore distressed cousins with the 'wambling trot'.[19] *The Welch-Mans Complements* (1643) relates how one soldier, newly returned from Edgehill, is described as a 'Welsh goat' by his sweetheart and is refused a final kiss because his breath smells of toasted cheese.[20] Four years later, *The Welsh-Mans Publique and Hearty Sorrow and Recantation* (1647), said to be by Shon ap Morgan, is presented as an act of contrition 'That ever her took up Armes against her cood Parliament'; here again the Welsh are represented as 'simple puppies', easily led blind-fold 'to make walks and perambulations out of her Countries of Wales, to kill and fight with her know not whom'; they are proud of their pedigrees and addicted to making wills, inventories, almanacks and prognostications; they are also dirty and flea-ridden, ragged, cowardly and dishonest. The political point is rammed home as Shon ap Morgan asks pardon for standing for the King and promises to defend the Protestant religion.[21]

The chapbook stories of the Welsh, probably dating from the 1670s, clearly reflect many of the attitudes and literary conventions of these and other pamphlets written thirty years earlier,[22] as if the political invective against the Royalist troops remained for decades afterwards a standard way of observing the Welsh. References to Kenton eventually disappeared but Taffy was still viewed in the popular press with a degree of contempt, even loathing, as in the offensive description of 'the vilest of Creatures' in *Wallography* (1682) by William Richards: 'But whether Welch-Men are the *Aborigines* of their Countrey, as Crab-lice are the Autocthones of theirs, and proceed only (like them) from the *excrements* of their Soil, we shall not here dispute.'[23] It seems true to say that the simple puppies who made 'walks and perambulations out of the Countries of Wales' in the Civil War pamphlets became the literary ancestors of the rogues and fools who take the road to London in the chapbook narratives and receive suitable punishments (ranging from imprisonment and mutilation in the verse tales to mustard in the eyes and natural death from a surfeit of bread and cheese in the prose tales) for being perennially silly and occasionally dishonest.

The events at Edgehill and Tewkesbury were not the only reason why the Welshman's 'perambulations' out of his own country were viewed with disfavour. Margaret Spufford comments on the xenophobia that characterizes the chapbooks and the way they reflect prejudice against immigrants, who are poor and therefore portrayed in the literature as invincibly stupid: 'The very real menace of the poor beggar was coped with by mockery.'[24] She points out that the historical background to the 'Welsh' chapbooks is the sixteenth- and seventeenth-century pattern of long-distance migration:

> In the Clee hills area of Shropshire there was only one Welsh surname in the 1524–5 subsidy returns. The parish registers indicate a steady flow of Welsh immigrants from the second quarter of the sixteenth century. The registers of Neen Savage record the highest number of Welsh immigrants between 1575 and 1616. Twenty-six new names were recorded, and eighteen of the people concerned were beggars. Many of the names occur once in the register, and so their owners presumably moved on eastwards into England.[25]

Spufford also refers to the steady flow of Welsh immigrants into Burford and Shrewsbury during the same period,[26] concluding that the effects of this immigration from Wales 'filtered through into popular consciousness and was reflected in the tradition of anti-Welsh jokes so freely used by the chap-books'.[27]

Taffy's wife and children escort him to London in a wheelbarrow: title-page of *The Pleasant History of Taffy's Progress to London: With the Welshman's Catechism* [1709?]

An early fictional example of one such Welsh beggar is to be found in *The Pleasant History of Taffy's Progress to London: with the Welshman's Catechism*. Given its striking similarities to *The Welch Man's Inventory* (a single sheet dated 1641 by Peter Lord),[28] it would seem likely that this eight-page pamphlet is much earlier than the copy in the British Library would suggest.[29] It consists of an interview with Taffy (the 'catechism'), followed by a brief narrative describing his ill-advised visit to London with his tattered family. Taffy explains to his interlocutor, clearly a Londoner, that the 'nasty thing' on his head (a leek) is worn in honour of St Taffy who headed twenty thousand Britons against five thousand Irish basket women and put them to rout.[30] Taffy has travelled to London to seek revenge against the people there who affront Goatlandshire on St David's Day by hanging out a bundle of rags in representation of a Welshman mounted on a red herring, with a leek in his hat. In order to satirize the Welsh obsession with genealogy, Taffy is given his full name – identical to that of the Shentleman of Clamorgan who appears in *The Welch Man's Inventory* – William Morgan ap Renalds ap Hugh ap Richard ap Thomas ap Evan ap Rice. The absurd list of his assets (very similar to the one given in the *Inventory*) together with the goods he has inherited from his cousin target the twin Welsh obsessions with inventories and wills and with their ubiquitous cousins[31] – and at the same time indicate his abject poverty. Taffy claims to be the owner of a four-year-old pig, two tablecloths (but no napkins), one grid-iron, two shoes, one pound of cow-butter, nine sprats, a good store of fowls, no towels, sheets or shirts, two gallons of sour cider, one bed of garlic and two of beans, and a Welsh Bible. The owner of the Bible then boasts of the great liberty of conscience in Wales and utters a little more gobbledegook in imitation of the Welsh language: 'our Teachers only go to the Top of a Mountain and cry's out *Toe ruglas togh hen a pie dogh*, that is, Come to Church, come, if not, stay at Home and be Hang'd.' He then lists a purse without money, one ladder, two ropes, one wife, two children, two dogs in pup, three cats, twelve mice, a bushel of fleas, three long clubs, a mousetrap (always good for a laugh in satires of the Welsh)[32] and a sword. From his cousin, Evan Morgan of Brecknock, Taffy has inherited six pairs of holland sheets made of canvas, one linsey-woolsey warming-pan, two woollen eel-skins, twenty-four egg-shells and sundry other items, all of them nonsensical, culminating in an owl which is near kin to the family. The will has been sealed and delivered in the presence of twenty goats now feeding on the mountains of

Penmenmoor [sic]. The historical image of the beggarly Welsh crossing the border into England is clearly projected in the brief narrative of Taffy's journey to London. He and his poverty-stricken family set out on 33 January 1890 (a satire on the Welsh method of computing dates), Taffy riding in a wheelbarrow pushed by his barefooted, leek-crowned wife who carries her baby on her back while another tags along behind.[33] They sleep in a barn at Leominster, beg for charity at Worcester and are whipped out of town. They reach London on the eve of St David's Day, 'Solemnis'd with so much Devotion as to get every *Welshman* Drunk by Night'. Taffy becomes 'pretty Boosie' and falls like fury to breaking the windows of every house where there is an effigy of a Welshman hung out; he is beaten by the mob and sent to Bridewell as an idle, drunken vagabond. After a flogging and a spell of hard labour, clearly intended to be comical, he returns to his own country with his family, grieving that he could not vindicate St Taffy and swearing 'hur would never see England again'.

The hapless Taffy of *The Pleasant History* reappears in the two verse chapbooks, *The Distressed Welshman, Born in Trinity-Lane: With a Relation of his Unfortunate Travls* [sic][34] and *The Welch Traveller; Or, The Unfortunate Welchman* (1671),[35] both probably written by Humfrey Crouch.[36] In each of these booklets of twenty-four duodecimo pages, written in rhyming couplets, Taffy is subjected to gross indignities of a peculiarly sadistic nature, nicely calculated (it would seem) to amuse Crouch's xenophobic readers. In *The Distressed Welshman*, Taffy ('If any ask hur what hur am, / hur is a Shentleman') goes to London where he is robbed by 'a sheating Quean'. When he is arrested for not paying his bill for a meal, the justice is inclined to be lenient until Taffy starts using threatening language; the death sentence is commuted to branding ('The People all did laugh out-right'), but when he refuses to sing 'God save the King' as instructed by the hangman, his arm as well as his hand is branded. He is too poor to pay his keepers their fee or feed himself ('Hur may buy no leeks nor sheese, / her substance is so small'), but he is freed anyway. When he becomes a lawyer's clerk, the people laugh and his master whips him. After bragging about dodging another bill, he is again flung into prison; he is put in the stocks, pilloried and has his ear cut off ('And bravely he [the hangman] his flesh doth carve, / whilst all the People laugh'). At the common butts, one of the archers almost splits his nose in twain; when he swears the classic Welsh oath of the period ('cots-splutter-a-nails') that he will break the arrow if he is shot at again, the archers 'could not refrain from laughter'. Driven by hunger to steal some leeks, he kills the dog that attacks him and is condemned to lose the other ear. However, the people persuade his accuser to let him go and he is charged to return to his own country. After several further misadventures, he goes to sleep in church and wakes with a start and a mighty 'f——' when the preacher says 'Awake, awake', whereupon he is at last driven out of town and made to swim the river. Not surprisingly, he is 'in a piteous case'. One can only say that it could have been worse: Shonny ap Morgan of *The Unfortunate Welch-Man*,[37] a single sheet of verses, is hanged 'in ragged array' after killing a bonny brisk Scot during a quarrel. Taffy of the second verse narrative, *The Welsh Traveller*, is another hapless itinerant. He is mockingly described as an astrologer as the Welsh were supposed by the popular press to have a penchant for prognostication:[38] this Welshman can tell how often the moon changes. In this story, Taffy escapes mutilation: he is merely mocked, cudgelled, burned while hiding in a chimney, stung with nettles, put in the stocks and pilloried, and run out of town with shovels, staves and stones. The scatological humour is strongly reminiscent of the Civil War pamphlets: Taffy escapes one beating by extracting 'A thing made of cheese and leeks' from his breeches and throwing it in his assailant's eyes, while on another occasion a scurvy quean and whore 'pisses in her hand, And threw it in hur face'. The tale ends with 'Taffy's Indictment', a long list of his misdemeanours, 'For which loose behaviour he was obliged to stand in the pillory; where we shall leave him till the next pranks he plays.'

The prose chapbook tales describe the adventures of Sheffery ap Morgan and his son Shon. As Peter Lord has pointed out, Shon ap Morgan is the stereotypical Welshman of seventeenth- and eighteenth-century woodcuts: 'His son is variously Sheffery Morgan or Morgan ap Shones, whose mother, Unnafred Shones, had a sister Marcate, "the old small-coal woman" in one version.'[39] Lord reproduces a number of illustrations of the family, including the splendid coloured broadsheets of Shon and Unnafred and their son Morgan, riding to London on goats.[40] In the chapbook stories, both Sheffery and his son practise as doctors; simple-minded and cunning, they suffer physical discomfort and petty ridicule, though they escape the sheer brutality meted out to Taffy in the verse tales and *The Pleasant History*.

In *The Life and Death of Sheffery Morgan, the Son of Shon ap Morgan*, the stupidity of the Welsh is lampooned in one episode where after coming down from university, Sheffery fails to obtain a living from the bishop because he is incapable of writing an appropriate sermon.[41] In another episode, after walking to London in the company of two cattle drovers, he mistakes a jackanapes chained to a counter for the shopkeeper's ancient father. The cunning of the Welsh is illustrated when Sheffery persuades an old couple that their sow has fallen in love with him and duly walks off with the pig, a dowry of twenty pounds and the old woman's best hat. Unlike Taffy, Sheffery eventually prospers when he marries a physician's widow and inherits his predecessor's prescription for a clyster, allowing for some mild anal humour. Sheffery escapes the physical battering that Taffy endures elsewhere though he does die – of a surfeit after eating seven pounds of bread and cheese. After telling this extremely silly story, the chapbook author displays an unusual degree of sophistication when Sheffery is mourned in a mock-heroic elegy which calls on St Taffy, ap Shink in Shones, cousin Price and all our near relations Hugh and Price:

> *Send forth your sighs, sad lamentation make,*
> *Until the very high* Welsh *mountain shake,*
> *With the fierce sobs ascending from the breath,*
> *Let all the* Welsh Goats *go mourn for his death*

Sheffery bequeaths his practice to his son, but in the sequel, *The Wonderful Adventures, And Happy Successes Of Shon ap Morgan. The only Son of Sheffry ap Morgan*,[42] Shon gives up medicine and, like all chapbook heroes, takes to the road. His naïvety is exposed with one or two examples of the humour characteristic of contemporary satires of the Welsh, metaphorically smearing the nation with excreta. Thus in a pastry-cook's shop he thinks that the mustard that comes with his roast pork is a child's 't—d'; when he is told that mustard is good for the eyes, he anoints his own with it; he carves a mutton pie against his breast, mistaking it for a loaf, so that the liquor runs all over his clothes; the maid misunderstands his order for spice posset and brings him piss in a basin ('who knows said the maid, but this may well be a well approved Welsh medicine for a queasy in the stomach'). These are relatively mild misadventures, however, and, like his father before him, Shon eventually prospers, despite or even because of his simplicity. A merchant at the Royal Exchange is 'taken with his honest and innocent behaviour' (a rare reversal of the 'Taffy was a thief' motif) and employs him in his business. Shon helps to bring about his master's marriage – and marries the lady's maid himself.

Although he is a mere caricature in a brief and foolish chapbook tale, Shon ap Morgan does combine in his person two of the strands that would run through many eighteenth-century fictions of Wales. The episodes concerning the mustard, the mutton pie and the spice posset demonstrate Shon's 'innocence' in its usual sense of the simple-mindedness of the Welsh. Here he is at one with Taffy and Sheffery ap Morgan and the other Welsh characters that populate seventeenth-century chapbooks, pamphlets and song-sheets, lampooning the nation 'whilst all the People laugh'. But Shon's later prosperity, predicated on his 'honest and innocent behaviour' in the vicinity of the Royal Exchange, demonstrates his 'innocence' in quite another sense, not least his probity in financial dealings. Thus it is that while Shon invites his readers to have a good laugh at the Welsh, as a number of his literary descendants would continue to do in eighteenth-century fictions, he is also – quite unexpectedly – an unlikely literary ancestor of those exemplary characters who inhabit what Penelope Aubin would later refer to in her own 'Welsh' novel as a place 'rich in Virtue'.

2
A place 'rich in Virtue'

THE LIFE OF MADAM DE BEAUMOUNT BY PENELOPE AUBIN

It is possible that *The Life of Madam de Beaumount* may be the first novel – or more properly novella – in English to be written with a Welsh setting, though relatively little is known about the author, Penelope Aubin. She was born about 1685 in London, the daughter of a French officer.[1] Her earliest recorded works are three odes written in praise of the Stuart monarchy during the reign of Queen Anne,[2] though the Abbé Prévost refers to 'diverses petites Brochures' brought out anonymously before she took the risk of publishing a novel in her own name.[3] It has been suggested that the death of her husband (probably a government official) left her in financial difficulties and that she wrote novels in order to support herself.[4] Prévost certainly claimed that she was ill-equipped to deal with poverty, though Aubin herself insisted otherwise: 'My design in writing, is to employ my leisure Hours to some Advantage to my self and others . . . I do not write for Bread.'[5] Between 1721 and 1729 she brought out seven novels as well as a number of translations from the French.[6] She may also have worked in the theatre during this period, possibly as an actress.[7]

According to Prévost's spiteful account, Aubin's first novel was a success simply because it was written by a woman, but once the novelty wore off her works were so poorly received that she destroyed her writing materials in a fit of spite, vowing never to use them again. He claims that when she turned to religion and began to compose sermons, there were preachers queuing up to buy them; after she made up her mind to become a preacher herself, her 'oratory' was soon full, with huge audiences willing to pay thirty *sols* for the privilege of listening to a poor address lasting only about three quarters of an hour. Like her books, Prévost continues, the oratory was successful only while it was a novelty.

It is known that by 1729, Penelope Aubin had set up The Lady's Oratory in Topham's Great Room at York Buildings near Charing

Cross[8] – an extraordinary venture for a woman at that period, nearly forty years before Dr Johnson's well-known strictures on female preachers.[9] It was presumably inspired by the Revd John Henley's notorious oratory, founded in 1726 as a place of public worship devoted (in its early days) to re-establishing the primitive church of the apostles and registered, according to the requirements of the Toleration Act, as a dissenting meeting house; since he had taken holy orders, Henley initially offered his own version of the liturgy of the Church of England but he also entertained the public with controversy, satire and burlesque in lectures and 'disputations' on a wide variety of topics.[10] It seems likely that Penelope Aubin's 'sermons' were also a species of public entertainment; she was involved in two 'concerts' at the oratory on 22 and 29 April 1729,[11] and in the same month she was pitting her wits against 'Orator' Henley himself,[12] who was lampooned that same year in *The Dunciad Variorum* ('Preacher at once, and Zany of thy Age!').[13] In August 1729 one commentator was refusing to 'interfere at all between the wonderful Mr. Henley and that other Candidate for the Town's Applause, Mrs. Aubin, or so much as hint an Opinion which of them excels in Oratory'.[14] According to Prévost, *The Grub Street Journal* took exception to the appearance of Aubin in a pulpit simply because she was ugly.[15] Even so, her venture seems to have been a money-spinner: Prévost claimed that she died before she could spend the profits gained in the space of a few weeks. In December 1730 'Mrs Aubin, the Oratrix' was at the Haymarket, speaking the Epilogue to *The Merry Masqueraders, or, The Humorous Cuckold*,[16] 'her surprizingly bawdy and flippant comedy'.[17] She died the following year.

Commentators on Penelope Aubin's work have generally made a connection between her preaching and the didacticism of her fiction, defined by John Richetti as 'positively exemplary Christian "realism"'[18] (*'My design is to persuade you to be virtuous'*[19]). It is also claimed that her efforts to moralize fiction in the 1720s provided Richardson with a precedent for a new species of novel, intended to promote the cause of religion and virtue,[20] though Stauffer offers a dissident view of Aubin's 'romances of salaciousness blended with preaching',[21] while Mary Anne Schofield's feminist reading insists that 'her plots present the negative side of the romance with its resultant dislocation, disorientation, fragmentation, and loss':

> The heroine is quintessentially beleaguered and harassed, disguised, seduced, and raped; the hero disguises and yet reveals (even masked) his

Mr Lluelling with Madam de Beaumount and her daughter outside their cave 'not far from *Swansey*': frontispiece and title-page of *The Life of Madam de Beaumount* by Penelope Aubin, 1721

THE LIFE

OF

Madam *de Beaumount*,

a *French* LADY;

Who lived in a Cave in *Wales* above fourteen Years undiscovered, being forced to fly *France* for her Religion; and of the cruel Usage she had there.

ALSO

Her LORD's Adventures in *Muscovy*, where he was a Prisoner some Years.

WITH

An Account of his returning to *France*, and her being discover'd by a *Welsh* Gentleman, who fetch'd her Lord to *Wales*: And of many strange Accidents which befel them, and their Daughter *Belinda*, who was stolen away from them; and of their Return to *France* in the Year 1718.

By Mrs. *AUBIN*.

Superanda omnis Fortuna ferendo est. Vir. Æneid.
Fortem posce animum, & mortis terrore carentem.
Juvenal. Sat. 10.

LONDON:
Printed for E. BELL, J. DARBY, A. BETTESWORTH, F. FAYRAM, J. PEMBERTON, J. HOOKE, C. RIVINGTON, F. CLAY, J. BATLEY, E. SYMON. 1721.

base, animalistic tendencies. Because the stories and characters are virtually indistinguishable, the entire Aubin corpus functions as a gigantic masquerade: only the costumes change; the plot remains the same, and the story is, essentially, a harrowing one for the woman.[22]

All these views imply that Aubin was exclusively concerned with the sexual adventures of her heroines. It can be argued, however, that while *The Life of Madam de Beaumount* takes account of the 'virtue' of her young heroine, Belinda, Aubin's 'Welsh' novel is essentially concerned with one of the more intractable moral issues of the age (though to discuss the text in these terms may in effect disguise both its brevity and the inconsequential development of its bizarre plot).

In the Preface to *The Life of Madam de Beaumount*, Aubin establishes Wales as a place '*rich in Virtue*':

> Wales *being a Place not extremely populous in many Parts, is certainly more rich in Virtue than* England, *which is now improved in Vice only, and rich in Foreigners, who often bring more Vices than Ready Money along with them. He that would keep his Integrity, must dwell in a Cell; and* Belinda *had never been so virtuous, had she not been bred in a Cave, and never seen a Court.* (p.vii)

By focusing on 'integrity' in this way, Aubin suggests that to live in Wales is to live a virtuous life far away from financial and political intrigue. Commenting on Aubin's 'immediate preoccupation with the felt moral and political reality she and her readers knew', Jerry C. Beasley points out that that, in criticizing the English,

> This jab is sharp and cutting, for Welshmen, like the Scots, were at the time popularly regarded as a species of romantic barbarians. And here Aubin is more than just vaguely topical, for a common charge against the Whig government turned upon its manner of sinking the nation into vice and infamy.[23]

The xenophobic reference to foreigners without ready money hints at the anxieties intrinsic to a society existing on credit – more so than anywhere else in Europe[24] – while there is also a reminder here that in the early eighteenth century, the court at Whitehall was still the centre of political power. Thus it comes as no surprise that the villainous Charles Owen Glandore, who attempts to seduce Belinda in the early days of her marriage, is represented as a Welshman who has been corrupted by the metropolis, described by Gwyn A. Williams as that 'unheard-of and monstrous capital city in London', created as part of the process that would make 'Great Britain into the greatest merchant empire in the world':[25]

> but alas! he lived too long in that curs'd Town, where Vice takes place of Virtue, where Men rise by Villainy and Fraud, where the lustful Appetite has all Opportunities of being gratify'd; where Oaths and Promises are only Jests, and all Religion but Pretence, and made a Skreen and Cloak for Knavery; a Place where Truth and Virtue cannot live. Oh! curse on my Credulity, to trust so rich a Treasure to a Wolf, a lustful *Londoner*. (p.102)

In the Preface, Aubin makes a gendered distinction between male probity ('*Integrity*') and female chastity ('Belinda *had never been so virtuous*'), and in similar vein reminds her readers that '*Wales has produced many brave Men, and been famed for the unshaken Loyalty of its People to their Princes, and Bravery in Fight, scorning to bow their Necks to Slavery, or to be conquer'd; why may it not produce a Woman virtuous and wise, as Men are courageous?*' (pp.vii–viii). Here, female chastity and wisdom are set against male courage and '*unshaken Loyalty . . . to their Princes*', possibly a sly reference beyond the Welsh princes to James Edward, the Old Pretender, waiting in the wings of the novel. Aubin ends the Preface by presenting her story '*to the true-born English, and Antient Britons, to whom I wish Increase of Sense and Virtue, Plenty of Money, good Governours, and endless Prosperity*' (p.viii), pointedly excluding those of foreign birth and reiterating her concern with the moral, financial and political welfare of her readers. In a novel published only six years after the Jacobite Rebellion of 1715 it is arguable that this concern with public morality and good government under the Hanoverian dynasty is translated in the text itself into a coded representation of the conflict between Protestantism and Catholicism. Indeed, it is possibly the great virtue of religious toleration that is ultimately 'preached' in the oratory of this small fiction.

The Life of Madam de Beaumount begins in May 1717, 'NOT far from *Swansey*, a Sea-Port in *Wales*, in *Glamorganshire*', where Mr Lluelling, a thirty-six-year old bachelor with an estate of about £500 per annum, is walking by the seaside. Ascending a hill and pausing to enjoy a lovely prospect of fields and valleys, he sees a beautiful maiden at an open door in the opposite hillside. He soon discovers that he is looking at the entrance of a cave and that the occupants, Madam de Beaumount and her daughter, Belinda, together with their servants, have been hiding there for fourteen and a half years. Mr Lluelling immediately falls in love with Belinda, who (despite her long incarceration) is wearing a cherry-coloured silk petticoat flowered with silver, a satin waistcoat with red and silver ribbons, green satin ribbon in her carelessly braided hair, and a fine straw hat lined with green and gold. The frontispiece shows him kneeling in front of the ladies in a lane leading down to the sea, with three sailing ships in the offing. He is given a guided tour of the cave, once a hermit's cell but now consisting of five rooms arranged in a circle, furnished with damask beds, scrutores and furniture, with a central pair of stairs leading to a skylight covered with a shutter and grate. This is clearly a five-star cave, at least as cosy as Robinson Crusoe's habitation which Defoe had introduced to the public only two years earlier.[26] Nevertheless, Madam de Beaumount points out rather plaintively that 'in Winter 'tis no pleasant Dwelling'; mother and daughter leave their hideout with alacrity when Mr Lluelling invites them to his seat and entertains them 'in a manner suiting the noble Nature and Hospitality of the Antient Britons' (p.19).

In order to ponder the contemporary significance of that cave 'NOT far from *Swansey*', described at a precise moment in history, May 1717, it is necessary first to suggest how the 'history' of Wales, as revealed in Aubin's fiction, intersects with the 'biographical time' allotted to three generations of women in the novel, each occupying an ambiguous position in relation to the Catholic church. In an inset autobiographical narrative, Madam de Beaumount explains that her mother 'came over [to France] with the unfortunate Queen of *England*, Wife to King *James* II. to whom my Mother's Father was a loyal, and faithful Servant, tho a Protestant' (p.20). The oddity of this conformation is compounded when the exiled young lady marries a French Catholic. The child of this mixed marriage, the future Madam de Beaumount (otherwise unnamed), is orphaned at an early age and although her father has left instructions that she should not be forced into a convent, her guardians shut her up in a monastery of the Poor Clares, ostensibly to convert her to Catholicism but in actuality to deprive her of her fortune. She manages to escape and, like her mother before her, marries a French Catholic nobleman. She is regarded as a heretic by her parents-in-law, but her husband tries to defend her: 'let not her Religion, which is not a fault in her, but the Misfortune of her Education, make you prejudiced against her' (p.26). When she becomes pregnant, however, instructors 'in the Truth' try to convert her; using the language of the Inquisition to describe her ordeal, Madam de Beaumount explains to Mr Lluelling how she resisted even her husband's eloquence to make her Protestant stand: 'not Racks, nor Flames, could move my Soul, so much as one of those tender things he said to me: and now I was daily visited by learned Priests, and such who, as Relations or Friends, thought themselves obliged to assist in my Conversion; but having been educated in an intire Abhorrence of the Church of *Rome*, I gave little heed to their Arguments, and resolved to continue firm to the Opinion I had been bred in' (pp.30–1). When her husband is sent into the army, he arranges for her to go to England to be cared for by an uncle; but she is shipwrecked on the Welsh coast and duly takes up residence in the cave 'NOT far from *Swansey*', where she gives birth to a daughter and remains in hiding for the next fourteen years.

At one level, the cave may signify no more than a shelter appropriate to the wild Welsh coast; designed perhaps as a female version of Crusoe's cabin, it is one of several primitive dwellings featured in Aubin's novels.[27] At another level, the cave may be subjected to the kind of feminist psychoanalytical interpretation theorized by Julia Kristeva, Claire Kahane, Luce Irigaray and others in relation to the Gothic novel, with the possibility that in Aubin's novel, as in Ann Radcliffe's *A Sicilian Romance*, there may be, as Alison Milbank puts it, 'moves towards a testing out of what it might mean to acknowledge the mother and to establish social networks built upon this Utopian project'.[28] It is also possible, however, that in this bizarre image of the cave, Aubin is making a significant reference to the space of history and culture beyond the text.[29] Madam de Beaumount's cave is quite specifically a refuge from religious persecution: she is described on the title-page as 'a *French* LADY; Who lived in a Cave in *Wales* above fourteen Years undiscovered, being forced to fly *France* for her Religion; and of the cruel Usage she had there'. The cave may thus represent a secure refuge for Protestantism under threat, a symbolic place of womb-like safety where Belinda can be brought up in her mother's faith, despite the fact that while she was (literally) still in the womb, her father announced that his child must be brought up as a Catholic.

Yet all is not quite as it seems. When the Protestant Madam de Beaumount flees to England to stay with her uncle, she is confident that 'there I shall enjoy my Religion without Molestation' (p.32); after her arrival in Wales, however, Madam de Beaumount hears that the same uncle 'was long since dead in *Scotland*, being forced to fly *England*, all his Estate being seized by the Government on account of his loyalty to King *James*, and carrying on Designs for his Service' (p.36). This same Jacobite uncle, very much alive, turns up later in the novel under a false name, Mr Hide, a pseudonym which suggests the covert nature of his political activities and perhaps deliberately echoes the family name of the Clarendons (Anne Hyde had been James II's first wife). There is no direct reference in the novel to the religious persuasion of Mr Hide and his friends – and one recalls that his father was a loyal and faithful servant of James II's queen 'though a Protestant'. Yet there is sufficient ambiguity in Aubin's presentation of Mr Hide and his Jacobite friends to suggest that this novel is not, after all, simply an exercise in Protestant polemic. Indeed, McBurney refers boldly to the 'sympathetic portrayal' of the Jacobites in *The Life of Madam de Beaumount*. He notes that Aubin's works 'take place against the exciting political and religious background of the great Anglo-French population exchanges of the late seventeenth century – the emigration of the Huguenots after the revocation of the Edict of Nantes in 1685 and the flight of the Jacobites to France with the last Stuart king and after the Battle of the Boyne' and adduces, from internal evidence in the novels themselves (including, for instance, the anti-Hanoverian tone of *Charlotta du Pont*),[30] that the author was writing from a Catholic perspective: 'If Mrs. Aubin is her own Belinda de Beaumont [sic] or Charlotta Du Pont (in anything but beauty), she too was a Catholic, by birth or conversion, for Huguenots fare as poorly in her fiction as Turks, Italians, Dutch, and Irish.'[31] McBurney is not alone in taking this view: R. B. Dooley has claimed Aubin as a forgotten Catholic novelist.[32]

The Jacobites first appear in the novel soon after Belinda's marriage to Mr Lluelling and her abduction by his cousin, the 'lustful *Londoner*', Glandore. He first attempts to seduce her in a summerhouse[33] and plans to incarcerate her in a ruinous castle, fifty miles from 'Swansey', inhabited by an old man and his family 'who spoke nothing but *Welsh*'. When Glandore is killed by brigands, Belinda is rescued by 'a company of Clowns' who are on their way to a fair with horses to sell, 'but they could speak nothing but *Welsh*, so that she could not make them understand one word' (p.64). She is directed to a house which (as it turns out) coincidentally belongs to her uncle, Mr Hide, who is absent in Ireland; after being entertained by his son, she sets out for home and is abducted for a second time by bandits. Employing what might now be considered a semantic distinction between terrorists and common criminals, Aubin insists that only three members of the gang are 'really Thieves' – indeed, Belinda has already met their captain as a fellow guest at Mr Hide's house:

> We have for our Royal Master's, and Religion's sake, been ruined; our Estates, or our Fathers, which was our Birth-right, confiscated; we have try'd to get our Bread abroad, but like the poor Cavaliers, were look'd on as burdensome wherever we came. Thus made desperate, since *Lewis* the Fourteenth dy'd, we return'd to *England*; we had most of us a Being when first we came, but our Friends are since impoverish'd: our Spirits are great, therefore we have chosen this desperate way to maintain ourselves. At the harmless Country Peoples, where we lodge in couples, we pass for Jacobites, and honest Tories, great Men disguised, &c. and when we have got a good Booty, and are flush of Money, they imagine we have receiv'd Supplies from abroad. (pp.111–12)

The gang is a ruthless one. Belinda finds herself incarcerated with two Frenchwomen who have been travelling in Wales on business; both have been robbed and raped. When the women manage to escape, they find themselves in an unforgiving landscape 'where they could discern nothing but dreadful high barren Mountains, and lonely Valleys, dangerous to pass' (p.117); so wild is this place that after three days' wandering, Belinda stabs a kid ('They lick'd up the warm Blood, and eat the raw Flesh, more joyfully than they wou'd Dainties at another time, so sharp is Hunger!' (p.120)), and the cold is so intense that the ladies nearly expire on the banks of the River Wie [*sic*] before they are rescued by some kindly fishermen. Confusingly, however, the Jacobites are treated sympathetically elsewhere in the novel, as McBurney claims. When Mr Lluelling and Belinda's father (now a Marquis) come upon Mr Hide and his Jacobite friends occupying a 'clay cottage' near Cork, they are regaled with venison pasty, wine and dried tongues. Most of the group are well known to the Marquis, identifying themselves as Sir C.O., Mr T.B., Sir A.D. and the two A-rs. At the end of the novel, Belinda's captors are embraced by Mr Hide as they embark for Barcelona (presumably to serve the Old

Pretender), armed with 'Letters of Recommendation' from the Marquis 'to some Great Men there, who were his Friends' (p.138). Perhaps their departure to Spain in 1718 is not entirely unconnected with the fact that three years after the first Jacobite Rebellion, the Spanish government sponsored another abortive invasion of Scotland in support of James III.[34]

How far the representational space devoted to Mr Hide and the Jacobite bandits can be shown to refer directly to events in Welsh history 'outside' the novel must remain speculative, especially as Aubin's description of the Jacobite brigands in Wales in 1717 is disconcertingly similar to her brief account in *The Life and Adventures of Lady Lucy* of James II's defeated supporters after the Battle of the Boyne (unless this too should be interpreted as a small aperture on a portentous moment in history).[35] According to John Davies, two-thirds of the Welsh members of Parliament in the late Stuart age had Tory sympathies, though only a tiny minority of the population of Wales were Roman Catholic. Most Welsh clergymen were natural Tories, though most of them swore the oath of allegiance to William and Mary, while surviving loyalty to James II among the gentry was undermined after the Battle of the Boyne.[36] Faithfully reflecting these views, the Revd Ellis Wynne produced his 'classic of Welsh High Anglicism',[37] *Gweledigaetheu y Bardd Cwsc* (1703), a version of Quevedo's political allegory, rewritten as a defence of the Established Church, with Queen Anne as 'the most beloved of heroines'[38] – the role in which she also appeared in Aubin's odes of 1707 and 1708:

> For where great *ANNA* rules the Church and State,
> *ANNA*, the Pious, Vertuous, Good and Great,
> All human Blessings must abound,
> And whilst brave *Churchill* fights for Thee,
> For Right Religion, and our Liberty;
> He ever shall, as now, victorious be.
> And all thy Reign still with new Glories crown'd,
> Your Fortune equal to your Godlike Birth;
> And all the Universe proclaim
> The Wonders of your matchless Fame,
> Confessing you the best, and greatest Queen on Earth.[39]

The Hanoverian succession in 1714 caused much anguish in conservative parts of the kingdom, including Wales; decades would pass before Welsh landowners and clerics abandoned their loyalty to the house of Stuart. In rather more picturesque language, Gwyn A. Williams has the Tory squirearchy slumping sourly into their Jacobite drinking clubs in response to 'all the sickening lurches between William III, Anne and the Hanoverians'.[40] Aubin's novel, published seven years after the accession of George I, indicates the remarkable level of tolerance shown by the 'harmless Country People' towards these same 'honest Tories', and also suggests that in the years immediately after the Jacobite Rebellion of 1715 there were still nests of activists living a double life in wild Wales and willing to resort to banditry in order to maintain themselves after the confiscation of their family estates.

It is possible to make some sense of the political and religious ambiguities in *The Life of Madam de Beaumount* by suggesting that the Protestant cave 'NOT far from *Swansey*' may be deliberately juxtaposed to the ruined house and ancient church (emblems perhaps of the exiled house of Stuart and its allegiance to the Old Faith) from which the Jacobite bandits make their sorties. Both places may be seen symbolically as offering a safe haven in the wilderness from religious and political persecution. Read in this way, the novel may suggest that although some of the unfortunates who have by necessity to hide from religious persecution may retain some of the accoutrements of their former lifestyle (Madam de Beaumount and Belinda keep possession of their fine clothes and furnishings), they are essentially cold, estranged, deprived of family, friends and community ('in Winter 'tis no pleasant Dwelling'); beyond the ruined house and old church occupied by the bandits lie 'dreadful high barren Mountains, and lonely Valleys, dangerous to pass'. In this novel, both Protestant and Catholic are given a refuge in wild Wales, a place symbolically rich (or so it would seem) in the virtue of religious toleration. It is perhaps worth noting that although the Declaration of Indulgence and the Act of Toleration were measures introduced during the reign of James II (to pacify in turn his Roman Catholic and Nonconformist subjects), Aubin claims in *The Stuarts* that Queen Anne also played an active part in encouraging the toleration of dissent:

> She heals our Discords, and we Friends become,
>   Tho' different Principles possess;
>   Dissenting from the Church; yet we agree
> To joyn in our Respect to Her and Loyalty.[41]

Aubin's claims for Queen Anne's desire to heal 'our Discords' may not be historically justified,[42] but the first person response in *The Stuarts* to the idea of religious toleration ('we Friends become') has particular resonance in view of what appears (opaquely) as an exploration of the same theme in *The Life of Madam de Beaumount* (and is also significant in view of the fact that it was probably as a dissenter herself that under the requirements of the Toleration Act, she would be licensed to open The Lady's Oratory some years later).

Yet for all her praise of the country, Aubin represents Wales as a strange and remote territory, as exotic and barbaric as Muscovy. When Madam de Beaumount's husband (referred to as 'the Marquis' after the death of his father) takes command of a regiment and fights on behalf of that brave and glorious monarch, the last king of Sweden, in his last campaign against the Tsar,[43] he is taken prisoner and accommodated in the household of a Russian general at Toropierz before escaping into a landscape very similar to that in which his daughter would find herself after fleeing from the Jacobite bandits in Wales: he too travels through 'dreadful Mountains and Hills, whose Tops were covered with Snow' (p.82) and is held captive by a band of Tartar robbers. Although there is a little more 'cultural coloration'[44] in the scenes set in Wales, Aubin's references to the Welsh language are dismissive: essentially, it is the language of 'clowns', while the festivities held at Mr Lluelling's seat to celebrate the marriage of Mr Hide's son and the Marquis's stepdaughter (acquired by a second marriage, contracted after Madam de Beaumount's disappearance) are viewed with a mixture of admiration and amused contempt:

> this Wedding was very splendid, all sorts of innocent Diversion, as Dancing, Feasting, and musical Entertainments, compleated the Festival. The Country-People had their share in it, and much pleased the Ladies with their odd Dancing and Songs: the *Welsh* Harpers came from all parts of the Country, blind and lame, and the Halls echo'd with the trembling Harps. The Marquiss, who had heard the most harmonious Concerts of Musick in *Rome* and *France*, confess'd he had heard nothing more diverting, or seen an Entertainment where there was less Expence, or more true Mirth; saying, 'Were the *Welsh* Language as agreeable and musical as their Harps, I should love to hear them talk, and prefer it to *French*.' (p.140)

The negatives stitched into this description of a Welsh wedding are obvious enough. While the ladies admire the 'odd' dancing and singing, the polite prevarications of the Marquis's sentence structure conveys the fact that he finds the Welsh language disagreeable and unmusical — and certainly inferior to French. This is not the crude disgust of the chapbooks but the urbanity of mere distaste.

It is not entirely unexpected, therefore, that at the end of the novel, France beckons. After the birth of Belinda's son on 17 March 1718, the Marquis and his lady return to their native country. The Hides depart soon afterwards. On 2 May, Belinda and her husband set off to spend the summer in Normandy and find France so charming that they decide to settle there permanently. The place 'rich in Virtue' is speedily evacuated and the last word given to Aubin in her guise as preacher:

> Thus Providence does, with unexpected Accidents, try Men's Faith, frustrate their Designs, and lead them thro a Series of Misfortunes, to manifest its Power in their Deliverance; confounding the Atheist, and convincing the Libertine, that there is a just God, who rewards Virtue, and does punish Vice: so wonderful are the Ways of God, so boundless is his Power, that none ought to despair that believe in him. (p.142)

Madam de Beaumount and her daughter, both paragons of virtue, are quite properly delivered from their cave. The Jacobite brigands are likewise delivered from their hideout, apparently unpunished by the 'just God' of Aubin's homily. (Robbery and rape, it seems, can be practised on unsuspecting female travellers in wild Wales without fear of reprisal, divine or otherwise — but, since the Jacobites are not 'real Thieves', perhaps they should not be seen as 'real Rapists' either.) Even so, we are exhorted to imitate the virtues of the worthy persons whose story we have read, 'since that is the only way to make us dear to God and Man, and the most certain and noble Method to perpetuate our Names, and render our Memories immortal, and our Souls eternally happy' (p.143).

3

'A Genuine Account of the Life'

૪

TRAVELLERS' TALES

'Is it true or a fiction?' asked the Revd John Eagles, the first editor of *The Journal of Llewellin Penrose* – and admitted that he could no more tell than anyone else who might read it.[1] An autobiography by – or said to be by – an eighteenth-century Welshman or Welshwoman may be of intrinsic interest whether the story s/he has to tell is fact or fiction or a judicious blend of both. But if one prefers to know which variety of autobiography is on offer, it can prove difficult to show conclusively how far the record is 'genuine'. Barrett J. Mandel has suggested that 'A reader who at first mistakes fiction for autobiography or vice versa feels cheated. One wants to know whether the book is one or the other: it makes a difference in terms of how the book is to be read.'[2] In the case of several 'Welsh' examples of that 'mass of travel literature that flooded Europe during the seventeenth and eighteenth centuries',[3] there can be no serious danger of feeling 'cheated': in *The Voyages, Travels and Adventures of William Owen Gwin Vaughan, Esq.* (1736)[4] or *A Genuine Account of the Life and Transactions of Howell ap David Price, Gentleman of Wales* (1752),[5] the reader is fully aware that we journey into the realms of fantasy, conveniently labelled 'Tunis' or 'Algeria', 'Monmouth' or 'Llandeglai'. *The Admirable Travels of Messieurs Thomas Jenkins and David Lowellin* (1783)[6] is perhaps a little more problematic: Stauffer, for one, more than half-believes that on 1 September 1770 Messieurs Jenkins and Lowellin did as a matter of historical fact drift on to the African coast.[7] However, it is the provenance of *The Journal of Llewellin Penrose* (1815),[8] attributed to William Williams, that is truly perplexing. The testimony of the great Benjamin West may convince most sensible readers that the *Journal* – styled by D. H. Dickason as 'very probably America's first novel'[9] – is the fictionalized record of William Williams's youthful experience as a castaway on the coast of South America. Yet the shade of Llewellin Penrose haunts the text as the possible author of his own amazing story. After the recent discovery that Mike Parker Pearson's archaeological work in Madagascar 'appears to have proved beyond the reach of literary critics that Robert Drury's Journal [1729] is the story of Robert Drury',[10] it seems justifiable at least to examine the possibility that Penrose's *Journal* may after all be the autobiography of a Welsh Alexander Selkirk rather than the fictitious record of a Welsh Robinson Crusoe.

The author's own claim to be 'telling the truth' is, of course, no conclusive guide to the reader in a period which routinely disguised fiction as history, even in novels dealing with captivity in Barbary which 'had achieved by Crusoe's time a European legend all its own, and was "familiar to English readers as a lively emblem of Hell" '.[11] Thus *The Voyages, Travels and Adventures of William Owen Gwin Vaughan, Esq.* claims on the title-page to include 'THE HISTORY *of his* BROTHER JONATHAN VAUGHAN, Six Years a Slave in *Tunis*. Intermix'd with the HISTORIES of *Clerimont, Maria, Eleanora*, and Others.' If the promise that the *Voyages* are 'Full of Various TURNS of FORTUNE' is contemporary shorthand for describing a plot full of fantastical twists and turns, the Preface to the Dublin edition of 1754 performs a similar function by alerting the reader to the fictional 'drapery' that clothes the essential 'truth' on which the story is 'founded':

> I Take Leave to inform the Reader, that the Facts and Incidents in the History of VAUGHAN, are founded upon strict Truth, therefore, if the very Marvellous is not to be met with, Truth is only to blame. The intercurrent HISTORIES have the same Blemish, and, therefore, perhaps, may not appear as entertaining as Productions founded on Fancy. Therefore, if you find *virtuous* and *vicious* Characters of both Sexes pencil'd here, be assured they are drawn from the Life, I have not any thing to answer for but the ill Choice of the Drapery.

In this edition, the author, W. R. Chetwood,[12] drops his anonymity and presents himself as the 'editor' of the *Voyages*, while his Dedication to the Hon. Edward FitzGerald, Knight of the Glinn, invites a humorous complicity in establishing the 'reality' of Vaughan as he introduces the Irish gentleman to the Welsh one:

> THOUGH Families and Names in different Kingdoms may be intire Strangers to each other, yet Conformity of Minds and Dispositions may

Will and Isabella rescue Sir Eustace from the lake on his uncle's estate 'but a short day's journey from *Monmouth*': frontispiece and title-page of *The Voyages, Travels and Adventures of William Owen Gwin Vaughan, Esq.*, by W. R. Chetwood, 1736

THE VOYAGES,

Travels *and* Adventures,

OF

WILLIAM OWEN GWIN VAUGHAN, Esq;

WITH THE

HISTORY *of his* BROTHER

JONATHAN VAUGHAN,

Six Years a Slave in *Tunis*.

Intermix'd with the HISTORIES of *Clerimont, Maria, Eleanora,* and Others. Full of Various TURNS of FORTUNE.

VOLUME *the* FIRST.

LONDON:

Printed for J. WATTS: And Sold by J. OSBORN, at the *Golden-Ball* in *Pater-noster-Row*.

MDCCXXXVI.

simpathize: Give me leave to assure you, Sir, that VAUGHAN is a Gentleman of an ancient Family, of strict *Honour* and *Probity*, with every manly Virtue, and therefore, I venture to introduce him to your Acquaintance . . .

Chetwood has had his admirers. Richetti gives a résumé of *The Voyages, Adventures, and Imminent Escapes of Captain Richard Falconer* (1720) as a popular work demonstrating 'how much the combination of the clichés of religious polemic and the attractions of travel literature were regarded as a profitable merger'.[13] This volume, together with *The Voyages, Travels and Adventures of William Owen Gwin Vaughan*, were two of only four books to which Henry Fielding subscribed in his lifetime.[14] (As prompter at Drury Lane, Chetwood was given a benefit performance of Fielding's *Tragedy of Tragedies* in 1732; later, he was introduced into the opening scene of Fielding's farce, *Eurydice*).[15] Sir Walter Scott, in his turn, recalled *The Voyages and Adventures of Captain Robert Boyle* (1726) with affection, describing it as one of the two books in the world he had most longed to see.[16]

The first volume of *The Voyages, Travels and Adventures of William Owen Gwin Vaughan* deals mainly with Will's relationship with his wicked stepmother, his visit to his uncle and his friendship with Isabella and her aunts. In the second volume, Will travels abroad with his tutor and, after being captured by a corsair of Tunis and rescued by Spanish coastguards, meets up with his brother Jonathan whose story is one of the inset 'histories' in Will's autobiography. Jonathan tells Will that after fighting in the Flanders campaign, he was captured by a French privateer and forced to take part in the siege of Tunis where he was taken into slavery. He resisted a master 'posses'd with the most hateful Passion Man can be guilty of' and was sold to a galley-owner. Freed at last after being taken by the Genoese, he has now been reunited with his sweetheart Fatima, whom he had met while he was in captivity. Little is made of Will's 'ancient Family' in the novel, though his uncle does tell him that 'We are originally *Welsh*: Many of our ancestors have flourish'd in the Church, as well as State, and left a sweet Scent of Virtue in their Ashes' (I, p.73), a sentiment that would have struck a cord with Penelope Aubin. Not until the end of the second volume does it become apparent that his uncle lives but a short day's journey from Monmouth, so that Will's pursuit of Isabella's captor, the villainous Sir Eustace, takes him down the River Wye from Monmouth to Chepstow (Chetwood provides brief footnotes on both towns). Isabella is found, safe and well, in 'Redcliff-street', Bristol. Despite this chase down the Wye, there seems little reason for Chetwood's choice of an extravagantly Welsh name for his title-page. If there is any 'truth' in this Welshman's autobiography, it is well hidden under ample folds of drapery.

Like Chetwood's novel, *A Genuine Account of the Life and Transactions of Howell ap David Price, Gentleman of Wales* exploits the popularity of travellers' tales set in north Africa. The *Genuine Account* ('Written by HIMSELF') claims to be 'A SERIES of most remarkable Occurrences during his Seven Years Travels Abroad; Five of which were spent with a Lady he had released from Slavery.' Howell's adventures abroad occupy a substantial part of his autobiography and are even more fantastic than those related by Chetwood. Soon after Howell joins the merchant navy, his ship is taken by a French privateer which in turn is captured by an Algerian corsair and like Jonathan he becomes a slave. He escapes with Cleone, a wealthy English widow (who has been seized by Algerian pirates after leaving Venice), and their travels take them with a caravan across the desert to Grand Cairo, with pilgrims to Mecca and with merchants from Aleppo to Aden from where they sail for home – an epic journey punctuated by a series of hair-raising misadventures and hair's-breadth escapes.

Like Chetwood's novel, however, *A Genuine Account* is not simply a travelogue. The tag 'Gentleman of Wales' on the title-page may alert the reader to the possibility that the *Genuine Account* is likely to be a satirical 'Life', a close relative of the chapbook attacks on the Welsh, and, curiously enough, Howell's adventures are indeed bracketed by an account of his family which belongs to a quite different literary genre. The intrepid traveller grows up in Llandeglai, Radnorshire, and by satirizing the genealogical obsessions and abject poverty of Howell's father, and describing his affection for his mother who comes from a family of Herefordshire shopkeepers ('and though she was so near a Borderer, my Father would often weep to think he should be the only one in his Family, who had ever crossed the ancient *British* Strain by a Foreigner' (p.3)), the author expresses once again the contempt for the Welsh that had long fuelled the hostile slapstick of the popular press. The Price family is unforgivably poor, producing little corn and keeping a few sheep and goats which provide them with coarse and clumsy clothing and meat only when an old ewe is past bearing, 'but yet (as if it was the only Necessity in Life) we were to regale upon the empty, misapplied Sound of our Gentility' (p.5). The family tree, derided here as in other contemporary satires of the Welsh, is the symbol of the Prices' gentility. It is an imposing document, composed of three parts, from Noah to Cadwallader to Howell himself – but the latter makes his mother laugh when he observes that 'upon Sight of the great *Cadwallader* in the Root, it seemed to be a well established Plant; but looking upwards, methought I seemed to stand but like an hungry Owl upon one of the Top Branches' (p.7).

The later chapters of the novel again target the poverty of the Welsh, together with their execrable language and ludicrous pretensions to gentility. When Howell returns from his travels, he visits the family seat, 'a small Hovel, covered with Thatch, coated with Lome, and for the most part glazed with Paper' (pp.257–8). Enriched by his marriage to Cleone, he travels in a coach and six with four liveried servants in attendance. Scorning the family offering of milk, cheese, brown bread and 'a brave Parcel of Offals', Howell supplies ham, fowls, sirloin, wine, ale and a basket of bread – a feast which attracts a multitude of visitors speaking 'half *Welch*, half *English*, and some shewing out in a Mongrel Tongue between both' (p.265). Howell's elder brother, ridiculed as a Welsh bumpkin, is taken to London to be cured of his country habits:

> I'll warrant *Rice,* you had rather be a Merchant of *London,* than a Gentleman of *Wales,* now. You are so far in the right, Brother, replied he, that to me, the Merchant of *London* seems the Gentleman, while the Gentleman of *Wales* is a Beggar. (p.287)

It is this dichotomy between the London merchant and the Welsh gentleman that reveals the ideology of the *Genuine Account*. Richetti suggests how travel literature reflected the concerns of the emerging modern world:

> In the broad sense, that is, the form and spirit of the travel book embodied the cultural values and assumptions summed up in such words as movement, variety, change, and originality, as opposed to the opposing conservative religious orientation suggested by ideals such as passivity, submission to authority, permanence, self-effacement, and voluntary restriction. The travel book could easily invoke a world where joyful and profitable movement was potentially unlimited; where there were, ideally, no boundaries; where there were many human and natural dangers, but where great rewards might be earned by those who moved with skill and speed.[17]

Richetti points out how, after his profitable first voyage to Africa, Robinson Crusoe's captivity in Barbary, a symbolic transformation from merchant to slave, is 'a compensation, in mythical terms, for the triumphant secular enterprise of commercial travelling on the high seas and into exotic places'.[18] In the *Genuine Account*, Howell undergoes a series of transformations, from commercial traveller in the merchant navy to Barbary slave and African traveller and ultimately City merchant. A poor Welsh gentleman has no argument to counter the spirit of the age. Ten years later, Howell's brother Rice, the former country bumpkin, returns to Wales in *his* coach and persuades his parents to move to London. His father demurs: 'Is the Name to be lost in this Country, no Trace, no Remains of the Blood and Family of the *Prices*?' (p.301). But his English wife (from the family of shopkeepers) wins the day and like Aubin's Lluellings before them, the Prices abandon Wales.

In comparison with this bizarre yoking of chapbook and traveller's tale, *The Admirable Travels of Messieurs Thomas Jenkins and David Lowellin* is a model of restraint and verisimilitude, and by the same token it is more difficult to know 'how the book is to be read'. Mandel is confident about the reader's ability to distinguish between fiction and autobiography: 'the intention in most novels is perfectly clear: the novelist's use of autobiographical devices serves an end that is purely fictional. No one takes *Robinson Crusoe* for autobiography.'[19] Stauffer's comments on *The Admirable Travels* demonstrate, however, that it is not always easy to distinguish between the two genres. He is candid about his own difficulties ('one wonders with some trepidation how many works of fact and works of fiction are incorrectly listed in this present volume'[20]), but his enthusiasm for the memoirs of eighteenth-century travellers is essentially predicated on his belief in the authenticity of their writing:

> They tell thrilling stories; they acquaint the reader with new regions and the strange customs of foreigners who are nevertheless men; they develop, directly or indirectly, the characters and careers of the narrators; above all, they show the almost infinite capacity, resourcefulness, resilience, and indomitable courage of the human spirit in dangerous and difficult new worlds.[21]

Stauffer initially includes the author of *The Admirable Travels* in his tribute ('For sheer enthralling narratives of action, the actual accounts of their own lives by Lowellin, Drury and Benyowski cannot be surpassed by fiction'[22]), though later a note of doubt creeps in — he is clearly in two minds about the author's veracity when he suggests that *The Admirable Travels* is a *Captain Singleton* yarn ('If we can believe Lowellin (and the comical misprints and Malapropisms seem genuine enough)'[23]). He also admits that good as is Lowellin's story, 'it is surpassed by one less questionably authentic adventure in Africa [Drury's *Pleasant and Surprising Adventures*], which forms one of the best travel narratives that has ever been written.'[24] Stauffer makes no reference to the various editions of *The Admirable Travels* though these cast further doubt on its status as genuine autobiography. The title-page of the 1783 edition claims that, during the course of his travels through unknown tracts of Africa, Lowellin 'lived five Years on an uninhabited Spot; and, having sustained many dangerous Attacks from wild Beasts and Savages, returned safe to London, in September, 1781, after having been eleven Years in those extensive regions.' To further authenticate the account, the title-page claims that the book has been printed from the original manuscript, with the author's consent, for the benefit of Robert Barker, an unfortunate blind man. Yet in the edition printed by A. Swindells in about 1800, Lowellin is said to have spent eight years in an uninhabited spot and returned to London in September 1784 after fourteen years in those extensive regions; no reference is made either to the original manuscript or to Robert Barker.

Whether or not *The Admirable Travels* is purely or partly fictitious, the inclusion of dates, place names and circumstantial details suggests authentic autobiography, in the style of Defoe. It opens with a brief but convincing sketch of Lowellin's Welsh background, quite unlike the crude satire of Howell ap David Price's family:

> I, DAVID LOWELLIN, was born near the spot where the castle of Methravill once stood, in the county of Montgomery, anno 1726. I removed thence, with my parents, to an hereditary estate of their own, situate between Aberistwith and Cardigan, on the sea-coast, when about three years old; and, having a full prospect of the vessels passing up and down the channel from my father's door, my early attention was from time to time engrossed by, and frequent enquiries were made concerning, them . . . (p.5)

Lowellin's parents allow him to take a trip to Liverpool, Dublin, Cork and Bristol with Captain Jones and his son, Griffith, but, after three months away, he still wants to go to sea. In May 1742, the family return to Montgomeryshire but David steals £120 from his father's scrutoire, arrives in Landerinye before daylight, gets a passage to Worcester on a timber barge and from thence to Bristol on a trow belonging to Broadstey. He sails to Antigua, Virginia (where he is apprenticed to a shoemaker) and the West Indies. Later, after inheriting the family fortune, he sails from Cardigan to London in Griffith Jones's sloop, meets a fellow Welshman, Thomas Jenkins, and loses £4,000 in reckless gambling. He goes to sea again, serving in the Royal Navy from 1757 to the end of the war. In February 1770 he joins a Danish ship bound for the East Indies and meets up again with Thomas Jenkins When Lowellin and Jenkins go aboard a bark whose crew seems to have been wiped out by the plague, the ship is struck by lightning and they drift helplessly on to the African coast. They are taken prisoner by 'some hundreds of Blacks, or Negroes, with short woolly hair, all well armed with bows, arrows, and lances' and delivered to their ruler, 'mild, humane, and gentle, to the highest degree, using us more like companions than slaves' (pp.20–1). With two thousand in the company, they travel east for four hundred miles to the capital; they proceed alone, covering over a thousand miles in a north-easterly direction. Later they give up their plan of getting to Ethiopia and turn westward, but are defeated by the desert where Jenkins eventually dies on 17 January 1775. Lowellin survives alone on the edge of the desert for four years, discovering gold and diamonds in the stream beds nearby. He is rescued at last by five well-dressed gentlemen who take him blindfolded to an utopian city consisting of ninety-six octagonal buildings built in a circle twenty miles in diameter with twenty-four capital streets running from its centre, the image of the sun on top of each. Eventually he escapes from the sacred city and reaches Grand Cairo on 10 May 1780. From thence he travels home, reaching Dover on 13 September 1781. Or so he says.

Without some kind of external evidence, it is impossible to decide in the case of *The Admirable Travels* whether one is reading a total fabrication from start to finish, or whether the text provides some 'genuine' insight into the life and adventures of an eighteenth-century Welshman. *The Journal of Llewellin Penrose* is even more difficult to 'read' since the search for its true author raises questions about the provenance of the text itself, given the potential existence of at least four manuscript versions of the *Journal* (two of them probably fictitious, two still extant): 1. the original journal, said to have been written by

THE JOURNAL

OF

LLEWELLIN PENROSE,

A

SEAMAN.

A NEW EDITION.

LONDON:
PRINTED FOR TAYLOR AND HESSEY,
93, FLEET-STREET,
AND 13, WATERLOO-PLACE, PALL-MALL.
MDCCCXXV.

Penrose drifts towards the coast of South America: title-page of *The Journal of Llewellin Penrose, a Seaman*, by William Williams, illustrated by Edward Bird, 1825

Penrose during his twenty-six-year sojourn on the South American coast, with a brief continuation by his son; 2. the copy of Penrose's journal said to have been made in Charlestown by John Waters and sent to England by Paul Taylor; 3. the manuscript now deposited in the Lilly Library, Indiana, given to Thomas Eagles by William Williams; 4. the bowdlerized copy of Williams's manuscript made by Thomas Eagles after Williams's death, with illustrations by Nicholas Pocock and Edward Bird (also deposited in the Lilly Library). Seven different writers (the first four probably fictitious) are said or known to have had a hand in producing the *Journal* – Llewellin Penrose and his son, Owen (diarists), John Waters (copyist), Paul Taylor (writer of the covering letter sent to London with the copied manuscript), William Williams (probable author), Thomas and John Eagles (early editors) and finally D. H. Dickason (twentieth-century editor). The *Journal* should almost certainly be read as a novel by William Williams, based in all probability on his own adventures as a young man, but perhaps Llewellin Penrose ought not be condemned to perpetual obscurity as a fictional character in his own autobiography without at least some examination of the available evidence.

When *The Journal of Llewellin Penrose* was first published in 1815, it was dedicated to the historical painter Benjamin West[25] by its editor, the Revd John Eagles.[26] The prefatory 'Advertisement' explained that the author was one 'Williams' – his name was nowhere given in full and did not appear at all on the title-page. Eagles, a Bristol clergyman, had a colourful tale to tell about Williams – so colourful that some of his early readers believed that it was a complete fabrication. In an essay written forty years later, Eagles admitted that it had been generally supposed that he himself was the author of the *Journal*:

> Indeed I know that, though I have so distinctly asserted, and now most distinctly assert the contrary, this work, 'Penrose's Journal,' has been given to me as its author; and that which I am about to narrate has been treated as a fiction, allowable in novel-making, and as patent an invention as a preface to the *Travels of Lemuel Gulliver*, or any of the numerous literary impositions which usually amuse the world.[27]

By conflating Eagles's two accounts, which rely on Benjamin West's testimony for much of their biographical detail, it is possible to give an outline of Williams's life, with amendments based on other sources, notably the extensive researches of D. H. Dickason.[28] Although

Benjamin West claimed that William Williams was born in Wales,[29] he was almost certainly born in Bristol in 1727 into a family of Welsh extraction.[30] There he 'imbibed' a love of painting but went to sea as a boy, sailing to Virginia on a ship commanded by Captain Hunter. Hunter later confirmed that some time after absconding from his ship, Williams was shipwrecked in the Caribbean and lived among Indians on the coast of South America for some years.[31] He was about twenty years old and a painter of 'cattle pieces' when the nine-year-old Benjamin West first met him in Philadelphia.[32] West remembered Williams as an excellent actor, often recounting his adventures among the Indians, which (he was to testify later) were exactly the same as those described in the *Journal*. West encountered Williams many years later when he returned to England and sat for a figure in *The Battle of La Hogue*.[33] Williams attempted to set up in business in Bristol but he was destitute when he approached Thomas Eagles,[34] a merchant of that city, and begged him for a pass to St Peter's Hospital.[35] Eagles relieved his immediate needs and supported him until he was found a place in the Merchants' and Sailors' Almshouse, probably in 1786.[36] Here Williams painted a portrait of himself wearing his almshouse dress of green cloak and red velvet cap,[37] and here he died on 27 April 1791 and was buried in the churchyard of St Augustine-the-Less on College Green.[38] He left all his possessions to his benefactor; according to Eagles, his father inherited the manuscript of the *Journal*, though it is not referred to by name in either of the wills Williams wrote while he was in the almshouse.[39]

John Eagles describes how the *Journal* was read with delight by every member of the Eagles family; he recalls that at the end of his school holidays he contrived to miss the coach so that he could finish reading the manuscript. Thomas Eagles made a copy in his own hand and had it bound with blanks for illustration by the Bristol marine artists, Nicholas Pocock and Edward Bird.[40] Dickason has amply demonstrated in *Mr. Penrose* how Thomas Eagles bowdlerized the original manuscript, destroying the vigour, colour and directness of the original. By what appears to have been a remarkable coincidence, Benjamin West happened to glance at the copied manuscript while calling on Thomas Eagles at his London lodgings on 10 July 1805 and was convinced that he recognized the author. West called again on 13 July and it is from the memorandum made by Thomas Eagles of these two visits, together with the letter West wrote on 10 October 1810, that John Eagles gleaned most of his own knowledge of Williams.

William Williams wearing the green cloak and red cap of the Merchants' and Sailors' Almshouse, Bristol: self-portrait

When his father died in 1812, Eagles inherited both manuscripts of the *Journal* and he was paid a handsome two hundred guineas when the bowdlerized version was published in 1815. The unexpurgated *Journal* did not appear in print until Dickason's edition of 1969. While scholarly opinion insists that the *Journal* is a fiction,[41] there remains the possibility that the manuscript which William Williams bequeathed to Thomas Eagles was not after all a novel based on his own adventures but a genuine diary originally penned by one Llewellin Penrose. At the beginning of the *Journal*, it is established that Penrose is a Welshman:

> LLEWELLIN PENROSE is my name; I was born near Caerphilly in Glamorganshire, in the month of May *anno dom.* 1725. My father, who was a Sailor, was cast away in a Ship belonging to the City of Bristol called the *Union* Frigate, commanded by a certain Capt. Williams (who was his own countryman), in the great January storm of the Texel in Holland . . . My mother, being left a Widow, with two children, (Viz) myself and a sister five years younger, after a time married a Schoolmaster and removed with him into Worcestershire, thence into Monmouthshire, and after that into Wales. (pp. 37–8)

A search of the relevant parish registers has so far yielded no Llewellin Penrose[42] – Eagles suggests that he was named after a Philadelphia shipowner, known to Williams while he lived in America. Young Penrose (like William Williams) has some talent for drawing, but in September 1744, when his stepfather decides to place him with a lawyer, he runs away from home, accompanied by a friend, Howell Gwynn. They head for Bristol, ignoring the young man they meet at Pile who has just returned from an unsuccessful cruise and tries to dissuade them from going any further. In Bristol, Gwynn enters the White Lion and Horseshoe on the quay, a rendezvous for privateers, and goes off to Hungroad to join his ship. (It is perhaps not without significance that on 30 June 1744, the *Oracle* had reported that the *Prince Charles* under Captain Charles Gwynn had sailed from Bristol and that, among its crew of one hundred and fifty men, '130 are Antient Britons, so great is the spirit of those people against the common enemy'.[43]) Penrose meets a cousin, goes to Ireland, works his passage to London and in 1746 joins the *Harrington*, a privateer bound for Jamaica. As a castaway on the Spanish Main, he spends the next twenty-seven years among people first identified in a contemporary review of the *Journal* as the Rama Indians of Nicaragua.[44] Penrose is married twice, to women of the local Indian tribe, giving Welsh names to three of his five children – Owen ('that being the name of my father'), Morgan ('which signifies born on the coast', suggesting that the author had some knowledge of Welsh), Rees and the twins Somer (after his Dutch friend) and America (his only daughter). After Penrose makes his last entry in his journal on 30 October [1773], twenty-six years after his shipwreck, his son Owen continues the record, describing his father's death on 21 July [1774]. The journal breaks off abruptly a year later.

Appended to the *Journal* is a letter from one Paul Taylor, informing an unnamed correspondent in England that in 1776 he was mate of a brig commanded by Captain Smith; while lying at Havana, he became acquainted with the mate of a Spanish sloop, late from the Main, who asked him to take care of a bundle of papers given to him by two Indians with a good command of English. Some time later, while unemployed in Charlestown, Taylor had the manuscript copied by John Waters, who had formerly sailed with Captain Dean. Taylor is sending the copied manuscript to his correspondent as some little return for many friendly services: 'You will find when You come to Read it many curious accounts of things which I Know to be matters of fact, altho I never knew any thing of ye Man' (384). It is dated from New York, 2 May 1783.

Not for nothing did Lord Byron stay up half the night to read the *Journal*. ('I never read so much of a book at one sitting in my life . . . It has all the air of truth, and is most entertaining and interesting in every point of view.'[45]) It is indeed a compelling narrative as it moves through the three phases of Penrose's life – his boyhood, his solitary life as a castaway, and the establishment after his marriage of an extended family which becomes in effect a small commune as friendly Indians, stranded Europeans and the runaway African slave, Quameno, join the group. The narrative is enlivened by some excellent dialect: like Williams himself (as West recalled), the author of the *Journal* is clever at imitating the 'voices' of his characters. In addition, the setting of the narrative on the Moskito Coast is brilliantly realized, with minutely observed descriptions of the flora and fauna of the locality, together with lively accounts of the daily round of hunting, fishing and gathering the fruits of the earth.

Dickason's analysis of the text of the *Journal* has established that Penrose's use of place-names is meticulous to the extent that a chart might be made of his voyages before he became a castaway on the Moskito Coast: 'Obviously, Williams might have gleaned much information by poring over the nautical maps of the period, but so many casual and minutely specific references are made in the *Journal* that the reader feels himself indubitably in the presence of a firsthand report.'[46] Dickason points out Penrose's knowledge of public events of the period and his references to actual ships and their officers, and after surveying the travel literature that was available to William Williams at the period, and some of the popular fictions of the day based on actual voyages, he concludes that the *Journal* is essentially a work of imagination, based on personal experience:

> Thus *Mr. Penrose*, although it does share details concerning habitat, physical activities, and domestic equipment with other typical and popular documents of travel and adventure, both repertorial and fictional, is essentially an original, independent and creative product of the personal experiences and private imagination of William Williams.[47]

Dickason is persuaded that '*Mr. Penrose* is not a book made from other men's foot-notes, but rather is a volume deserving critical study and appreciation as an unique and original fictional narrative cast in a popular mode'.[48]

Having settled this question to his own satisfaction, Dickason barely glances at the possibility that the author of the *Journal* may have been Llewellin Penrose himself. Even John Eagles made no direct reference to Penrose when he posed the key question about the authenticity of the *Journal*:

> And what is this story? It may be asked. That is a question I doubt if I should answer. Is it true or a fiction? I can no more tell than any one else who may read it. I can only say, if not true, it is a most ingenious invention, and I should add, that many dates and events spoken of incidentally in the journal have been inquired into and examined and found correct.[49]

Yet his query is an ambiguous one. When he asks whether the *Journal* is a 'true' story, it is not clear whether he is suggesting that it may be an authentic, autobiographical record of Llewellin Penrose's sojourn on the coast of South America, or simply a fictionalized account of 'real' events in the life of William Williams. He certainly recognizes

Memorial to the Revd John Eagles, Bristol Cathedral

the possibility that as 'a most ingenious invention', the *Journal* may simply be a complete fabrication.

Since an archaeological expedition to the 'Moskito Coast' is not immediately in prospect, any consideration of the true authorship of the *Journal* has to be based on biographical evidence (still inconclusive despite West's testimony and Dickason's research on William Williams), together with the limited evidence provided by the text itself. The generic nature of the travelogue, with its careful documentation of names, places and dates, sets out to persuade the reader that we are reading an original document, and, if in Eagles's edition the elegance of the prose style scarcely suggests the immediacy and provisional nature of a genuine diary, the less polished version edited by Dickason is much more convincing as the journal of a Welsh seaman, real or imaginary. The leisurely recall of Penrose's early years as a castaway is 'explained' by the fact that by his own account he did not acquire paper and ink until the shipwreck of the *Dertroost* in the seventh year of his residence, when he was able to get a precise date from surviving members of the crew on Monday 5 August 1754. After this date (which was indeed a Monday), the act of writing becomes one of the measures of Penrose's superiority over the Indians who crowd round in fascination to watch him write but jump back in terror if he points his pen at them. Penrose is acutely aware of his own skill as an autobiographer: 'one day as I was reading it over to Somer Harry said that now he was sure I was a very cunning man for that I could make all my old words speak again quite new, and that I could make dead people talk' (p.166). He then proceeds to write up the experiences of the past six years:

> I had been for a considerable time at my Journal day by day before I could bring it down to this period of time; and as to what has preceded it has been all collected as I could best remember. But I persuade myself nothing of any note has escaped, remembrance having been carefull to retain all I thought any way worthy. (p.167)

He writes with a single purpose: that eventually his journal will be read by his own countrymen 'and Brother Tars', and with that end in view, he stresses (in an entry made during his sixteenth year in South America) his complete veracity:

> Many extraordinary things which are absolute curiosities of Nature have escaped my memory, especially such as fell under my observation

in the first years of my residence here, for want of means to record them as in those days I little expected to become master of materials for that purpose. Yet whatever came within reach of my speculation never escaped my inquisitive inclination, having from a Child ever taking much delight in prying into the works and wonders of Nature. Now what ever I have or shall advance, I declare has passed within my view; and as thousands have passed or traversed over many part of this vast continent they may confute me easily if I advance falshoods. But where could a Man, scituated as I am expect to recieve a benefit from by imposing untruths on the World? – especially as I have but a scant expectation that what I write may ever fall under the inspection of my own Nation and Brother Tars, for whose information in chief I thus amuse my time. As to the lerned, I stand not in any dread of their sensure, being a man of no Education my self, therfore beneath their scrutiny and Envy. Yet may I venture so far as to think they will not carp at what may be honestly advanced by me, who am but an Illiterate Sailor. (p.267)

Penrose does not normally write daily entries in his diary: once he has acquired pen and ink and written up his early experiences as a castaway, he writes only occasionally, and usually retrospectively, of notable events: 'Nothing happened worth my notice for some time so that I but seldom went to my book' (p.178), or 'I think it quite unnecessary to recite over all our ordinary customs as they are in general one and the same round, in order to avoid being too tedious' (p.197). His consciousness of being 'tedious', as elsewhere he is aware of the scrutiny of 'the reader', suggests perhaps a literary anxiety unlikely in 'an Illiterate Sailor'. (On the other hand, he certainly has access to literary models: in his twelfth year as a castaway he acquires a box of books from an Irish sea captain, Dennis (H)organ.) His frequent use of the past perfect can seem inappropriate in a journal, though when he shifts to the present tense within a single sentence he merely appears to have an uncertain grasp of the rules of English grammar, as likely in a Penrose as a Williams: 'And now another year had revolved since I first came on this foreign shore, but I am content' (p.197). There are, however, points in the narrative where the retrospective journal becomes a convincing present-tense diary, for instance, in his twentieth year as a castaway when he finds out that the Spanish authorities have discovered his whereabouts: 'Matters are now changed greatly; at this my Once peaceful dwelling a general confusion reigns . . .' (p.332). Significantly, he spares a thought for his journal during this anxious time:

> My Son Owen is made privy to the manner of my bestowing my Journal so that if things turn not out as I wish he may perhaps find a means one day or other to convey it into the hands of some Subject of Great Britain, to whose care I charge him to deliver it unless Providence may direct his Course that way himself. – Not that I entertain any thoughts of its material use to my fellow Mortals, But it may shew the world the manner I Spent my time in, and what became of the Schooner *Recovery* and poor Lewellin Penrose. But If Providence so order it that I remain where I am unmolested, I shall continue my narrative as long as my strength and materials last. (p.334)

The journal reverts to a present-tense diary in the final entries made by Penrose himself, when his health is failing, though it must be acknowledged that the dying man's style seems self-consciously literary, especially his last entry: 'There must be a last time for every Mortal Man . . .' (p.379). Even so, whether these entries represent a metafiction by William Williams or Llewellin Penrose's self-conscious definition of his role as a writer, 'I can no more tell than any one else who may read it', as Eagles would put it.

It is something of a paradox that one of the factors that seems particularly unlikely in a castaway's journal is the writer's sense of himself as Rousseau man, exemplifying in his simple life among the Indians of the Moskito Coast the great eighteenth-century ideal of man in harmony with nature, living contentedly among 'noble savages' in the Edenic beauty of their native land. Making no reference to the long history of the noble savage in English literature, Dickason maintains that in the *Journal*, Williams shows himself to be far ahead of his time in his themes and attitudes:

> One such fundamental focus is on the romantic ideal of the 'natural man,' the virtues of the unspoiled, uncorrupted folk culture and *mores*, and therewith the concept of the escape of a white protagonist to a pastoral utopia. When a sardonic Irish sea-captain asked Penrose how it was possible for him to live so many years 'among these dung-coloured Savages,' the castaway curtly retorted that they had indeed proved themselves to be his 'true and experienced friends'; he was so well content with his situation that he 'would not of a choice change it'; and

the 'happy state of Innocency' in which they lived more than compensated for the lack of worldly, sophisticated contacts. Here Williams (perhaps in Rousseau's train, though no evidence is extant that he had read him) antedates Freneau and Cooper in their stress on the virtues of their wilderness figures, and Melville's portrayal of his Polynesian natives before their corruption by European influence.[50]

Dickason makes no comment on the fact that while Penrose does indeed value his Indian friends for their 'innocency', his behaviour towards them nevertheless exemplifies an endemic sense of racial superiority. His benevolent rule over his little colony is absolute. From his earliest meeting with Ayasharre (Harry) and his sister Yaluta (Luta), he is determined to establish his authority:

> These poor innocent young cretures became every day more and more the delight of my mind, being always eager to obey me in all I desired or directed them to do, and I Industriously strove to gain their regard by every means I could study. Nevertheless I carried my self so as that they should regard me as a kind of superior to them. (p.88)

When three 'canoas' full of Indians arrive during the feast held to celebrate Penrose's seven years as a castaway, he deliberately arranges a tableau meant to impress the visitors with the unmistakable symbols of his role as chief in his community (his 'best attire' like the motley garments described elsewhere in the *Journal* is one of its more amusing features):

> first my Sambraro on my head with two fine Maccaw feathers stuck in it, my Tigers skin then made into a jackket the hair side out, round my waist a belt of bass rope in which hung my hatchet, at my back my bow and arrows, with a Mascheet in my hand; and in this garb I seated myself abaft, Harry and Noonawaiah as my two mates. (pp.144-5)

Penrose's high-handed disposal of the Indian girls – 'married' with little more ceremony than jumping over a broomstick (with no reference to their own tribal customs) – is predicated on a sense of their racial inferiority. This is made explicit when Owen (the son of Penrose's first marriage to Luta) falls in love with a picture of the Virgin Mary: 'to obtain the booby a White Wife as We were scituated was next to impossible and then what White Girl could be procured so indelicate as for to contaminate with an Indian?' (p.371). (Eventually Owen marries an Indian girl, Bashada, and names his firstborn Lewellin.) Such attitudes coexist in this eighteenth-century text with Penrose's undoubted kindness as a husband, his affection and courtesy towards his Indian friends, and his sympathy for the African slave, Quameno, who ends his days peacefully as a member of the miniature colony. Such attitudes might, of course, belong to William Williams on behalf of his (possibly semi-autobiographical) hero, the fictitious Llewellin Penrose – or equally to a real life Penrose, setting up his small colony in South America.

The travellers whose tales are told in the four novels reviewed in this chapter are all Welsh or of Welsh extraction. In each case, the title of the work draws attention to the nationality of the protagonists, offering the reader the adventures of William Owen Gwin Vaughan, Howell ap David Price, Thomas Jenkins, David Lowellin and Llewellin Penrose. Whether this corresponded to an eighteenth-century stereotype of the Welsh as a nation of seafarers and intrepid adventurers can only be a matter for conjecture, though young Lowellin's upbringing on the Cardiganshire coast 'having a full prospect of the vessels passing up and down the channel from my father's door' nicely catches the maritime activity of a country bound on three sides by the sea, while Llewellin Penrose and his friend Howell Gwynn provide fictitious examples of those 130 'Antient Britons' who, as a matter of historical record, set sail from Bristol on the *Prince Charles* in 1744 ('so great is the spirit of those people against the common enemy') – just as James Parry, author of *The True Anti-Pamela*, had become master-at-arms on the *Revenge* in 1742. Even Penrose, ruling his little colony of Rama Indians of Nicaragua in his 'Sambraro' and macaw feathers, might be seen as a worthy representative of those Welsh men and women who had sailed west and played their part in exploring and settling North America: the legendary Madog ab Owain Gwynedd, said to have discovered and colonized America three hundred years before Columbus and given 'the very first pre-eminence' in Hakluyt's *Principall Navigations, Voiages, and Discoveries of the English Nation* (1589);[51] Robert Mansel of Margam and Thomas Button of St Lythan's, whose attempts to find the north-west passage were commemorated in Mansel Island and New Wales in Hudson's Bay; Robert Vaughan, who attempted in vain to establish a Welsh colony in Newfoundland between 1616 and 1632;[52] then, after the Restoration, several waves of Nonconformist settlers, including Quakers from central Wales who joined the 'Holy Experiment' in Pennsylvania and the Baptists of Ilston who settled in Swanzey, Massachusetts.[53] As Gwyn A.Williams puts it, 'Welshmen were everywhere in the New World, from the West Indies to furthest Canada.'[54]

While the present chapter may point in this way to fictional examples of stereotypical Welsh seafarers and settlers, it has been more immediately concerned with establishing questions of authorship, in order to add a name or two to the tally of Welsh writers of fiction and autobiography in the eighteenth century. On balance, it seems unlikely that in *The Admirable Travels*, David Lowellin was telling his own story of African adventure. Almost certainly, the same must be said of *The Journal of Llewellin Penrose*, though in this case the question of authorship is of more moment, since it is a work of considerable quality. If, as argued above, the *Journal* cannot after all be claimed as the diary of one Llewellin Penrose, born and bred in Caerffili, a bibliographer of eighteenth-century fictions of Wales has probably to settle for a novel written by William Williams, a Bristolian 'of immediate Welsh extraction'. Common sense suggests that Llewellin Penrose is a literary creation, not unrelated to those other intrepid Welsh adventurers of eighteenth-century fiction, William Owen Gwin Vaughan, Howell ap David Price and Messieurs Thomas Jenkins and David Lowellin. But, in the unlikely event that Llewellin Penrose has in fact suffered the fate of Robert Drury (now happily identified as the author of his own story), it may be prudent to recall the opening words of the journal so readily attributed to William Williams:

> If ever the following lines should reach my dear country the Reader is not to expect to meet with any persuasive Arguments to enforce belief or language to adorn the story, as the Author never recived more learning than what a common country school affords. (p.37)

4

A revenge tragedy

THE TRUE ANTI-PAMELA BY JAMES PARRY

The True Anti-Pamela, or, Memoirs of Mr. James Parry, Late Organist of Ross in Herefordshire. In which are inserted, His Amours with the Celebrated Miss – of Monmouthshire (1741)[1] suggests a brisk riposte to Richardson's novel. Faster on the draw than Fielding in *Shamela* (1742) or *Joseph Andrews* (1742) and pre-empting Eliza Haywood in *Anti-Pamela, or, Feign'd Innocence Detected* (1742),[2] Parry was quick to profit from the success of *Pamela* (1740–1). The epithet 'True', however, together with the subtitle, *Memoirs of Mr. James Parry*, claims autobiographical status for the text and it is not difficult to establish that certain events in the *Memoirs* are authenticated by other historical records. Nevertheless, as an autobiography transparently masquerading as a novel for commercial gain, the text invites the kind of critical approach outlined by James Olney:

> Did he, for whatever reason, deliberately and consciously alter details in that body of historical facts that lay there in a clear and objective light to be revered accurately by the author's memory and to be transmitted faithfully to the reader as the *bios* [the 'life'] of the autobiography? What Gusdorf and others argued, however, was that the *autos* [the 'self'] has its reasons and its truth (which, in terms of historical fact, may well be false) that neither reason nor a simple historical view of *bios* can ever know.[3]

Parry's autobiography poses a problem of interpretation that is different in kind from the question of authenticity raised by the texts attributed to Owen Gwin Vaughan, Howell ap David Price and David Lowellin. In *The True Anti-Pamela*, the fundamental issue that has dominated recent theoretic and critical approaches to autobiography – the nature of autobiographical truth – becomes significant in an unusually provocative way. If it is admitted that is difficult (or impossible) for the reader to know whether (or how often) Parry tells lies, this cannot be glossed over in the single-minded pursuit of autobiographical truth which is said, in Gusdorf's terms, to be somehow different from (or 'beyond') literal truth:

> The significance of autobiography should . . . be sought beyond truth and falsity, as those are conceived by simple common sense. It is unquestionably a document about a life, and the historian has a perfect right to check out its testimony and verify its accuracy. But it is also a work of art, and the literary devotee, for his part, will be aware of its stylistic harmony and the beauty of its images.[4]

Gusdorf explains that beyond the historian's task of checking the accuracy of the narrative and the critic's task of demonstrating its literary value lies the task of attempting 'to draw out its innermost, private significance by viewing it as a symbol, as it were, or the parable of a consciousness in quest of its own truth.'[5] Such an approach certainly has positive results when applied to Parry's text: here, the *autos* certainly has its reasons – a castration complex originating not in the Freudian darkness of early infancy but in a commercial proposition put to a choirboy with an outstandingly beautiful voice. However, the task of checking its testimony and verifying its accuracy is also of the utmost importance. Leigh Gilmore parodies the manner in which a critic like Philippe Lejeune might 'police' an autobiographical text, authorizing

> a mobile readership of detectives who concern themselves with verifying the facts. One imagines them running credit checks rather than knocking on doors and demanding documentation, gathering and generating more paper as they track the facts to the truth. What do these inquiring minds most want to know? What really happened.[6]

Nevertheless, if Parry's autobiography is not policed in this way, his Parthenissa (unlike Pamela) does not remain simply a fictitious character inscribed in the text: in effect, the 'real' historical Mary Powell of the Great House, Llantilio Crossenny (her oval memorial tablet is still there for all to see in the parish church), is still held to be guilty of lasciviousness and breach of promise.[7] This runs counter, of course, to the idea that the death of the author implies the death

Frontispiece and title-page of *The True Anti-Pamela, or, Memoirs of Mr. James Parry*, 1741

THE TRUE ANTI-PAMELA:

MEMOIRS

OF

Mr. James Parry,

Late ORGANIST of *Rofs* in *Herefordfhire*.

In which are inferted,

His AMOURS with the Celebrated Mifs P——— of *Monmouthfhire*.

WRITTEN BY HIMSELF.

In Two PARTS Compleat.

PART I. MEMOIRS of his LIFE and AMOURS.
PART II. Genuine LETTERS of *Love* and *Gallantry*.

> *Beware the dangerous Beauty of the Wanton;*
> *Shun their Enticements; Ruin, like a Vulture,*
> *Waits on their Conquefts: Falfhood to.'s their Bufinefs;*
> *They put falfe Beauty off to all the World;*
> *Ufe falfe Endearments to the Fools that love them:*
> *And when they marry, to their filly Hushands*
> *They bring falfe Virtue, broken Fame and Fortune.*
>   OTWAY.

LONDON,
Printed for the AUTHOR, and fold by the Bookfellers in Town and Country. 1741.

of the autobiographer: 'The self, then, is a fiction and so is the life, and behind the text of an autobiography lies the text of an "autobiography": all that is left are characters on a page, and they too can be "deconstructed" to demonstrate the shadowiness of even their existence.'[8] According to this view, Parry's memoir ensures that both he and Mary Powell exist only in the shadowlands of a deconstructed autobiographical text – and are certainly not to be confused with the 'real' Parry ('buried in the sea manner' off the Canaries) or the 'real' Mary Powell (come to dust in the family vault at Llantilio).

Despite its mischievous title, *The True Anti-Pamela* is not (or not primarily) a fiction. In his Dedication of the book to 'Dr Galen', identified in the Beinecke Library copy as Mr Rogers of Ross, Parry's insistence on his truthfulness may be indistinguishable from similar claims by Chetwood and company: 'As for fine Language or Wit, it must not be expected from me, both for my Want of Capacity and Education; but you will peruse in these Memoirs *Truth*, and that without Disguise.' But, for Parry, there was genuinely much at stake. As one who had already stood in the dock and gone to jail for intemperately storming the Powell household, he was passionately determined to persuade his readers that in *The True Anti-Pamela* he was quite literally telling the truth, the whole truth and nothing but the truth. In Parry's case, any drapery he cared to arrange over his relationship to Mary Powell thus scarcely counts as 'fiction'. Unlike William Williams who (mysteriously) had the right to utilize or vandalize his own experience to produce a novel which 'pretends' to be autobiography, James Parry had no right – legally or morally – to tell lies about Mary Powell. Autobiography must not be mistaken for fiction – or vice versa: 'It makes a difference in terms of how the book is to be read.'[9]

Parry states his purpose in publishing his book by contrasting Richardson's heroine with his own Parthenissa:

> If *Pamela* is a virtuous Character, I think *Anti Pamela* (alias *Parthenissa*) the Reverse. For *Pamela*, a poor innocent Virgin, withstood all the Attacks of a Person of Fortune; the Reverse, *Anti-Pamela*, is rich, and kept me for her Pleasure several Years, still leading me on with the Thoughts of marrying me, till I was almost ruined, and then she jilted me. (p.v)

If the link with *Pamela* is ludicrous (especially the idea of the self-confessed womanizer, Parry, in the role of 'a poor innocent Virgin'), there is no mistaking the avowed intention of the author: this is the testimony of a man who claims that he has been the victim of a breach of promise. He goes on to make it clear that he will not be deflected from his purpose by threats of prosecution and he rejects the claim that the letters published with the memoir are counterfeit. He insists that he would have printed the memoir sooner, 'but my Friends might have looked upon it as wrote out of Revenge, for being disappointed, which I do assure you it was not' (p.v). Here, at least, he can be detected in a falsehood. If there is one emotion that colours *The True Anti-Pamela* — even more than lust or personal vanity — it is revenge.

It is possible to 'verify the accuracy' of *The True Anti-Pamela* on a number of occasions where historical records exist of James Parry's activities, though predictably enough the available documentation throws little light on the intimacies of his relationship to Mary Powell. The existence of historical records can indeed have a distorting effect on a critical reading of the text: if it can be 'proved' that he appeared, say, in a court of law on the date he said that he did, it is tempting to read the whole record, including private meetings with Mary Powell, as if it is historically accurate in every detail. Similarly, it is possible to consider *The True Anti-Pamela* as at least a literary artefact if not a work of art. But when one considers, in Gusdorf's terms, making an attempt to see Parry's autobiography as a 'parable of consciousness in quest of its own truth', one comes up against the limitations of what one can only describe as Parry's sense of himself. This is partly a matter of history — Rousseau's *Confessions* had still to be written and the Romantic sense of the self was as yet unborn. It is also partly a matter of the man himself. As Roy Pascal points out,

> The value of an autobiography depends ultimately on the quality of spirit of the writer. I do not mean, in a simple sense, the quality of truthfulness . . . I mean a capacity which differs according to the nature of the personality and life, and which succeeds in creating in us the consciousness of the driving force of this life, what Montaigne calls a man's 'master form'.[10]

The arrogance of judging both the autobiography and the man in such terms has been clearly recognized,[11] yet the temptation to judge

Parry as the embodiment of a chapbook Welshman, a rogue and (probably) a thief, is difficult to withstand. As W. J. T. Collins put it so memorably, 'The coarseness of the *Memoirs* is really appalling, almost incredible – but they were coarse times, and Parry was a cad with a vile mind, bent on revenge.'[12]

However inappropriate such moral judgments may be, any consideration of Parry's truthfulness has to take account of Mary Powell – not only as a 'character' inscribed in the text but as a real person who would have been incalculably harmed by its publication. A critique of *The True Anti-Pamela* may quite properly attempt to identify the parable by which Parry expresses the 'truth' about himself, independently of the literal accuracy or otherwise of what he has to say. But it remains the case that if indeed Parry told lies, if he invented an affair with Mary Powell (or elaborated on it), if he counterfeited (or tampered with) the correspondence said to have passed between them, this cannot be dismissed as a mere matter of literary inventiveness. Conversely, even if Parry is in fact telling the strict truth about their relationship, one cannot ignore the fact that he clearly intended using his autobiography as an explosive device to destroy Mary Powell. In either case, he is revealed as 'a cad'.

By his own account, James Parry wrote the first version of his memoirs while languishing in Monmouth gaol in 1736. Beginning with the day of his birth, 'I wrote every minute Action that I had been concern'd in, till I was 15 Years old; and if it had been finished, it would have been a great deal more tedious than this Book is' (p.275). He had completed thirty-nine sheets when the gaoler's wife destroyed the manuscript, fearing that she might make a personal appearance in its pages – and thus at a stroke deprived posterity of an eighteenth-century 'Welsh childhood'. The published version of *The True Anti-Pamela* begins with a relatively brief account of Parry's boyhood and, while this may appear to have little connection with his later 'Amours', it is possible to trace in these early pages a paradigm of the tale he has to tell about his dealings with Mary Powell.

James Parry states that he was born in Carmarthen on Thursday 20 March 1712, the son of 'a Hair-Merchant'. As he had a fine voice, he entertained a number of gentlemen in the locality, including Sir Richard Steele (who, in Swift's immortal lines, 'From Perils of a Hundred Jayls, / Withdrew to starve, and die in Wales'[13]), and sang with the daughters of Dr Smallbroke, Bishop of St

David's.[14] At twelve years of age he was bound apprentice to Nathaniel Priest,[15] organist of Bristol Cathedral. Known as 'the Welch boy', he drew people from all over the city to hear him sing and was much in demand at concerts in Bath. Parry claims, however, that Priest appropriated his earnings, refused to teach him to play the harpsichord and generally neglected his welfare. Parry also claims that his master ('Knowing my Voice to be so good, and having some Years to serve him') advised him to be castrated; he names both the anatomist, Dr Rousse, and the surgeon, Mr Sam Pye, who were prepared to perform the operation 'with the utmost Safety and Secrecy'. He was deflected from this course of action by a young lady of seventeen who 'gave me such strong Reasons for not suffering myself to be made an Eunuch, as dissuaded me entirely from it'.

The young lady in question was presumably Winifred Doning (D–n–g in the text) who had taken a great fancy to 'the dear little *Welch* Boy'; her family, owners of the Purton Ferry (P–t–n in the text) across the Severn estuary, had taken lodgings on College Green near the Cathedral.[16] In thus establishing his attractiveness to women and drawing attention to his virility, Parry provides a prologue to his later 'Amours'. He also demonstrates that thirst for revenge that would later impel him to wreak terrible vengeance on Mary Powell. In this early episode, his victim is Nathaniel Priest. An advertisement in *Farley's Bristol Newspaper* (Saturday 25 February 1727)[17] represents the point at which James Parry, the character inscribed in the autobiographical text, enters the historical record:

> WHEREAS James Parry, a Native of Caermarthen, between 14 and 15 Years of Age, and a Chorister or Singing-Boy in the Cathedral Church of Bristol, did, on Sunday the 19th of this Instant, run away from his Master, Mr. Nathaniel Priest, Organist of the aforesaid Church, and hath not since been heard of: These are therefore to caution, or forewarn all Persons from harbouring or entertaining the said James Parry, forasmuch as he is an Apprentice to the said Mr. Priest, who hereby declares, that he will prosecute such Person or Persons, to the utmost Rigour of the Law: But if any one will discover the said Parry, so that he may be brought again to his Master's aforesaid, near the College-Green, he shall be well rewarded for his Pains. N.B. The said Parry is a thick well-set Lad, speaks very fast and shrill, has a Wart on one side of his Nose, wears a Peruke,

and when he went from his Master had on a light Drab Coat, with little Sleeves, and a blue Shagg great Coat.

Parry is silent about this episode but his own record shows that later that same year, he absconded again. (This is to assume that there were *two* episodes; perhaps he simply got the date wrong.) He might have attributed his decision to go to America with the Donings to a boyish sense of adventure or to undying love for Winifred; instead, he explains his defection as a means of paying out Priest, who 'brought no Thought into my Mind but that of Revenge' (p.19). Claiming that he walked out of the cathedral on 11 November 1727, he points out that 'Putting me in the news-papers would have been of no manner of signification' (p.27), though he includes details appropriate to a press report, explaining that he was wearing 'a fustian frock with black velvet sleeves, and a white waistcoat, and nothing else but what I usually wore' (p.21). He joined the Donings aboard the *Two Friends* – a party which included Mrs Doning, Winifred, and two of her brothers – and sailed for America. But his revenge was short-lived: at the request of the dean of Bristol, the Secretary of War sent orders to the governor of South Carolina to return the boy to England. On 22 February 1728 he was put on board the *Old Carolina* and restored to his master – who immediately released him from his apprenticeship as his voice had broken.

Parry survived by performing with the Bath Company of Comedians. Characteristically, he claims that he taught them the music of *The Beggar's Opera* ('they had the particular advantage of having Mr. *John Gay*, the Author, to teach them the action') while omitting to mention that most of their performances took place in a fairground booth.[18] He took organ lessons from Mr Swarbrick at Hereford, sang in Shrewsbury as Signor Perini and on 12 December 1729 was elected organist at the parish church of Ross-on-Wye. On 1 May 1730 he began giving music lessons to Mary Powell.

James Parry's record of his affair with Mary Powell is highly circumstantial, providing a carefully dated account of his comings and goings at her mother's house in Ross-on-Wye and her half-brother's house in Llantilio Crossenny, a village half way between Monmouth and Abergavenny. His total recall of the trivia of daily life, with conversations recorded verbatim, suggests several possibilities: that he had an unusually retentive memory, that he was able to refer to an exceptionally detailed diary, or that he was not averse to inventing some of the events of this period of his life. He also prints fifty-eight letters, the majority said to have been written to or received from Mary Powell; he claims that some were written 'in Characters', some backwards, some in lemon juice and some in urine. He also makes the extraordinary claim that he kept copies of every letter he wrote to Mary Powell and steadfastly denies that he was capable of counterfeiting her handwriting.

While one would accept Mandel's careful distinction between autobiography and fiction,[19] there is much to admire in Parry's narrative style: his story 'reads' like a novel. It is carefully paced (or plotted): the young music teacher grows fonder of his pupil over the course of four years, thus carefully establishing the fact that he can scarcely be accused of being an over-eager fortune-hunter. But there are also 'peaks' in the narrative, the first occurring on Tuesday 7 March 1734, when the pair go through a symbolic marriage ceremony – an account which also provides evidence, in a peculiarly colourful way, of Parry's contention that Mary Powell was guilty of breach of promise. The ceremony takes place after Mrs Powell has gone to church and the servant girl has been sent out for a pennyworth of Scotch snuff:

> I immediately lock'd the Street Door, went to the Kitchen, where Miss was sitting by the Fire-side; I took her by the Hand, and led her into the Parlour. *Dear Miss*, said I, embracing her, *now is the time to make your Yesterday's promise good; nay, I now will be so free as to insist upon it.* She would have deferr'd it, but I was too much in Love to be put off any longer, and insisted upon the Performance of her Promise at that very Time; upon which, she ran up Stairs, and brought down a very remarkable Ring, (it had been formerly lost by [her] Mother, for seven Years, and upwards, and afterwards was found in a Dunghill) with which we married each other, reading over the Ceremony, Word for Word, as it is in the Common-Prayer-Book. I need not tell the Reader what happen'd after the marriage-Ceremony between us; but before the old Lady, together with the Girl, return'd, I possess'd all that my Soul could wish. (pp.98–9)

It is impossible to know whether this episode is fact or fiction but the detail of the wedding ring retrieved from the dunghill, whether true or false, points to the irresistible urge of the storyteller to embellish his text with the telling comic detail. Throughout *The*

True Anti-Pamela there is a sense that Parry the writer positively enjoys the business of creating a humorous narrative – in counterpoint to the deadly serious business of destroying Mary Powell's reputation. Thus his attempt, a year later, to arrange a secret marriage at Dingestow is described with a number of amusing details. He is entrusted with eleven of Mary's rings so that he can have a wedding ring (marked J.P.M.) made by Mr Price, a goldsmith in Gloucester. He then makes arrangements for the wedding ('you shall be married in a masque'), to be carried out by the Revd Mr Davis of Bryngwyn. When Mary fails to keep her appointment with destiny on Monday 30 June 1735, her excuse has at least the virtue of novelty:

> 'For God's sake, my Dear, *said she,* don't put yourself in a Passion, before you hear what I've to say for myself: The greatest Part of our Hounds were bit by a mad Dog and Bitch; *James* and *Coone,* the Huntsman, with *Jacob George,* the Gardener, agreed last Night (unknown to me) to take the Pack this morning, and dip them in the Salt Water. They will be at Home to Night: and I do assure you if there had been any Body at Home to ride out with me, nothing should have prevented my coming; so that, I hope, you will not be angry with me. I am satisfied you know very well, that I never did, nor could ride out alone.' 'When will you come then, my Dearest?' *said I,* She replied, 'To-morrow, if I am alive.' (p.153)

On the following day there is more comic business as Parry grows tired of waiting for his bride and rides over to the Great House to fetch her (he accept a glass of Lisbon wine but refuses an invitation to 'dine upon a Roasted Pig'), managing to miss Mary who has already set out for Dingestow, walking very slowly and pretending to be on her way to collect the rent from a tenant 'at the *Parloo*'. Her immediate excuse for not marrying on this occasion is her fear that her brother would shoot them both ('I think that is reason enough, *says Miss*') – but her later explanation has potentially more sinister implications: after leaving for Dingestow, 'I found the F – s [Fluxes] coming upon me, and then I was sure of not being with Child' (p.164). In a text dedicated to destroying Mary Powell's reputation, it suits Parry's purpose admirably to suggest (truthfully or otherwise) that Mary Powell had left him standing at the altar – and that she was prepared to admit that she might have been pregnant.

Parry claims that three months later, on 8 October 1735, Mrs Powell caught them 'in an indecent Posture' at the bottom of the great staircase in the Great House and that this incident in effect brought to an end his relationship with Mary Powell. But even here there is a comic note as he provides a footnote on the 'trowzers' of the day (worn over the coat and breeches to keep 'those that ride post down into the North' warm and clean), in order to explain his disarray as he pushes Mary up the great staircase and slips down the garden stairs 'with my Trowzers at my Heels'. He sees Mrs Powell look pale, confused and out of temper: 'So, thinks I, I have done my Jobb here, and I would that the Devil had had the Trowzers, before I had seen them: For I was certain that my Trowzers were the strongest Evidence against me' (p.189).

Parry was subsequently denied access to Mary Powell and gossip began to circulate that she was about to wed her cousin, Dicky Jeffries.[20] At Monmouth on 22 February 1736, Parry 'drank more Negus than I could well bear' and there followed an incident which is a matter of historical record as well as the subject of a comic narrative in *The True Anti-Pamela*. The process book for the Court of Quarter Sessions in Monmouthshire records that at Chepstow on 14 July 1736 James Parry, late of Ross in the County of Hereford, was 'Indicted for entering the Dwelling House of Mathew Powell Esq. at Llandilo and disturbing the family and putting them in fear of their Lives and for assaulting Jane the Wife of Ambrose Greyswood'. At Caerleon on 6 October 1736 he was fined one shilling.[21] In his memoirs, Parry describes how Ambrose Greyswood, the innkeeper at the Ostrey in Llantilio Crossenny, refused to serve him and pushed him down the steps, claiming that he was carrying out Mrs Powell's orders. Parry then proceeded to the Great House, intending to ask Mrs Powell what she meant by using him in that vile manner. The innkeeper's wife, Jane Greyswood, ran across the garden to warn the household of Parry's approach and it was she who answered his knock on the door. When the servants refused to allow him to see Mrs Powell, he vowed to speak with her or else die on the spot:

Mrs. P[owell] and her Daughter were in a little Parlour, guarded by old and young J[effries], and some Men, armed with Swords and Pistols. I was going towards the Room they were in, when three or four Women, and some Ploughmen, push'd me back; and the more they disswaded me from going there, the more I was bent upon it. The Parlour Door was barricado'd, and the three stout men that guarded the Ladies were in great Eagerness for coming out to cut me in Pieces. But Mrs. P[owell] kept them in by mere Strength, notwithstanding the Strugglings of these Dunghill Heroes to the contrary . . . In the mean Time, the People in the Kitchen were stirring to push me out of the House. 'Hold d–n ye, said I, I have a Wife or something worse here, where is she' If you have a Wife here, says the House-keeper, come in a peaceable manner for her, &c. The Champions in the Parlour cried, turn him out, turn the Rascal out. Hearing Mr J[effrie]s's Voice, put me if possible, into a greater Passion than ever. I d–d them for a Pack of W–; and thought I was ill used, considering that I had enjoy'd the best of the Family with an intent to have begotten an Heir, &c. to the Estate. However I was forc'd to march out of the House, where I flatter'd myself to have spent some Part of my Life in, one Time or other. (pp.216–17)

In this instance, Parry's racy narrative, complete with comic embellishment ('Dunghill Heroes') and direct speech, is at least a version of what 'actually' happened; later, he gives his own account of the indictment at Chepstow and the hearing at Caerleon, the latter including a verbatim account of the evidence given by Jane Greyswood. It seems clear, both from the partial evidence of the process book and from Parry's own account of his appearances in court, that the charges laid against him were for forcible entry, stealing and assault.[22] Parry himself admits that his sixteen-week sojourn in Monmouth gaol in 1736 came about because he could not find bail after his appearances at Newport Quarter Sessions in May and Chepstow in July. Fornication and breach of promise had no part to play in the proceedings, though Parry claims that he blurted out scurrilous accusations against his former pupil while giving evidence in court.[23] Thus, even where the historical record intersects with the autobiographical account, Parry's claims about his relationship with Mary Powell remain a matter of his own testimony alone.

Early in 1737, a few months after his court appearance in Caerleon, Parry wrote his memoirs; the additions he makes to the narrative after that date are sketchy and his comments on Mary Powell's sexual appetite more scurrilous. Even so, the brief account he gives of his movements between 1737 and 1741 establishes another intersection between his autobiography and other historical records. He claims that in 1740 he was recommended to Mr Rich of Covent Garden 'where I continued during the long Run of his Grand Entertainment, *Orpheus and Euridice* [*sic*]' (p.316). Other records suggest that his theatrical career at this period almost certainly included an appearance in *Tom Thumb* at Covent Garden on 30 April 1740 when 'Parry' took the part of King Arthur. He may also have been the 'Parry' who performed in Lee and Phillips's booth at Tottenham Court Fair on 4 August, playing Jupiter in *Jupiter and Juno* and the Spaniard in *Harlequin Happy*, and at Bartholomew Fair on 23 August, playing a Conjurer in *Harlequin Restored* and the title role in *Cephalus* (which included 'A Song by Parry in Praise of Admiral Vernon upon his Taking Chagre Castle'). On 9 September, 'Parry' was again playing Cephalus at Southwark Fair.[24] On 10 October 1740, the musician who had grandly taught the Bath Company of Comedians to sing *The Beggar's Opera*, now appeared in Rich's 'Grand Entertainment', *Orpheus and Eurydice*, as one of the villagers: 'Perry' appeared in the pantomime again on 5 January and 24 February 1741 but 'seems not to have had any other roles'.[25]

The final paragraph of *The True Anti-Pamela* explains why the theatrical career of the elusive 'Mr Perry' came to an end:

> I am now, *May* the 9th [1741], made Master of Arms on Board the *Revenge* Privateer, Capt. *James Wimble*, in order to sail upon a Cruize against the *Spaniards*, and if the Almighty should spare my Life a few Years longer, I hope to give my Friends, *&c.* a farther Account of myself. (p.316)

As Olney comments, 'no autobiography as conceived in a traditional, common-sense way can possess wholeness because by definition the end of the story cannot be told, the *bios* must remain incomplete. In effect, the narrative is never finished, nor ever can be, within the covers of a book.'[26] That being so, James Parry seems to contrive – after the 'false ending' of his story at the Caerleon Quarter Sessions – a remarkably apt conclusion to his memoirs. After all, what can possibly be a more fitting ending to his own revenge tragedy than to have the *Revenge* bear him out of sight on the tide of a narrative that, by definition, 'is never finished, nor ever can be, within the covers of a book'?

But even as James Parry (having completed his memoirs) sails into the sunset on board the *Revenge*, only weeks later (in a manner of

Illustration in *The Life and Surprizing Adventures of James Wyatt*, 1748.

speaking) he sails into the full glare of history – or more precisely is metamorphosed into a 'character' in the text of another autobiography, *The Life and Surprizing Adventures of James Wyatt* (1748).[27] The author, born near Exeter in 1707, was a woolcomber and dyer by trade but he had spent some years at sea and had also played trumpet for James Churchill's puppet show and Motet's collection of wild beasts at various venues in the west of England. In May 1741 he became Trumpeter on board the *Revenge*. In his address 'TO THE READER', he refers to the kindness and courage of Captain Wimble, 'And all the other Officers behav'd in a Gentleman-like Manner, except one, *viz.* Mr. *James Parry*, whose ill Treatment I have mention'd at the Beginning of my Life, who nevertheless I freely forgave long before he was kill'd.' Wyatt is referring to an incident at Catwater, Plymouth, which they reached on 10 July. The master-at-arms, who is referred to as sometime organist of Ross and author of *Memoirs of the Life of Mr. James Parry*, had 'some Words' with Wyatt and challenged him to a fight with the small sword. When some of the ship's company insisted that if they were determined to fight, it should be with hanger and pistol, Parry backed down. A few hours later he tried to prevent Wyatt from going ashore, although he had obtained the captain's permission to do so. When Wyatt pushed off the boat, the 'Centry' refused the order to fire, whereupon Parry himself 'took the Musquet from him, and immediately fir'd at me, which went through one of the Oars, and took off a Piece of the Rollock' (p.12). When Wyatt and Captain Wimble returned to the ship, Parry was found in his hammock, asleep and very drunk. Later, he swore that he remembered nothing of what had happened and was heartily sorry for what he had done. Wyatt was magnanimous: 'I assur'd him I freely forgave him.'

Wyatt's account not only draws attention to Parry's violent and drunken behaviour but, more significantly for a reading of *The Anti-Pamela*, demonstrates his readiness to take revenge for what he must have seen as a humiliating climbdown, one that no doubt called into question his 'manhood': he had refused to fight with hanger and pistol and later shot at Wyatt. Indeed, this incident provides an invaluable clue to the 'innermost, private significance' of Parry's autobiography, the genre which in Gusdorf's terms operates as a 'parable'. The revenge enacted by the choirboy, 'the dear little *Welch* boy', against his master was at least partly prompted by the threat of castration, just as the revenge enacted by the poor music master against his rich pupil was activated by her rejection of him as a husband: for all his boasting about his sexual prowess ('I look as much like a man as any one can, and she knows I am no Eunuch: I do tell you once more that I have carnally known her as often as any man in the County has a single Womrn [sic], for these two Years past and upwards'), he was not considered good enough to marry her. He had clearly believed that his potency would persuade his Parthenissa to overlook his social inferiority and marry him privately – but (by his own account) she jilted him. The illustration which accompanies the text in Wyatt's *Life*, of Parry standing on board the *Revenge*, firing a musket at the trumpeter who had once more unmanned him ('Mr. *Parry* refused to fight me with those Weapons'), represents in graphic form the 'innermost, private significance' of his memoirs.

By 12 September 1741, the *Revenge* was in the Canaries and a boat with eleven hands was sent to take the Spanish sixty-ton *Barcolonga*, anchored half a cable length from shore. Wyatt describes how he and several others boarded the bark and cut the cable, Parry and the rest remaining in the boat:

> By the Bark's swinging round, our Boat was expos'd to the Fire of the Enemy; upon which Mr. *Parry*, our Master at Arms, order'd the three Men in the Boat to row off. We call'd after them, but they did not regard us. In less than a Minute I saw Mr. *Parry* drop to the Bottom of the Boat; this I then thought he had done to avoid the Enemy's Shot, which was continually firing at them, but have since heard he was that Moment shot through the Heart. (p.44)

The so-called 'second' edition of *The True Anti-Pamela* (1770) attempts to complete the narrative by appending an account of Parry's adventures on the *Revenge*, together with a brief account of his death and burial at sea. There is, of course, a singular appropriateness in his being 'shot through the heart'. The reader also senses a certain ghoulish relish, a hint perhaps of 'good riddance to bad rubbish', which in effect becomes James Parry's only epitaph: 'Mr. Parry was shot through the heart and died immediately . . . The Captain ordered the corps of Mr. Parry to be buried after the sea manner, viz., being sewn up in his hammock, with a large bullet sewed into each end, and then thrown into the sea.'

As an eighteenth-century secular autobiography of a Welshman, *The True Anti-Pamela* is a rare literary phenomenon. Ultimately, it is the chapbook tradition rather than, say, the spiritual autobiography of one of Howel Harris's Welsh Methodists that may be silently invoked in the editor's note to the second edition. For Parry, that living embodiment of a chapbook Taffy, meets an entirely appropriate end. By his own account, the 'little Welch boy' with the outstanding singing voice became an unscrupulous music master with designs on both his pupil's person and her fortune; Wyatt's memoir, from which the editor presumably derived the details of Parry's death, revealed him to be a drunken bully and a coward. It was the fate of those hapless victims of chapbook malice — the Distressed Welshman and the Welsh Traveller in particular — to suffer mutilation and humiliation at the hands of the London mob. Indeed, a literary cousin, the Unfortunate Welch-Man, did not escape hanging. Like one of his fictitious forebears who suffered the final indignity of being thrown into the river, Parry is doomed — another Welshman 'in piteous case' — to be thrown into the sea. He may have been shot through the heart by the Spaniards — but it is, after all, his editor who provides the hammock with *large* bullets sewn into each end.

5
'Ye chaste Abodes of happiest Mortals'

THE HISTORY OF OPHELIA BY SARAH FIELDING

When Penelope Aubin declared that her heroine '*had never been so virtuous, had she not been bred in a Cave*', she was giving voice to that controlling idea in Western thought that became particularly active from the Renaissance to the end of the eighteenth century: 'Nature' may have been a word 'contrived in order to introduce as many equivocations as possible into all the theories, political, legal, artistic or literary, into which it enters',[1] but this did not deter writers from using the idea to suit their own literary purposes: 'All down the eighteenth century, both in England and France, there had been a succession of novels, plays, poems, and treatises exalting the natural over the artificial man, the primitive (as being fresher from the hands of God or Nature) over the sophisticated, the rustic over the urban.'[2] Sarah Fielding's *The History of Ophelia*[3] (1760) is rooted in the idea of Wales as a place of virtue, demonstrating the moral superiority of the natural over the artificial (wo)man by establishing the adamantine innocence of the heroine after an upbringing in a remote and hidden location near the Welsh border. Yet it can also be argued that in *Ophelia* Fielding makes an early contribution to radical feminist thought by making a covert attack on the institution of marriage, as she had already done in earlier novels, most provocatively in *The Cry*: 'Fielding is perhaps the first of the British women writers who have *consciously* "long used a wide range of tactics to obscure but not obliterate their subversive impulses" by "presenting acceptable facades for private and dangerous visions."'[4]

Sarah Fielding was born in 1710; she was the younger sister of Henry, who wrote a Preface for her first novel, *The Adventures of David Simple* (1744), with a notorious comment on her minor errors of grammar and style '*which no Man of Learning would think worth his censure in a Romance; nor any Gentleman, in the Writings of a young Woman.*'[5] Mrs Piozzi reported that after Sarah had made herself a competent Scholar, so as to construe the sixth Book of Virgil with Ease – the author of Tom Jones began to teize and *taunt* her with being a literary Lady &c. till at last She resolved to make her whole pleasure out of Study, and becoming justly admired for her Taste and Knowledge of the Greek Language, her Brother never more could perswade himself to endure her Company with Civility.[6]

Some years after Henry's death, Sarah did in fact publish a translation of Xenophon.[7] If this was unusual literary activity for a woman at that time, her collaboration with Jane Collier, notably on *The Cry*, was an early example of shared female authorship.[8] She was acquainted with the bluestockings, Elizabeth Montagu, Sarah Scott and Elizabeth Carter, and in 1767 was involved in plans to set up a community of unmarried gentlewomen at Hitcham, a real-life variant on the female communities described in her own *The Governess, or, Little Female Academy* (1749) and Sarah Scott's *Description of Millenium Hall* (1762).[9] The plans did not materialize and Sarah remained in her cottage in Bath, possibly bought from the proceeds of *Ophelia*.[10]

It is possible to view all Sarah Fielding's novels as theses in which realism is subordinated to ethical and philosophical argument. She herself described *The Adventures of David Simple* as 'a Moral Romance'[11] and, despite his strictures on his sister's grammar, Henry Fielding had nothing but praise for the structure of *The Adventures of David Simple*: '*there is one Beauty very apparent which hath been attributed by the greatest of Critics to the greatest of Poets, that every Episode bears a manifest Impression of the principal Design.*'[12] *Ophelia* is another highly schematic novel which demonstrates Shaftesbury's notion, propounded in his *Characteristicks of Men, Manners, Opinions and Times* (1711), of the divine perfection of Nature and the natural goodness of human beings, who are born with an innate sense of right and wrong that is antecedent to and independent of any religious beliefs. In a sense, *Ophelia* can be read as an extended and elaborated version of the fictions Shaftesbury inserted in the *Characteristicks* to enliven his philosophical arguments.[13] In Fielding's novel, Ophelia's aunt and lover enter into an astonishing conspiracy that systematically denies her any knowledge of the existence of evil. With a fine stroke of irony, the author rewrites the contemporary novel of seduction by ensuring that Ophelia's virtue is patently *not* subjected to temptation. Fielding creates a heroine whose perfect goodness flourishes in a state of moral ignorance, an Eve who is at no point offered the fruit of the tree of the knowledge of good and evil, though unwittingly she tempts Adam with its luscious fruit.

But it can also be argued that, as well as imposing a rigorous 'moral scheme' on her novels,[14] Sarah Fielding was also constrained to make use of what Patricia Meyer Spacks refers to as 'the necessities of disguise', that mechanism by which tedious and improbable novels written by women in the eighteenth century 'affirm as energetically as the fictional masterpieces of the period the inevitability with which fiction conveys psychic truth, and they affirm a particular kind of truth nowhere directly stated until the end of the century [in Mary Wollstonecraft's novels]'.[15] If Sarah Fielding was permitted in the 1760s to give her heroine a deistic light within the breast (ensuring virtuous behaviour even when she has not been taught conventional Christian morality, with its insistence on the idea of original sin), it was quite unthinkable for her to use the tenets of Shaftesbury's natural religion to suggest a radical reinterpretation of female virtue and the defence of free love as an alternative to marriage. Yet the 'psychic truth' of *Ophelia* seems to lie precisely in this bold version of deism, suitably draped in the ample folds of fictional disguise.

The novel begins at the point where Ophelia's aunt, discovering that her marriage to an army officer is bigamous, salvages what remains of her fortune and precipitately leaves the West Indies with her two-year-old orphaned niece. Determined 'to fly all human kind', she chooses Wales as a suitable place for indulging her 'romantick despair':

> We landed in the west. My aunt's romantick despair led her into Wales; where she found a small cottage, situated on the side of a hill, commanding a beautiful, though a wild and mountainous, prospect. At the foot of the hill was a delightful valley; to which, from our cottage, we were led by a fine grove of trees: on the side of the grove ran a clear brook, with several small cascades intermixed, descending into the valley; where it flowed, in beautiful meanders, till it lost itself in a little wood. This place was too well suited to a love-sick despair not to excite my aunt's envy. (p.7)

The author's thesis requires that Ophelia is brought up far from the haunts of men and that she is systematically denied all knowledge of the existence of evil; the cottage is therefore 'situated above twenty miles distant from any other house'. Its situation in Wales appears to have offered contemporary readers a credible image of a trackless wilderness in which one might be completely hidden from one's kind for years on end: just as Madam de Beaumount and her daughter were concealed in a cave near 'Swansey' for fourteen years, Ophelia is hidden away in her aunt's Welsh cottage until she too is of marriageable age. If *Ophelia* is to be interpreted as a moral fable, it is perhaps appropriate that the place is unnamed. This is Wales and Nowhere, a purely symbolic place of absolute virtue. It is probably no accident that later in the novel, when Ophelia is abducted by Dorchester, she makes no effort to contact her aunt because quite literally she does not know where she has come from. It is also a slightly chilling fact that her aunt and mentor, like the place she inhabits, has no name.

In Shaftesbury's dialogue, *The Moralists: A Philosophical Rhapsody* (1709), Theocles invokes the 'quiet Sanctuarys' of fields and woods and verdant plains:

> Bless'd be ye chaste Abodes of happiest Mortals, who here in peaceful Innocence enjoy a Life unenvy'd, tho Divine; whilst with its bless'd Tranquillity it affords a happy Leisure and Retreat for Man; who, made for Contemplation, and to search his own and other Natures, may here best meditate the Cause of Things; and plac'd amidst the various Scenes of Nature, may nearer view her Works.[16]

At their own quiet sanctuary in Wales, the aunt organizes life for herself and her young niece according to the best principles of self-sufficiency, purchasing a garden, grove and pasture and learning to milk her goats. Later in the novel, the Garden of Eden becomes an important motif in Dorchester's eloquent argument for free love; here, the Edenic quality of life at the cottage is hinted at in the way the animals who give them sustenance are compared to the infant Ophelia, 'then as ignorant of evil, and almost as dumb, as they' (p.8). Ophelia describes her childhood as a blessed time:

> There I lived, blessed indeed in innocence; all that was dear to me within my sight; I had nothing to regret, nothing to sigh for, no thought, no wish, to suppress; actuated by virtue, with virtue alone I loved my single friend; happy in knowing no more, I enjoyed a constant sense of contentment. (p.112)

She remains entirely secluded; educated by her aunt, her reading is confined to divinity and history of a kind which instructs without informing her of the existence of vice, 'which a pure imagination, untaught by observation and experience, cannot represent to itself' (p.8). It is one of the weaknesses of *Ophelia* as a philosophical argument that nowhere does the author attempt to explain how her heroine can be denied all knowledge of wickedness in this way while at the same time enjoying the 'moral sense' celebrated in Shaftesbury's writings, the natural capacity to recognize the difference between good and evil – a conundrum which becomes particularly baffling later in the novel when theoretically Ophelia still has no knowledge of evil yet fully understands and deplores the threat that Dorchester poses to her virtue.

Into the Eden of their secluded life in the cottage bursts Lord Dorchester while exploring the 'wild and natural beauties' of the Welsh countryside, much as the hero of Jane Austen's *Love and Freindship* would later descend on Laura's cottage in 'the Vale of Uske'. He appears one evening while Ophelia is walking by the brook with her aunt and admiring the reflection of the full moon on the water. The scene is presented as a meeting of angelic beings: the young man's clothes 'outshone the gentle lustre of the moon' and his first words are, 'Stay, beauteous angel! – stay!' as the moon shines full upon him – an encounter that may well shed some lustre, later in the novel, on the lyrical defence of free love and the identification of Dorchester and Ophelia with Adam and Eve. As she continues to set out her thesis, the author is not at all concerned with realism: the wildly improbable circumstances of Ophelia's upbringing are now compounded by the conspiracy between Dorchester and the aunt, who persuades him that he must say nothing to lessen her niece's 'ignorant simplicity'. He complies with this but feels free to repay their hospitality by abducting Ophelia, taking her first to his country house and then to London where he poses as her guardian. With an ignorance which she later admits is 'almost incredible', she finds his behaviour an 'inexplicable mystery', but gives him her full co-operation, explaining to the reader that 'Some knowledge of the world was necessary to make me believe any one could wish to injure another' (p.40).

This is no ordinary seduction tale, though. At first, Dorchester's strategy seems clear enough: when Ophelia is decked in all the glories of lutestring, gauze and garlands, he is understandably delighted that his plans for 'corrupting by glaring follies a mind bred in simplicity and reason, had succeeded so well' (p.18). Strangely, this is where Dorchester's role as seducer begins and ends. Not once during the

The History of Ophelia by Sarah Fielding

Lord Dorchester meets Ophelia and her aunt: illustration in Sarah Fielding's *Ophelia*, 1785 edition

following months does he try to tempt her from the path of virtue. On the contrary, he enlists the help of Lady Palestine to continue in effect the role of Ophelia's aunt, and between them they contrive that even in the midst of London high society she continues to be totally ignorant of the existence of evil. She might still be in Wales. The moment of truth for Ophelia occurs when she overhears a conversation between Dorchester and his friend, Lord Larborough, in which he reveals his libertine views on marriage and claims that, although he has been waiting to take advantage of Ophelia at an unguarded moment, he now doubts whether that moment will ever arrive: 'I thought I had only a woman to resist me. Who would have expected that an angel should be hid in a cottage, while we frail mortals inhabit palaces?' (p.110). Outraged and grief-stricken, Ophelia immediately leaves his protection and although he swiftly proposes marriage, she refuses him (apparently speaking as a Welshwoman): 'I have lost all my confidence in you, and detest the rest of your nation . . . trust me, so corrupt a people cannot be taught virtue but by suffering' (p.122). In desperation, Dorchester goes down to Wales to try to persuade her aunt to intercede on his behalf. Astonishingly, she does so. Full of misgivings, Ophelia eventually capitulates and agrees to marry him. She is, after all, in love.

In his edition of *The Adventures of David Simple*, Malcolm Kelsall suggests that, for all her schematic plotting, 'Miss Fielding failed to keep control of her material' – a shortcoming which he attributes in part to what he calls 'the irresistible pull of romance'.[17] In the case of *Ophelia*, it is possible that the 'happy ending', together with other rifts and dislocations in the structure of the novel, indicate that here too the author fails to 'keep control of her material'. It is also possible that these apparent disjunctions in the logical development of her argument signal important 'hidden' comments on her material. How is the reader to understand the self-confessed rake who abducts the heroine and then takes infinite pains to ensure that she retains the innocence of a child of nature? How does one explain a tempter who does not tempt – or an aunt who brings up her niece in total ignorance of evil and then persuades her to marry a libertine whose reformation has to be taken on trust? Some of these questions may be tentatively answered by a reading of the text which takes full cognizance of 'the necessity of disguise' in female writing of the period – an approach by which one might *expect* to discover contradictions between what Fielding desired to write and what she felt constrained to write.

This tension between desire and constraint seems particularly apparent in Fielding's treatment of philosophical and religious ideas in *Ophelia*. As a child of nature, the heroine's views on religion are perilously close to deism, that is, to a theology which rejects biblical revelation, celebrates the God of creation and locates morality in Nature itself, so that every human being has an inborn sense of right and wrong. While staying at Dorchester's house in the country, Ophelia agrees to attend church, 'though I had been taught to look on all space as the temple of the great Creator' (p.18). She concedes that the building is pretty – but too much calculated to please the eye where the suppliant soul should be entirely filled with the adoration of the Supreme Being. If Ophelia has been taught by her aunt to eschew the practices of the Church of England in this way, it follows that Dorchester's views on marriage (one of 'our vile customs' as he describes it to Larborough) are not likely, in essence, to be too distant from her own deistic ideas. Not realizing that Ophelia is listening in, he points out to his friend that Adam and Eve did not have the sanction of a priest for their union: 'I and my Ophelia will, like our first parents, love by our own and Nature's licence, with more warmth, more tenderness, sincerity, and constancy, than the obedient servants of the church, the slaves of custom, can boast' (p.108). Ophelia, he argues, ought more than anyone to obey that first parent:

> She who still enjoys her natural innocence, who has made uncommon progress in the knowledge of all good, and yet remains as ignorant of evil as on the day she was first numbered among the species she was born to eclipse, has no occasion to be confined to political rules, made to keep those in order who have not a better guide within their own minds. (p.109)

Dorchester's reference here to what Shaftesbury in his *Characteristicks* called the moral sense or what Adam Smith in his *Moral Sentiments*, published only a year before *Ophelia*, called 'the demigod within the breast – the great judge and arbiter of conduct',[18] chimes only too harmoniously with Ophelia's own religious ideas. Dorchester speaks not only with highly persuasive lyricism but also, in terms of the ideas about Nature which Ophelia has been so strictly brought up to respect, with incontrovertible logic.

One reading of the text suggests, therefore, the barely articulated possibility that under her aunt's tutelage, Ophelia, no less than

Dorchester himself, embraces the principles of deism. On this reading, that idyllic state of nature in which Ophelia has been brought up is seen to be a potentially dangerous one: the aunt is revealed as one suffering a morbid state of mind ('romantick despair'), isolating her niece from all social contacts while pursuing a fanatical theory of education based on principles perilously close to those peddled by Dorchester himself – indeed, so close that she readily gains his co-operation in keeping Ophelia in ignorance of the existence of evil. Lord Larborough articulates the counter-argument, taking his friend to task for his share in the scheme: 'Is there any virtue in not knowing the evil she has never seen? You have spread the veil which has concealed it all from her eyes; and then, like a true irrational lover, admire her for not seeing what was not visible to her' (p.109). In other words, Ophelia would have been *more* virtuous if she had been educated in the world and learned to recognize the power of evil. Later, Lord Larborough reminds her, rather brutally, that it is fortunate that no one in polite society suspects that she is penniless and maintained at Dorchester's expense, 'otherwise innocence could not have preserved you from infamy'.

If Ophelia is indeed on dangerous ground, the reader might be expected to 'blame' the aunt and Dorchester who are shown, at the beginning and end of the novel, to be collaborators. Yet there is another way of reading the text. It is possible to argue that far from being an attack on the deistic ideology peddled by the aunt and Dorchester, the 'psychic truth' of the novel is hidden after all in those first descriptions of Ophelia's Edenic childhood in Wales as well as in Dorchester's transfiguration by moonlight and his lyrical evocation of Adam and Eve as he later argues his case against marriage: 'I would receive her as the gift of Love alone. Her heart must give her to me, and mine receive her, as the pure votary of Love; mine, and only mine, exclusive of all prudential, all lucrative views. This is the truest bliss my heart can know' (p.109). One acknowledges the dangers of what Terry Eagleton refers to as 'the cavaliers, deconstructionists and debunking liberals' moving in on an eighteenth-century text once (in the case of *Clarissa* at least) 'the spicy news is out that the madonna has feet of clay'.[19] Nevertheless, it seems at least a possibility that in defiance of contemporary orthodoxy (and for that matter in defiance of *Clarissa*), the hidden agenda of *Ophelia* is a deistic rejection of orthodox Christianity together with a muted celebration of free love and a nervous attack on the institution of marriage itself.

This reading of the text can be illuminated by turning to *The Cry* (1754), another of Fielding's highly schematic novels (possibly written in collaboration with Jane Collier),[20] in which realism is eschewed even more comprehensively than in *Ophelia*. Described by Jane Spencer as a 'sharp feminist analysis of the shortcomings of romance',[21] it includes an extraordinary account (given the date of its composition) of a highly intellectual young woman, educated in the classics, an avid reader of moral philosophy and one who instigates and manages her sexual relationships entirely to suit her own needs. Cylinda learns early 'that women of understanding, and a superiority of parts, ought not to be tied in fetters by the rules of honour or the forms of established custom' (II, p.266) and judges that the God of Nature would not restrain free love:

> *Oh Amaralli, Amaralli,* &c. would I often repeat; and highly was I pleased with my own wisdom in discovering the folly of those people, who would imagine that nature, or the God of nature (for I always considered them as synonymous terms) would give laws to restrain those passions which were as natural to us as to the feathered race . . . (II, p.268)

Even in *The Cry*, however, it would seem that the 'necessities of disguise' require that a woman should be converted to Christian orthodoxy, a process which involves a detailed refutation of passages from Shaftesbury's *Characteristicks*, the core text of deistic philosophy.[22] (It is sometimes claimed that Dr Collier wrote the critique of Shaftesbury for *The Cry*.[23]) Even so, Fielding evades the conventions of romance: as a punishment for her immoral and irreligious life, Cylinda is condemned to a single life. Even if the author's own single state is disregarded, Richardson's 'Sally Fielding' makes it quite clear in her *Remarks on Clarissa* (1749) why Lovelace must be rejected: 'She thought a single Life, in all Probability, would be for her the happiest; cherishing in her Heart that Characteristic of a noble Mind, especially in a Woman, of wishing, as Miss *Howe* says she did, to pass through Life unnoted.'[24] The heroine of *Ophelia* is at best only a half-hearted recreation of Cylinda. When Dorchester improves her education by teaching her philosophy, the process occupies only one paragraph of the novel and if there are clear indications that Ophelia herself may have deistic tendencies, these are slight indeed compared with Cylinda's lurid unorthodoxy in the earlier text. Unlike Cylinda, condemned like her creator to a single life, Ophelia is married off to Dorchester in 'conformity to the laws of God and man'. It might even seem that Sarah Fielding suffered from a loss of nerve so that, just as the clever and sexually liberated young woman of *The Cry* had necessarily to be silenced and punished before the end of the novel, by the time *Ophelia* came to be written six years later, only the faintest, rubbed-out sketch of Cylinda remains in her depiction of the innocent child of nature.

When Dorchester travels down to Wales in order to persuade the aunt to plead his cause with Ophelia, his objections to marriage lack the lyrical quality of his earlier declaration to Larborough: according to the aunt, he believes that marriage robs social life of its charm, love-making loses its merit once it is no longer a crime, many wives behave badly, love does not last long once it is formalized and marriage banishes freedom and equality between lovers. There is another awkward disjunction in the logical development of the plot when the aunt, man-hater and devotee of Nature, now argues vigorously *for* the married state — and it is, of course, essential that she does so if the 'necessary disguise' of conventional attitudes to matrimony is to veil the true agenda of the novel. She has two main counter-arguments: insisting on 'conformity to the laws of God and man' (with no direct reference to Nature) and emphasizing (like Larborough) the importance of a woman's reputation. When Dorchester stages a tearful repentance, the aunt finally agrees to urge Ophelia to marry him out of compassion, though she is fully aware that his sincerity is in question. In London, she succeeds in her mission, fully admitting that she has persuaded her niece to marry a man whose principles she has always considered an infallible source of unhappiness. Ophelia too has serious misgivings though she tries to convince herself that a mind naturally good may be clouded for a while but can recover its original lustre. Ultimately, she accepts Dorchester purely and simply because she loves him: 'I was insensible to any dangers with which my peace was threatened by his principles, while I had the infinite satisfaction of imparting happiness to one that was dearer to me than myself.' Even so, she admits that 'mine was a dangerous trial' (p.132).

Having thus made a perfectly open attack on one version of the romantic idea of marriage, Fielding clearly feels constrained to provide a conventionally happy ending. At the end of a novel in which she appears to wrestle with the contradictions between orthodox and subversive ideas about the nature of female chastity and the institution of marriage, there is perhaps a final authorial shrug of the shoulders when Ophelia claims that Lord Dorchester 'rendered the rest of our lives a scene of bliss' – even extending the cottage in Wales and spending three months there every year. Alternatively, the ending of this highly ambiguous novel may have quite different implications: the moral geography of eighteenth-century fiction may suggest instead that the cottage in Wales, symbolically enlarged to accommodate Dorchester, might indeed be 'a scene of bliss' appropriate for the angelic beings who met and fell in love in the silvery moonlight at the beginning of the novel – a place 'rich in Virtue' (in Aubin's phrase) where the mind of the young husband might readily recover its 'original lustre'.

6

'*O Rus, quando te aspiciam!*'

HUMPHRY CLINKER AND OTHER SATIRES OF LONDON

In the first lines of *London, a Poem in Imitation of the Third Satire of Juvenal* (1738), the poet, Samuel Johnson, stands on the banks of the Thames 'Where Greenwich smiles upon the silver flood', waiting with the friend he calls Thales[1] for the wherry that will take the latter on the first stage of his journey to become a 'hermit' in Wales:

> Tho' grief and fondness in my breast rebel,
> When injur'd Thales bids the town farewell,
> Yet still my calmer thought his choice commend,
> I praise the hermit, but regret the friend,
> Who now resolves, from vice and London far,
> To breathe in distant fields a purer air;
> And, fix'd on Cambria's solitary shore,
> Give to St. David one true Briton more.[2]

For a while the friends wait in silence. Then, moved by the sight of the palace of Greenwich, the birthplace of Queen Elizabeth I, they both kneel and 'kiss the consecrated earth'. This homage to Britannia's glorious past is, however, but a moment of 'transient calm': Thales turns his gaze on 'the neighb'ring town' and with a 'contemptuous frown' launches into the scathing attack on the iniquities of city life that forms the body of the poem. As Boswell points out in his account of the poem, Boileau had already applied Juvenal's Third Satire to Paris and Oldham had done the same for London: 'all which performances concur to prove, that great cities, in every age, and in every country, will furnish similar topicks of satire'.[3] For himself, Thales prays that in leaving London he will find a place 'Where honesty and sense are no disgrace', though at the end of the poem, he promises that if the poet himself eventually flees the city, he will leave Wales and join him:

> Farewell! – When youth, and health, and fortune spent,
> Thou fly'st for refuge to the wilds of Kent;
> And tir'd like me with follies and with crimes,
> In angry numbers warn'st succeeding times;
> Then shall thy friend, nor thou refuse his aid,
> Still foe to vice, forsake his Cambrian shade;
> In Virtue's cause once more exert his rage,
> Thy satire point, and animate thy page.

In *London*, the poet is scarcely wholehearted about Thales's retreat to rural life. Although Johnson's own passion for social justice goes without question, he was famously addicted to London life: not only does he have mixed feelings about his friend's departure ('grief and fondness in my breast rebel') but 'the wilds of Kent' denote – perhaps with unexpected humour – the furthest one might expect even a disenchanted Johnson to distance himself from the city.[4] Thales is given a messianic role: he will return. He promises that if he is needed, he will 'forsake his Cambrian shade' in order to assist Johnson to attack 'In angry numbers' the follies and crimes of the age. In a curious conflation of identity, Thales becomes Johnson's alter ego as he promises that on returning to London, he will 'once more exert his rage, / Thy satire point, and animate thy page'. The narrative framework of Johnson's poem thus offers a number of locations from which to view and denounce the city. Thales's satire, as pronounced in the text of the poem, is uttered from a point only a few miles down river, but significantly from the 'consecrated earth' of Greenwich in order to effect a contrast between the glorious, Elizabethan past and the decadence of modern times. In a second satire, promised in some future text, as yet unwritten, Thales will view the city after a sojourn on 'Cambria's solitary shore'.[5] After Johnson's retreat to Kent, both will have placed themselves at a suitable critical distance from the object of their 'rage'.

In a cluster of prose fictions published between 1765 and 1771 – *The Parasite* (1765),[6] *Letters from Altamont in the Capital, to his Friends in the Country* (1767) by the Revd Charles Jenner,[7] *The Contemplative Man, or, The History of Christopher Crab, Esq. of North Wales* (1771), attributed to Herbert Lawrence,[8] and *The Expedition of Humphry Clinker* (1771) by Tobias Smollett,[9] a number of sojourners on 'Cambria's solitary shore' make the long journey to London and, like Thales, observe the vices and follies of the city, sometimes with the jaundiced eye of the experienced traveller but more usually with the innocent eye of the newcomer to the city. Philip Jenkins has described the peregrination of the Glamorgan gentry to the fashionable squares of London in the 1730s,[10] while Geraint H. Jenkins's account of the mid-eighteenth-century flow of gentlemen, masterless men and middling sorts towards London focuses on the lower end of the social spectrum: 'Isolated and often frustrated by the lack of economic opportunities in Wales, they ventured to London in search of new and exciting challenges.' Not everyone was capable of making his own way in the city: 'To Lewis Morris, London was "a bush of thorns" . . . a devilish world of scribblers, cheats, drunkards, prostitutes, and pickpockets. Those who failed to profit financially were either obliged to master evil habits, live on their wits, or return to their native land.'[11] In *The Expedition of Humphry Clinker,* Tobias Smollett drew a similar picture, deploring through the mouthpiece of his Welsh squire both the migration of the gentry and the exodus of the lower orders to the metropolis:

> The tide of luxury has swept all the inhabitants from the open country – The poorest 'squire, as well as the richest peer, must have his house in town, and make a figure with an extraordinary number of domestics. The plough-boys, cow-herds, and lower hinds, are debauched and seduced by the appearance and discourse of those coxcombs in livery, when they make their summer excursions. They desert their dirt and drudgery, and swarm up to London, in hopes of getting into service, where they can live luxuriously and wear fine clothes, without being obliged to work; for idleness is natural to man – Great numbers of these, being disappointed in their expectation, become thieves and sharpers; and London being an immense wilderness, in which there is neither watch nor ward of any signification, nor any order or police, affords them lurking-places as well as prey. (p.87)

In the fiction of the 1760s, it is to this 'immense wilderness' that Dick Swallow of *The Parasite* and Altamont of the *Letters* migrate from north Wales, the former to seek work as an apprentice apothecary, the latter to take up an appointment in the Post Office. In the next decade, the fictional Welsh are mere sojourners in the wilderness: the Crab family of *The Contemplative Man* take in the Welsh border, Birmingham and Oxford on their modest trip to the capital, while for Matthew Bramble and his party in *Humphry Clinker,* London is a stopover of several weeks on a tour which has already taken them to Bath and will eventually take them to Scotland. Swept towards London on what Smollett characteristically refers to as a 'tide of luxury', workers and holiday-makers alike allow their authors to reveal – with polite deprecation or towering rage or simple glee – the follies or wickedness of life in the capital.

In *The Parasite*, the account of Dick Swallow's early life in Wrexham includes some conventional satire of the Welsh, targeting the family's poverty and delusions of grandeur. His father is an honest parson, living on the income of a small curacy; he can trace his ancestry back to King Edgar, though his royal blood has never procured a living above forty pounds a year. The parson's verbosity is as ridiculous as his meagre diet; whenever he is moved to utter ten strings of quotations to support the necessity of Greek and Latin, he is immediately summoned to dinner, when 'the Fumes of the Barley-Broth dissipated every Shred of Learning, and left no other Subject of Investigation or Dissection than a Neck of Mutton and Turnips' (I, p.8). Dick's education is found wanting: having attended 'the best Writing-School in all *Wrexham*', he is tutored by his father and apprenticed as an apothecary to an uncle, and, since his distaste for the classics may be offensive, several Shandian pages are left blank so that the reader can insert his own quotations. Dick absconds when the maid becomes pregnant ('*Wrexham* echoed with *Kate*'s Shame / Till *Offa*'s Dyke rebellowed with the Din' (I, p.7)), and, like the chapbook heroes before him, he takes the road to London, a rogue in the making. Having engaged in an affair with an actress on the road to London, Dick finds work as a journeyman apothecary and seduces his master's wife; he falls among billiard sharks, attempts to become an actor and writes a comedy; he becomes a gigolo to old Lady D– and renews his affair with the apothecary's divorced wife, now a common prostitute; he procures a worthless medical degree and finds a place among the sycophants at rich men's tables; he dabbles unsuccessfully in a project to grow saltpetre and, after Kate's reappearance in London 'in her red Cloak and brown Camblet Gown' (II, p.192), sells remedies for hunchback and contraception. Eventually he reaches the nadir and turns pamphleteer: the novel ends with a specimen of his writing on toad-eating.

The anonymous author[12] describes with apparent relish Dick's sexual immorality, his corrupt medical practice and unpleasant toadying to the great, inviting the reader to laugh with him. The mild disgust generated by the novel is derived from an intrinsic failure of moral vision: the satire, if such it is, in no way matches Johnson's lofty denunciation of the vices of the city. As a reviewer would write much later of Disraeli, 'He loves a trickster; the picaresque amuses him'.[13] Yet, while there seems to be no attempt in *The Parasite* to attempt any kind of 'moral fable', the author does contrive to make Wrexham a foil of sorts for the dissipations of the capital. Early in the novel, Dick is invested with a certain provincial naïvety, amusingly so in connection with the black lead comb that he uses on Sundays to dye his hair 'a tolerable Brown':

> These may be looked upon as the fundamental Principles of Coxcombism in *Denbighshire, North Wales*: No such Thing – *Dick* had as much of the Rustic in him as Parsons or their Sons for the Generality have. He never dared ogle the Girls at Church, and he had never attempted an Intrigue with any but *Kate* in *Wrexham*. But let it not be imagined that his Ideas were naturally confined to so humble a Sphere . . . though *Dick* was no Coxcomb in *Denbigh* (save the black Lead Comb) he was not without Hopes of being a Fop in *London*. (I, p.40)

Similarly, when he meets Lady D– in London and begins in earnest his career as a parasite, Dick still has the air of a rustic innocent, though in this novel his lack of 'Effrontery' is not a moral category but an indicator of social class. He is, therefore, fair game for the predatory Lady D–:

> Our Hero was somewhat confused to find himself in such good Company – his Over-eagerness to divest himself of the Plebeian, would have made him appear uncommonly ridiculous in any Company except the present, where the Rusticity of his Manners was his greatest Recommendation; and the native Bashfulness of *Denbighshire*, which frequently overspread his Cheeks with Blushes, communicated more agreeable Expression than all the most well-timed Repartee uttered with all the Effrontery of Politeness. (I, p.104)

The irony is double-edged; neither party emerges with any credit, as the blushing young man from Denbighshire gratefully accepts the post of toy boy to the Duchess. In a more subtle use of Denbighshire as a standard against which to measure the life of the city, it is hinted that in trivial pursuits like billiards standards of play in Wrexham may not be as high as in the capital (Dick comes to grief precisely because he has been 'reckoned a tolerable Proficient at this Game in *Denbigh*' (I, p.66)), whereas in more important matters Wrexham may be a shrewder judge of a man's abilities ('though *Dick* was not looked upon in any classical light at *Denbigh*, he passed for a very profound critic at *George*'s and the *Bedford*' (II, p.136)). Even so, standards of behaviour prevalent in Wrexham operate only intermittently as a satiric norm in *The Parasite*. If the novel is to be read as a satire of city life, the author provides very little evidence that a virtuous life may be lived elsewhere – not even in Denbighshire.

Two years after the publication of *The Parasite*, another fictional account of a young man's first journey from north Wales to London in search of work appeared as *Letters from Altamont in the Capital, to his Friends in the Country*. Published anonymously, it is known to be the work of the Revd Charles Jenner, a former winner of the Seatonian Prize for Poetry at Cambridge.[14] Unlike Dick Swallow, prototype of the Welsh rogue, and as such a literary descendant of the chapbook tradition, Altamont is a virtuous young man, quite untouched by the moral squalor of the city. Like the Welsh heroines depicted by Penelope Aubin and Sarah Fielding, he is the representative of a land rich in virtue, one who might be expected to view the vices of the city with a clarity of vision and moral awareness conspicuously missing in the portrait of Dick Swallow. Yet here too Jenner's satirical purpose seems to waver so that by the end of the novel, he has summarily dispensed with the idea of Wales as the gold standard against which life in London should be evaluated.

Letters from Altamont has been described as a volume of sketches and essays rather than a novel[15] and as such can be related to Goldsmith's *The Citizen of the World* (1760) in using fiction as a framework for what is essentially a discursive account of London society. In what was to become a commonplace of eighteenth-century fictions of Wales, readers are made aware at the beginning of the novel that Altamont's father has retreated from society to seclude himself in 'the farthest and most inaccessible part of North-Wales' (p.vii). His reason for doing so, however, is not the usual plea of poverty or a broken heart but a direct response to the loss of his army commission when he refused to fight a duel (as a matter of principle) with a fellow officer. His son, Altamont, is brought up in this remote region with Henry and Charlotte, son and daughter of the parish priest, as his only companions. When Sir William B– finds him a situation in the Post Office, Altamont's letters to his father and friends at home provide the occasion for a critique of London society.

His first letter, written to Henry while he is still on the road to London, measures the distance he has already travelled from the world of his childhood, the epistolary form allowing the author to adopt the naïve persona needed for his satire of city life:

> Heavens! With what rapidity have we measured what, to me, appears an immense space! No sooner had we got clear of those mountains which render our country (alas! why do I say our country? I seem to have left it for ever) almost inaccessible, and gained a more cultivated part of the world, than we changed our method of travelling; we quitted our horses, and proceeded in vehicles, which having changed horses every ten or twelve miles, conveyed us with a swiftness wholly unknown to me, whose whole travels never exceeded a few miles, and that over rugged rocks. How new does every thing appear! . . . To-morrow we reach the capital. Can London be larger, more full of people, than the last town we were at, Chester? (pp.[1]-2)

The journey out of north Wales, described before the building of the turnpikes facilitated travel to and from the capital, emphasizes the remoteness of the area and its suitability as a location for an 'innocent' who (like Sarah Fielding's Ophelia) can be conveyed to the city with no prior experience of urban life. There is a certain irony implicit in Altamont's grumbling second letter, given the fact that it is precisely his upbringing in wild Wales that now enables him to view the follies of London life so clearly:

> The sequestered way of life which my poor father's chagrin drove him into, and, of course, imposed upon me from my cradle, has rendered me as unfit for society, and as ignorant of the customs of the world, nay even of the island in which I was born and bred, as an inhabitant of another planet. (p.3)

After sending home a series of letters which offer a relatively mild but comprehensive exposure of the artificiality, affectation and ignorance of London society, Altamont is still questioning the way in which he has been educated, and hinting at the difficulties of withstanding the temptations of city life:

> My life has, hitherto, been wholly in extremes: for the greatest part of it I have been only conversant with men in their most simple state, just as they came from the hands of nature: in this state your wise instructions easily gave me a love for virtue, which, joined to an ignorance of temptation, made me think it impossible for any man, who had the use of his reason, to swerve from his duty. The notice of my generous patron, has all at once hurried me into the opposite extreme, and introduced me to all the misguided wisdom, and all the dangerous refinements of the most polished society. My own genius, be it more or less, is all I have to trust to, for a knowledge of the intermediate state between these two extremes . . . (p.198)

The reference to 'men in their most simple state, just as they came from the hand of nature' looks forward to the language of the Preface to the *Lyrical Ballads*; Altamont's acknowledgement of the 'virtue' of such a society is rather grudging, however, even though he is fully aware of the 'temptation' and the 'dangerous refinements' of city life. In this respect, he could be seen as an inspid literary ancestor of the tortured Romantic souls brought into being by Mary Robinson and William Godwin more than thirty years later. Despite his indictment of London life, Altamont acquires a house near the city, proposes to Charlotte, and invites his father and Henry to live with them. Having thus subverted the very basis on which his hero's view of the city is grounded, Jenner proceeds to move all his dramatis personæ up to London. Wales, seen initially as a place where a child may grow up imbued with 'a love of virtue', is ultimately rejected as a place of moral extremism.

Unlike Dick Swallow and Altamont, who migrate to the city to make a living, Mr Crab of *The Contemplative Man* visits London on vacation and indulges in little more than a mild grumble about the expenses incurred during his short stay in the capital. The author has been identified as Herbert Lawrence, whose main claim to fame was his relationship to Hester Lynch Thrale,[16] and his position as medical adviser to her family.[17] Mrs Thrale records the fact that he wrote witty verses though she makes no reference to him as a writer of fiction.[18] The author of *The Contemplative Man* claims that he is Welsh ('for I am *of the noble Race of Shenkin*' (II, p.189)). However, beyond a brief description of the St David's Day celebrations, which begin 'in the most hospitable Manner imaginable' and end, after a truly Cambrian discourse upon the antiquity of their families, 'in broken Heads and bloody Noses' (II, pp.188–90), there is little in the novel to suggest an intimate knowledge of life in north Wales. The progress to London of Mr and Mrs Crab, with their lodger, Captain Gorget, and their son, Christopher, collected from Oxford after four years of medical studies, is essentially an unremarkable holiday trip, though Mr Crab in particular finds the city an unpleasant place to stay. He criticizes the ale and the manners of a carman ('Between you and I, zounds! If this be your *London* Breeding, God send us safe and soon in the Country' (I, p.229)), and swears softly to himself when his wife falls for sales talk and buys an expensive tippet ('Pox take it . . . what a Blockhead was I to come to this damn'd Town!' (I, p.232)). When Gorget's man only narrowly avoids being pressed into the army at Charing-cross, Mr Crab fetches a sigh ('Zounds! What a dangerous Place this *London* is. I wish we were well out on't' (I, p.237)), and he is scandalized by the price of beef at Vauxhall and the expense of the music:

> In the country we never give one of those Fellows more than a Shilling and a Mug of Ale, for playing Country Dances a whole Night; and as for Singers, there's *Will Price* of our Town sings better and louder than any of these squealing Creatures, and I'm sure he's be glad to come for seven Shillings a' week and his Victuals. (I, p.242)

When he grumbles all the way to the Gardens, Mrs Crab vows that she will never be seen with him in a public place again and is resolved to leave London rather than be put out of countenance before strangers. They duly set out next day 'for the *Rock* in *North Wales*'.

Lawrence has the temerity to devote a whole chapter of *The Contemplative Man* to a grudging review of *The Expedition of Humphry Clinker*,[19] in which moral vision and satiric purpose are never in doubt as Smollett's Welsh squire rages intemperately and entertainingly against the iniquities of the city. Until Matthew Bramble and his family arrive in Scotland and their travels there become a eulogy of Smollett's native land, the satire of English urban life depends almost entirely on the a priori existence of Brambleton-hall, near Abergavenny, as the criterion of the good life. In this novel, written in Italy in the last years of Smollett's life, the satire is not much concerned with the sexual mores of the city. ('A man without skin runs few risks of the flesh', as Ann Jessie Van Sant comments *à propos* Matthew Bramble and the body of the man of feeling.[20]) Here, Wales is no longer that symbolic place where young people – an Ophelia or even an Altamont – imbibe the 'virtue' that will be tested (triumphantly) against the 'vice' of the city. It is by no means a depopulated or primitive society, inhabited (like Altamont's Snowdonia) almost entirely by 'men in their simple state, just as they came from the hand of nature'. It is certainly not typified by a town like Wrexham where a young man like Dick Swallow receives only a limited education and a provincial veneer of blushing innocence. The symbolism in *Humphry Clinker* is of a different order: Brambleton-hall exists as an organic vision of a benevolent, patriarchal rural community, to be set against 'the folly and the fraud' of city life. Apart from the preliminary matter, which includes a letter, ostensibly written from Abergavenny by the Revd Jonathan Dustwich to a London bookseller, Henry Davies (with references to cousin Madoc, 'an Almanack and Court-kalendar' and toasted cheese), none of the letters in *Humphry Clinker* are actually sent from Wales. With consummate skill, however, Smollett ensures that his correspondents evoke the life of Brambleton-hall in sufficient detail to ensure that it serves as a satiric foil to the places they visit on their tour. 'We need not be shown the estate in Monmouthshire, for we have seen its plenteous image', as John Sekora puts it.[21] Although the details are often comic, they never subvert the ultimate purpose of the satirist, to express his terminal disgust with the life of the city.

Although the Welshness of Smollett's party of travellers is never in doubt, it is managed by literary sleight of hand, a matter of some judiciously placed phrases and the attribution of a few stock national characteristics. Thus Matthew Bramble Esq., formerly Matthew Loyd of Glamorgan, once a student at Jesus College, Oxford, and sometime member of the borough of Dymkymraig (literally 'No Welsh' and relying for its humour on the reversal of the monoglot Welsh-speaker's routine response to English, 'Dim saesneg'),[22] is named, according to his sister Tabby 'after great-uncle Matthew ap Madoc ap Meredith, esquire, of Llanwysthin, in Montgomeryshire, justice of the *quorum*, and *crusty ruttleorum*, a gentleman of great worth and property, descended in a strait line, by the female side, from Llewellyn, prince of Wales' (p.192). The genealogical joke is good-humoured – Smollett was fully aware of the similarity of Welsh and Scottish nomenclature[23] – but he was ready to make capital out of Welsh names, as in the absurd denouement in which Humphry Clinker is revealed as Bramble's illegitimate son and Tabby discovers that the young man 'has got the trick of the eye, and the tip of the nose of my uncle Loyd of Flluydwellyn' (p.319) – presumably a coinage which conflates Lloyd and Llewellyn for comic effect. According to his nephew, Matthew

Bramble is characterized by an acute sense of honour ('one of those who will sacrifice both life and fortune, rather than leave what they conceive to be the least speck or blemish upon their honour and reputation' (p.285)), while Jerry's own national trait is a 'passionate temper' – his uncle observes that is 'as hot and hasty as a Welch mountaineer'. Tabitha's national characteristic is conveyed in her use of simile ('patience is like a stout Welch poney'), in her shrewd dealing in cheese and Welsh flannel, and in the fact that her beloved Chowder is 'a filthy cur from Newfoundland, which she had in a present from the wife of a skipper in Swansey' (p.62). Win's Welshness is expressed in her figures of speech ('All the towns that ever I beheld in my borndays, are no more than Welsh barrows and crumlecks to this wonderful sitty!' (pp.107–8)), in her pronunciation (*firchin, disseyfer* and *pyebill* for *virgin, decipher* and *bible*) and a mode of address ('Hey for London, girl!') still heard in Wales today in the familiar speech of matrons who are forever girls to one another. Likewise Lydia, 'reared among woods and mountains' and toasted in Edinburgh as 'the Fair Cambrian', betrays her nationality when she tells Miss Willis that the Pump-room at Bath is 'crowded like a Welsh fair'.

In contrast to these stereotyped national traits of Bramble and his party, Brambleton-hall itself is given few specifically Welsh characteristics. The squire is patently not a 'poor gentleman of Wales' (though he devoutly wishes one of them would carry off his sister[24]), and far from being a 'mountaineer', whose cattle are as meagre and stunted as their peasant owners, his estate manifestly belongs to 'the rich counties of South Britain'.[25] But, in the satiric scheme of the novel, Brambleton-hall is more than this. It is, as Sekora puts it, 'the most perfect and salubrious place in all of Britain',[26] a place in which Smollett 'posited the values of an *earlier society* – one where life was simpler, and where order, station, and identity were more firmly established and respected'.[27] As Lewis Knapp observes, 'Smollett himself loved an Arcadia'.[28] Many of the details of Brambleton-hall are revealed through the comic irony of Tabby's letters, in which she attempts, *in absentia,* to run the household on a shoestring – but succeeds only in conveying the superabundance of her brother's estate. Smollett achieves this outcome in a variety of ways, by insisting, for instance, on her dependent status in her brother's household: 'These sums she has more than doubled, by living free of all expence, in her brother's house; and dealing in cheese and Welsh flannel, the produce of his flocks and dairy' (p.61). He also ensures that her parsimony is thwarted by her brother: when Bramble gives orders for Morgan's widow to have the Alderney cow ('I'll make her pay when she is able' (pp.5–6)), Tabby is astonished that it has been given away 'without my privity and concurrants', but the very terms of her complaint, the loss of four gallons a day ever since the calf was sent to market, emphasizes the productivity which her brother describes elsewhere: 'my dairy flows with nectarious tides of milk and cream, from whence we derive abundance of excellent butter, curds, and cheese; and the refuse fattens my pigs, that are destined for hams and bacon' (p.119). Tabby's notorious misspellings and grotesque characterization as a frustrated old maid – no feminist novel this[29] – ensure that her instructions for the discipline of the servants and the restriction of their diet are disregarded by the reader, who perfectly understands that in attempting to deprive the staff of butter, meat and beer, she merely demonstrates that they are used to consuming these items in full measure. Indeed, the servants are more than capable of subverting her authority: the mysterious claim that the gander has broken a clutch of eggs, a 'phinumenon' she fails to understand as the previous year the same gander hatched the eggs and 'partected' the goslings like a tender parent, together with the equally mysterious fact that thunder has soured two barrels of beer in the 'seller', suggest that goose eggs and a plentiful supply of beer certainly featured in the servants' diet – but also point to the productivity of the household and estate; this is reinforced by Tabby's references to the spinning of wool, the winecellar ('Let the ould hogs-heads be well skewred and seasoned for bear, as Mat is resolved to have his seller choak fool' (p.274)) and by Bramble's own instructions by letter for taking his corn to market and harvesting the hay.

It is this fair and prosperous image of rural Wales that is set against the sordid deprivations of city life. It is one of the comic ironies of the novel that Matthew Bramble, the most benevolent and long-suffering of men, should define himself as a misanthropist. As his nephew observes, 'He affects misanthropy, in order to conceal the sensibility of a heart, which is tender, even to a degree of weakness' (p.28). His benevolence and the nature of social relations at Brambleton-hall are apparent in his correspondence with Dr Lewis as he directs him to deal generously with his dependants, with Morgan's widow, with Davis who cannot pay his rent, with the poacher, Higgins ('I suppose, he thought he had some right . . . to partake of what nature seems to have intended for common use' (pp.14–15)), and with 'poor Joyce' who has been inoculated against smallpox and is to be provided with necessaries as soon as she is fit for service. Bramble, however, is a man peculiarly of his times. In his nephew's words, it is his 'morbid excess of sensation', 'his soreness of mind', that is responsible for the diatribes of disgust with which he surveys urban life. Even before he reaches the capital, Bramble assures Dr Lewis that his misanthropy increases daily: 'The longer I live, I find the folly and fraud of mankind grow more and more intolerable – I wish I had not come from Brambleton-hall' (p.47). In another letter written from Bath, he lists the odours arising from putrid gums, imposthumated lungs, sour flatulencies, rank arm-pits, sweating feet, running sores and issues, plasters, ointments, embrocations, hungary-water, spirit of lavender, assafoetida drops, musk, hartshorn, sal volatile and a thousand frowzy steams: 'Such, O Dick! Is the fragrant æther we breathe in the polite assemblies of Bath – Such is the atmosphere I have exchanged for the pure, elastic, animating air of the Welsh mountains – O Rus, quando te aspiciam!' (p.66).[30]

In a later letter, written from London, Bramble offers a carefully organized comparison between life in the city and life in the country. He gives a long list of the advantages of life at Brambleton-hall, beginning with elbow room indoors, fresh air, refreshing sleep, and good food and drink 'in great measure, furnished from my own ground'; he extols the pleasure of indoor amusements and the satisfaction of superintending his farm, seeing his tenants thrive and bringing employment to the poor; he acknowledges the blessing of friendship and the fact that he lives in the midst of honest men and trusty dependants. 'Now, mark the contrast at London', he tells his correspondent, and goes through the same items, from the air he breathes to social relations, in order to express his extreme aversion to the capital. Thus, the water he drinks at Brambleton-hall, 'the virgin lymph, pure and crystalline as it gushes from the rock' (p.118), is replaced in London by 'the maukish contents of an open aqueduct' or by river water from the Thames:

> Human excrement is the least offensive part of the concrete, which is composed of all the drugs, minerals, and poisons, used in mechanics and manufacture, enriched with the putrefying carcases of beasts and men; and mixed with the scourings of all the wash-tubs, kennels, and common sewers, within the bills of mortality. (p.120)

He thanks heaven that he is not so far sucked into the vortex but that he can disengage himself without any great effort of philosophy:

From this wild uproar of knavery, folly, and impertinence, I shall fly with double relish to the serenity of retirement, the cordial effusions of unreserved friendship, the hospitality and protection of the rural gods; in a word, the *jucunda oblivia vitæ*,[31] which Horace himself had not taste enough to enjoy. (p.123)

Wales as a place where one might, in Horace's words, enjoy the happy forgetfulness of life's cares, has necessarily to remain in *Humphry Clinker* in a state of infinite becoming: once Bramble reaches home, his letters will cease, the fiction reach vanishing point. But Smollett has the happy knack of creating a paradise (for which both characters and readers yearn) at once blissful and prosaic. The squire himself tells Dr Lewis that he has got an excellent fowling-piece from his new brother-in-law, Lismahago, 'and we shall take the heath in all weathers' (p.351). Tabby, in all the glory of her married state, orders the housekeeper, Mrs Gwyllim, to 'take great care to have the blew chamber, up two pair of stairs, well warmed . . . Let the sashes be secured, the crevices stopt, the carpets laid, and the beds well tousled' (pp.351–2). The last word goes to Win Jenkins in a letter to Molly Jones, her fellow servant at Brambleton-hall until her recent marriage to Humphry Clinker (under his new appellation as a Loyd) and elevation 'to a higher spear': 'Now, Mrs. Mary, our satiety is to suppurate – Mr. Millfart goes to Bath along with the Dallisons, and the rest of us push home to Wales, to pass our Chrishmarsh at Brampleton-hall, – As our apartment is to be the yallow pepper, in the thurd story, pray carry my things thither.' We never quite reach either the 'blew chamber' or 'the yallow pepper' but, as Sekora might have said, we have seen their image.

7

'God has called us into Wales'

THE SPIRITUAL QUIXOTE BY RICHARD GRAVES

As I am myself a Welchman by my mother's side, and am possessed of a pedigree of the *Morgans'* family five yards long; and can prove my descent from a knight of King Arthur's round table; no one I trust, will suspect me of any disrespectful intention, towards that ancient race of Britons.[1]

So wrote Richard Graves (1715–1804), chiefly remembered today for his entertaining satire of Methodism, *The Spiritual Quixote*. His biographer, Clarence Tracy, notes that the pedigree cannot now be traced, but it may well have been imaginary, yet another airing of the well-worn genealogical joke which never failed to amuse the eighteenth-century reader. His mother, Elizabeth Morgan, daughter of Thomas Morgan Esq., died in 1723 and was mourned by her husband[2] and remembered affectionately by her son.[3] According to Graves, his elder brother Morgan was adopted by a distant relative, Richard Morgan of Warlies, after the death of their father,[4] but apart from this, nothing is known about his mother's family. Tracy notes that 'The glow with which he [Richard Graves] always wrote about Wales must reflect the tenderness of his memories of his mother and his Welsh relations.'[5] Three of his four novels included Welsh scenes:[6] *The Spiritual Quixote* (1773), the focus of the present chapter, includes an account of Geoffry Wildgoose's adventures as an itinerant Methodist preacher in south Wales; *Eugenius* (1785) describes the early years of the Industrial Revolution in north Wales; in *Plexippus* (1790), the hero makes a brief foray into the Vale of Glamorgan to visit his Methodist parents. Graves also wrote (though scarcely with 'tenderness') another version of Holdsworth's *Muscipula*.[7]

Richard Graves was born in Mickleton, Gloucestershire, and educated at Abingdon and Oxford. He was an undergraduate at

Pembroke College where he began his celebrated friendship with the poet, William Shenstone. Curiously, Tracy makes no reference to the fact that George Whitefield, one of the great founders of Methodism – and a motivating force behind Wildgoose's 'ramble' in *The Spiritual Quixote* – was Graves's exact contemporary at Pembroke.[8] In 1736 Graves was elected to a fellowship at All Souls. It is not known whether he was ever a member of the Holy Club, though Charles Wesley's *Journal* suggests that he might have had leanings towards Methodism.[9] In 1737, Graves's younger brother, Charles Caspar, an undergraduate at Magdalen College, came under the influence of Charles Wesley who claimed that the young man had been 'carried away by his friends as stark mad' and clearly blamed 'Dicky Graves' for his brother's state of mind.[10] Peace was eventually restored between Wesley and Charles Caspar's 'friends',[11] but the young man's problems were by no means over. He became an itinerant preacher in 1738, only to 'renounce the modern practice and principles of the persons commonly called Methodists' in December 1740, declaring his conformity to the liturgy of the Church of England and his 'unfeigned assent and consent' to the Thirty-nine Articles.[12] In August 1742, however, after meeting the Wesleys in Bristol, he wrote to the Fellows of Magdalen, reasserting his Methodist principles (particularly his belief in the lawfulness of 'preaching the gospel in the fields') and lashing out at the 'oppressive men' who had been responsible for 'that scandalous paper, so un-Christianly imposed upon me'.[13] He remained an itinerant preacher until 1759 when he became the incumbent of Tissington, Derbyshire. Whether or not Wildgoose of *The Spiritual Quixote* was a satirical portrait of Charles Caspar, Richard Graves was certainly not averse to utilizing one of his brother's more spectacular adventures for comic purposes. During a missionary tour of Cornwall in 1746, Charles was seized in his bed and shanghaied on board a man of war,[14] an incident which is used with comic embellishments in *The Spiritual Quixote* when Wildgoose and Tugwell are forcibly transported from Bristol to Cardiff (on a ship bound for the St Lawrence) and thus inadvertently set out on a brief missionary tour of south Wales.

Although *The Spiritual Quixote* was not published until 1773, two years after *The Expedition of Humphry Clinker* had made fun of Tabby's comic conversion to Methodism under the spell of Clinker's sermons, Graves had probably begun the novel twenty years earlier. After his marriage to Lucy Bartholomew, he had resigned his university fellowship, obtained the living of Claverton near Bath, and set up a school where the pupils (among them Thomas Malthus) were educated alongside his own six children. It seems that the novel was Graves's response to 'a brush with the Methodists': 'One of their itinerant preachers, an unordained journeyman shoemaker, had invaded his parish, preaching and singing psalms in defiance of the rector, and had drawn off part of his congregation.'[15] In Graves's novel, the young hero, Geoffry Wildgoose, is converted to Methodism and sets out from his Gloucestershire village, accompanied by the local cobbler, Jerry Tugwell, in search of George Whitefield who was currently residing in Bristol:

> he [Wildgoose] resolved to visit the society in that city,[16] and confer with them upon the subject of the cause in which he was now a volunteer; and to take instructions for the better discharge of the mission, to which, he flattered himself, he had a divine call. (p.32)[17]

As they 'ramble' through Gloucester and Bath and eventually arrive in Bristol, Wildgoose is confident that 'God will send his angel before us, as he did before Mr. Whitfield [sic] in Wales',[18] and here they find Whitefield, resplendent in a purple nightgown and velvet cap, with 'a good bason of chocolate, and a plate of muffins well-buttered, before him' (p.229).

Before setting out on his first mission to the poor colliers and lead miners in the north of England, Wildgoose makes the acquaintance of Mrs Cullpepper, wife of a wealthy Alderman, and dines at her table with Captain Gordon, commander of a frigate about to sail for America, and 'a Welsh grocer', who has just seen a play for the first time in his life at Bristol fair:

> Being asked, 'how he came to return so soon, and whether he did not like the Play?' he said, 'It was fery goot Plaa; they plaad three bouts upon the fiddles, and the harps, and the pipes; but there were some Great Shentlemen came in, who had some private business to talk of together, and hur thought it was not goot manners to stay any longer.' (p.244)

As naïve as any chapbook hero, this poor Taffy 'as it has probably happened to other country gentlemen' had mistaken the music before the play for the play itself and had come away when the actors ('some great Shentlemen') made their first entry. Meanwhile, Captain Gordon grows jealous of Wildgoose's success with Mrs Cullpepper and arranges to have him put him on board his ship, along with Tugwell. When they are driven off course by a storm in the channel and anchor in the Bay of Cardiff, the Captain decides that he has carried the jest far enough and gives leave for Wildgoose and his Sancho Panza to be set ashore. They land about three miles from Cardiff and so begins their mission to Wales.

Sitting at the foot of a rock at sunrise, the pilgrims share two rolls and a slice of 'mutton-pye'; after a nap, in which he dreams of nothing but spiritual conquest, Wildgoose rouses Tugwell:

> 'Come, Jerry,' cries he, 'this is no time for sleep; up, and be doing: the whole land of Canaan lies before us; we must subdue the idolatrous nations, the Hivites, the Perizzites, and the Jebusites. God has called us into Wales; and I make no doubt but he will send his angel before us (as he did before Mr. Whitfield [*sic*]); and we shall go on from city to city (like Joshua); and the Devil's strong holds will fall down at our preaching, as the walls of Jericho did at the sound of the Rams-horns.' (p.264)

There is no evidence that Graves had any special knowledge of the Methodist movement in Wales. To a greater or lesser extent, both George Whitefield and John Wesley contributed to the rise of Methodism in Wales and Graves duly pays lip service to their influence. But this does not inhibit him from a cavalier use of their published journals for his own satiric purposes. Here, as elsewhere in the novel, he plunders Whitefield's diaries for comic detail, quoting at random (as Tracy demonstrates in his notes on the text), alluding to events that happened outside Wales and generally showing a blithe unconcern for historical accuracy. In Wildgoose's rallying call to Jerry after they have had their nap, Graves conflates at least three entries in Whitefield's *Journal* for 1739,[19] though the comic bathos of 'God has called us into Wales', among the sounding names of the Old Testament, is entirely his own. Predictably, Tugwell wants to leave 'this heathenish country' while Wildgoose, in his role as Don Quixote, positively welcomes the prospect of the desolate coast and the possibility of 'a little persecution'. His instinct for martyrdom is typically short-lived, however, and he is soon reassuring Tugwell that they are not far from Cardiff where they will find better accommodation and 'a Society of true Christians, which, I believe, Mr. Whitfield [*sic*] established there, when he visited the Principality of Wales'. (In fact, the Cardiff Society was in existence before the Methodist revival, and was closely associated with John

Wesley, not Whitefield.[20]) Within half an hour they are approaching the town and Tugwell, in chapbook mode, is looking forward to 'a cup of good ale and a slice of toasted cheese, which, now he was in Wales, he hoped to have in perfection'. (p.265).

The chapbook version of Wales persists. The Bristol attorney who nearly comes to blows with Tugwell is staying at the inn in Cardiff for familiar reasons: 'As the Cambro-Britons are a nation of gentlemen, jealous of their honour, and impatient of affronts, they are engaged in frequent litigations' (p.266). Similarly, while Wildgoose's adventure in the middle of the night, when Nan the Cook is discovered half-undressed by his bed (usually occupied by the Hostler with whom she has 'a nocturnal intrigue') is pure Fielding, Tugwell's adventure depends entirely on the notion that goats are ubiquitous in Wales, even in Cardiff, when he sees at the foot of the bed a diabolical figure with glaring eyes, a long beard and a monstrous pair of horns. Early the next morning, when Wildgoose and Tugwell go down to the stable yard, 'a great shaggy he-goat, drawn by the smell of Jerry's wallet [in which he always carries a plentiful supply of food], came running towards them' (p.272), though Tugwell remains stubbornly convinced that he saw 'nothing but the Devil himself'.

Since Graves's satire of Methodism in 'the Principality' is embedded in this chapbook version of Wales, his statement that 'both Mr. Whitfield [sic] in his Journals, and also Howel Harris, had represented the inhabitants of Wales as sweetly prepared to receive the Gospel (going frequently twenty miles to hear a sermon)'[21] is presumably ironic, a jeer at the spiritual potential of the people of Wales. Even so, the sketch of Harris in *The Spiritual Quixote* is disappointing in its lack of a satiric cutting edge. Lyles points out that 'In general, the satire of the minor Methodists seems curiously lacking in originality and force', but incidentally reduces Harris to the status of a 'minor' figure in the history of Methodism, along with William Romaine, Martin Madan, Sir Richard Hill, Augustus Toplady – and Daniel Rowland.[22] Harris may have been called the greatest Welshman of his age,[23] yet, as Geoffrey Nuttall has pointed out, 'to English students of the history of the Church in these islands Harris is virtually unknown'.[24] The lack of 'originality and force' in the representation of Howel Harris in *The Spiritual Quixote* is disappointing precisely because, historically, he was a figure of such towering proportions.[25] Graves was perfectly capable of taking pot-shots at the great Methodist leaders of the day, but there is nothing in his sketch of Harris to rival the vignette of Whitefield eating muffins in his purple dressing-gown, or Wildgoose's brief but memorable meeting with John Wesley on the road to Birmingham – a felicitous make-over of an entry in Wesley's own *Journal*.[26] Perhaps Harris was simply an unknown quantity – there is no evidence to hand that Graves had any personal knowledge of the Welshman and he certainly had no access to his voluminous diaries which have remained largely unpublished to this day.

At the inn in Cardiff, the waiter tells Wildgoose that 'Preacher Howel Harris' is in town and explains that he is a young fellow who goes all over the country to revels and fairs, preaching two or three times a day: 'He does a great deal of mischief amongst the country people; but I hope somebody or other will beat his brains out one of these days' (p.268). Fortunately, the tapster has nothing to say against Harris and gives Wildgoose directions for finding his lodgings. Wildgoose has heard Whitefield 'make honourable mention of Brother Howel Harris' (in this instance, Graves does appear to be aware of the rapport established between the two Methodist leaders in the early days of the movement[27]) and finds, bathetically, that the Welshman readily accepts his account of his nocturnal adventures with the fat cook: 'As people who are good themselves are not apt to suspect ill of others, Mr.Wildgoose found no difficulty in convincing his Brother Howel of his innocence' (p.273). Graves denies his readers the opportunity to hear 'Brother Howel' preach: Wildgoose is immediately engaged to speak from the judgement seat at the town hall and duly proceeds 'without Judge or Jury, to *arraign* and *condemn* the whole race of Mankind' (p.268). Characteristically, Graves utilizes an entry in Whitefield's *Journals*[28] to turn the occasion into slapstick comedy:

> Many were very attentive; but some mocked: and some jolly fellows, who had been drinking at the inn, one of whom kept a pack of hounds in the neighbourhood, having had intelligence of Wildgoose's intention by the Drawer, got a dead fox, and trailed him round the Townhall, and laid on his dogs to the scent. The music of the hounds, and the noise of the sportsmen, were so loud and vociferous, that they almost drowned the voice of the Orator; and the chearfulness of the sound had such a mechanical effect upon the minds of many of the Cambrians, that they ran out to join them . . . (pp.268–9)

In order to make Whitefield's account applicable to an event in Cardiff, Graves includes monoglot Welsh-speakers among the crowd, claiming that 'that part of the congregation seemed most affected, and bestowed the most hearty benedictions on the Preacher, who did not understand a word of English' (p.269). The satire is, of course, crude and unfair – there is evidence that the early Methodists were well aware of the needs of Welsh-speakers in their congregations, even if this was expressed as a lament ('O what a heavy curse was the Confusion of Tongues! And how grievous are the effects of it! All the birds of the air, all the beasts of the field, understand the language of their own species. Man only is a barbarian to man, unintelligible to his own brethren!'[29]). Certainly John Wesley tried to ensure that a Welsh-speaking congregation was given a summary of his sermon by an interpreter or provided with an alternative sermon in Welsh – on occasion by William Williams Pantycelyn himself.[30] In *The Spiritual Quixote*, Howel Harris dismisses the assembly and sits an hour with Wildgoose at the inn in order to settle their plans for the following morning. The pilgrims then retire early, 'highly satisfied with the adventures of the day; which Wildgoose said (in the style of the Journals), "was a day of *fat things*;" to which Tugwell (applying it in a literal sense to his rashers of bacon and Welsh ale) heartily assented' (p.269). Wildgoose's efforts to convert the Welsh are thus confounded with a merry combination of slapstick, authorial irony and Tugwell's exclusive concern with the inner man.

Although Harris cannot persuade Wildgoose to remain in Cardiff any longer, he sends the pilgrims on their way by accompanying them to Newport. Here he introduces them to a parson who has recently allowed Whitefield to preach from his pulpit. In this brief episode, the critical perspective shifts in order to give a view of Methodism from the vantage point of an orthodox Church of England parish priest:

> 'I have already,' continued the Doctor, 'found the ill effects of my complaisance to Mr. Whitfield [*sic*]. My own people, who are very well disposed, and who were before entirely satisfied with my plain doctrine, now, forsooth, give out, that I do not preach the Gospel, because I do not always harp upon the same string, of the New Birth, Faith without Works, and the like. They also expect me to have private meetings two or three nights in the week, and compliment them with private expositions of Scripture, extempore prayer, psalm-singing, and what not; though, I really believe, if I were to give them the very same sermons in a private room, lighted up with candles like a play-house,

the very novelty of the thing would content them for a while, as well as the best of your itinerant preachers.' (pp.273–4)

No doubt 'the Parson of Newport' speaks for the author himself: his indictment of Methodism, uninflected though it is, is a comprehensive statement of its pernicious effects on his 'very well disposed' parishioners. It is also characteristic of Graves's method that although the Doctor is 'not disposed to enter into the views of our Spiritual Adventurers', he nevertheless gives his guests a good breakfast of coffee and hot rolls before Wildgoose and Tugwell set out for Monmouth and Harris returns to Cardiff. One might even say that, despite its crudities and occasional unfairness, the whole novel is a symbolic offering of 'a good breakfast' to the Methodists.

In an incident said to take place at a village in the Usk valley (though the cascade, the ruined monastery and the hanging woods forming a natural amphitheatre suggest the scenery of the Lower Wye valley), Graves brings the comic stereotype of the poor Welsh clergyman into play in order to identify, in all seriousness, one of the root causes of the rise of Methodism in Wales. The walk up the valley prompts Wildgoose to admire the sequestered situation of the ruins, observing that 'if a true primitive spirit reigned amongst those people, they must be the happiest of mortals' (p.275). When they reach the parson's house, it appears to be the prototype of the picturesque cottages that would eventually become ubiquitous in Welsh fiction:

> The first cottage they came to was a tolerably neat one, and appeared the constant residence of peace and tranquillity. A little wicket, painted white, led through a small court to the house, which was covered with honey-suckles and sweet-briar: the windows were glazed; and the chimney rose, with a truly ancient British magnificence, two feet above the thatch. (p.275)

But having laughed at the 'truly ancient British magnificence' of the chimney, Graves goes on to reject the rural idyll that readers might justifiably expect in the remote and beautiful valley of the Usk: 'Peace does not always reside in a cottage.' Wildgoose and Tugwell are saluted with the confused noise and squalling of children, while 'a female voice, with a Welsh accent (which is alway expressive of anger)' (p.275) bids them go about their business as they have beggars enough in their own parish and 'that they never bought any thing of

Pedlars; that her own father, who was a gentleman born, kept a creditable shop at Newport; and she would not encourage people who travelled about to the prejudice of the fair trader' (pp.275–6). When Wildgoose and Tugwell look into the kitchen, they see a number of children with their mother (far advanced in pregnancy) and their father, the poor Welsh clergyman. Having used well-worn 'chapbook' references to beggars and gentlemen born, Graves clearly makes use here of the print of *The Welch Curate*, published by Bowles and Carver circa 1770:[31]

> The Master of the house, who was no other than the Vicar of the parish, was sitting down in his band and night-gown; but so far from being idle, that his eyes, his hands, and his feet, every limb of his body, and every faculty of his soul, were fully employed: for he was reading a folio, that lay on a table to the right; was hearing his little boy read, who stood by him on the left; he was rocking the cradle with his foot; and was paring turnips. (p.276)

Graves then offers his own comic version of the popular print. In exchange for a cup of small beer, a piece of bread and cheese and a pint of ale, Tugwell takes over the duties of the 'Welch Curate', rocking the cradle, paring the turnips and blowing the fire, while the master of the house sits at the door with Wildgoose and explains his plight, which is far from comic.

The plight of the poor clergy was a national scandal in the mid-eighteenth century.[32] Clerical poverty in Wales had long been a particular problem, with about a quarter of the benefices of the established church worth less than £50 per annum in 1704, so that 'the "mean and hard circumstances" of the clergy often prevented them from discharging their spiritual functions effectively'.[33] The poverty of the diocese of Llandaff – 'the Cinderella of all brides' – was exceptional.[34] In a chapter entitled 'Ecclesiastical Pride in the Diocese of Llandaff', Graves's poor parson tells Wildgoose that, in addition to a rectory of about thirty pounds a year, he earns another twenty pounds from 'the small tythes'. But this source of income encourages dissent in his parish:

> because I cannot afford to let them cheat me out of half my dues, they represent me as carnal and worldly-minded, and as one who regards nothing but the good things of this life, and who is always making

The Spiritual Quixote by Richard Graves

The Welch Curate, published by Bowles and Carver, c.1770

disturbances in the parish. And this prejudice against me prevents my doing that good amongst them which I sincerely wish to do. One man has left his church, and walks three miles to a Methodist-meeting, because I took one pig out of seven, as the Law directs; another has complained to the Bishop of my extortion, because I would not take three shillings and six pence, in lieu of tythes for a large orchard, as my predecessor had done. In short, Sir, here are two or three Dissenters in the parish, who give out that all tythes are remnants of Popery; and would have the Clergy consider meat and drink as types and shadows, which ought to have been abolished with the Levitical Law. (pp.277–8)

Wildgoose exhorts him to try regaining the people's goodwill by 'little popular acts of beneficence' and the inculcation of 'the *true* Gospel', but the vicar is afraid that nothing is likely to succeed with people who would risk their eternal salvation for the sake of a groat.

With this sideswipe at Welsh dissent, Graves reverts to comic mode by suggesting that the villagers are neglecting their business in order to attend Methodist meetings. Wildgoose and Tugwell observe an old tailor 'sitting on his board, with spectacles on his nose, and with more devotion than harmony quavering one of Mr. Wesley's hymns' (p.279). But once he knows that Wildgoose is going to preach, he leaps nimbly off his board, leaving a suit of clothes which he had promised to finish that evening. Similarly, the blacksmith leaves the farmer's horses half-shod, the farmer's wife slips on her shoes and stockings and leaves her cows unmilked and her child dangerously ill in the cradle. These, with half a dozen more, leave their several employments to join 'the devout cavalcade'.

From this point onward, Wildgoose's mission to Wales descends into genial farce. At a village three miles further on, 'a considerable thorough-fare to Monmouth', Wildgoose preaches to more than two hundred people. There is palpable nostalgia for what Prys Morgan refers to as 'Merrie Wales',[35] and a hint that Methodism is seeking to abolish this traditional way of life, as Wildgoose holds forth 'at the door of a little inn, being mounted on a horse-block, under a shady elm, which had long been sacred to rustic jollity and tippling, and thoroughly perfumed with the incense of ale and tobacco' (p.280). Graves utilizes an entry from John Wesley's *Journal* as the basis of a comic disaster which overtakes Wildgoose outside the inn – the collapse of an orchard wall on which a considerable part of the congregation are seated.³⁶ In his description of one of Wesley's converts, 'galloping through the street, upon a little poney, about the size of a jack-ass, hallooing and shouting, and driving men, women, pigs and children, before him', Graves blatantly rehashes the *Journal* in the diction of the chapbooks as the poor fellow cries out, '*Got* bless you! Master Wesley; hur is convinced of sin; and Got has given hur revelations, and visions, and prophecies; and has foretold, that hur shall be a king, and tread all hur enemies under hur feet' (p.281).³⁷ Graves adds to the joke by extending the metaphor of the New Birth when Wildgoose observes that the convert 'only wants the obstetric hand of some Spiritual Physician, to relieve him from his pangs'. The preaching ends with more slapstick comedy as Tugwell's efforts to sing a psalm (his voice being 'as unharmonious as the falling of a fire-shovel upon a marble slab') attract the beating of a drum and the discharge of three addled eggs, one of which flies 'directly into the aperture of Jerry's extended jaws', and, to add insult to injury, Wildgoose has to pay five shillings for the dilapidations to the wall.

In order to represent the effects of Wildgoose's preaching on the people of Monmouth on the following day, Graves conflates separate records by Wesley and Whitefield.³⁸ Thus, when Wildgoose is woken at two in the morning, he goes up to the 'Society-room' to find that the people have worked themselves up to such a pitch of religious frenzy that some have fallen on the floor, screaming, roaring and beating their breasts, in agonies of remorse for their former wicked lives. Others are singing hymns, leaping and exulting in ecstasies of joy, that their sins have been forgiven. Among them, a three-year-old is acting the part of a contrite sinner. When they eventually calm down and Wildgoose goes back to bed, Tugwell sleeps on some hop sacks in the corner of the assembly room (p.294). The next morning, before leaving Monmouth, Tugwell pronounces on the absurdity of Methodistic enthusiasm: 'Gad-zookers!' says he, 'these Welsh people are all mad, I think; I never heard such rantipole doings since I was born; a body cannot sleep o' nights for 'em' (p.295).

8

The first Welsh industrial novel?

EUGENIUS BY RICHARD GRAVES

Although *The Spiritual Quixote* deals very entertainingly with one of the great religious movements of the eighteenth century, it is essentially a retrospective novel, harking back at least thirty years to the early days of Methodism, when Howel Harris could be described as 'a young fellow' and both Wesley and Whitefield were out and about, in the first heady days of itinerant preaching up and down the highways and byways of the country. Only fleetingly in this novel is there any sense of the coming together of the beginnings of Methodism and the stirrings of the Industrial Revolution; Wildgoose's visit to the fearsome Kingswood miners is a tame affair, while his mission to the lead mines of the High Peak degenerates into farce. In contrast, *Eugenius, or, Anecdotes of the Golden Vale* (1785)[1] looks to the future; it reads as a fictionalized essay on the virtues of industrialization, hymning the individual entrepreneur as an economic saviour of the poor and showing little awareness of the potential ill effects on the life of a north Wales valley.

Graves makes it clear on the title-page of *Eugenius* that the golden age has passed: 'Subiit Argentea Proles, Auro deterior fulvo, pretiosior Aere.' According to Book I of Ovid's *Metamorphoses,* once Saturn was consigned to the darkness of Tartarus and the world passed under the rule of Jove, 'the age of silver replaced that of gold, inferior to it, but superior to the age of tawny bronze'.[2] For Graves in *Eugenius,* the golden age is represented by the aptly named Golden Vale in its romantic state of natural beauty, while the silver age comes into being with the industrialization of the valley. But there is nothing elegaic about the tone of this novel: from his parsonage near Bath, the seventy-year-old author looks eagerly to the future, creating in Eugenius a young Englishman who fully approves of the Industrial Revolution as it begins to gather momentum in the green valleys of

Wales. In doing so, he shared the optimism of his times, exemplified in Joseph Priestley's *Lectures on History and General Policy* (1788), composed for delivery at the Warrington Academy but enlarged and revised before publication. Priestley expresses a decided preference for modernity but he is even more radical than Graves in his rejection of the 'primitivism' of the period which saw civilization as a degeneration from an age of gold or as a departure from Nature's holy plan: 'Idleness, treachery and cruelty are predominant in all uncivilized countries; notwithstanding the boasts which the poets make of the *golden age* of mankind.'[3] In line with his reading of Adam Smith, Priestley presents a case for economic as well as moral individualism, arguing that under the beneficent sway of Nature, wealth will increase and be diffused through 'the lower ranks of society' as education and enlightenment teach the wealthy to use their riches for the good of the whole: 'If only we will allow free scope to "this natural course of things", commerce will bring international peace, and "the world would in time recover its pristine paradisal state".'[4] If Graves ignores the headier utopian implications of 'commerce', his industrialist, Mr Hamilton, is nevertheless a man after Priestley's own heart, exercising economic and moral individualism in order to banish idleness and diffuse wealth through the lower orders in a pristinely beautiful valley in north Wales.

This preference for the modern is established at the beginning of the novel when Eugenius and an old schoolfellow compare the manners which prevailed in England in their younger days with those of the present time; Eugenius emphatically prefers those of the present age and his story of the Golden Vale is intended to illustrate this view. He explains to his friend that, as a boy of 'enthusiastic imagination', he was of 'a romantic turn of mind'. While he was at Oxford, his 'passion for romantic views, and the wild beauties of nature' (I, p.26) prompted a college friend, Williams of Jesus College, to invite him to spend the vacation with his family 'in a sequestered vale, in the most mountainous part of North Wales; whither hardly any Englishman, till within these few years, and very few Welshmen, had ever penetrated; and which had escaped the sagacity of even the inquisitive and philosophical Mr. Pennant himself' (I, pp.26–7). The reference to the recently published *A Tour in Wales*[5] is a significant one, given Pennant's inclusion of not only the picturesque scenery of north Wales but also graphic descriptions of industrial developments such as the vast copper mines at the Parys Mountain in Anglesey ('NATURE hath been profuse in bestowing her mineral favors on this spot' (II, p.281)) and his emphasis on the economic benefits for the miners and their families.[6] Even before arriving in the 'sequestered vale', Eugenius establishes his own attitude to the economic potential of the country. Four days after leaving Oxford on horseback, the young men turn off the great road, wind along a valley for a few miles, then begin to climb a very steep and lofty range of hills from which they obtain a view of an extensive vale opening to the sea, at the mouth of which there seems to be a small sea port or fishing town, and only here and there a couple of farmhouses – or rather cottages – shaded by a few hawthorns on the hillside. Although Eugenius finds this landscape disappointing, he politely admires the noble view of the sea. He also concedes that although the mountains are not very fertile or alluring, 'they *might* probably contain some *rich* veins of lead or copper in their bowels' (I, p.30), an unexpected observation in a romantic youth but, as it turns out, appropriate enough in the mouth of a budding capitalist.

On this first visit to Wales, however, it is the romantic vision of the country in its age of gold that prevails. When the travellers turn inland 'amidst a vast ridge of craggy rocks, which seemed to be the very boundaries of creation', Eugenius discovers that instead of terminating in Milton's chaos, they open suddenly into 'a terrestrial paradise':

> But what imagination can conceive, or what language express, the beauties of this vale! I shall greatly injure by endeavouring to describe it; I will only say, that nature had assembled all her beauties in this sequestered spot. It seemed to extend, in a wavering line, about three miles; a small river ran winding through the bottom, the regularity of whose meanders was frequently broken by groups of poplars, elms, or alders; and the meadow on its banks enlivened by herds of cattle. The woods on the side of the hills seemed only to have cleared away to make room, every half mile, for tolerably neat buildings, farms, or cottages, which gave the whole an habitable, and yet a retired, romantic air. Toward the extremity of the valley, a small parish church appeared, above which the mountains rose in a circular form, and bounded the view. (I, p.32)

Williams explains that the Welsh name for this beautiful valley is Llandryffyd Dwr Llwifen, 'which the gentlemen lately settled there not being able to pronounce, they had given it the name of THE GOLDEN VALE' (I, p.33). The change of name is presented neutrally. Graves appears to have no axe to grind (even for satiric purposes) on behalf of the Welsh language. The Williams family represent the indigenous freeholders of the valley. They live in a substantial farmhouse with barns and ox-stalls shaded by oaks of antediluvian appearance, an oblique allusion perhaps to those descendants of Noah who had lived in north Wales during the Druidic age of gold.[7] In the old-fashioned parlour, most of the furniture dates from the previous century, with a brown-rubbed oak table and Turkey-work chairs, together with a glass in a gilt frame, elegant china and a mahogany tea table sent down from London by Mr Williams's sister. Instead of the jessamine that would flourish in later fictions of Wales, the small windows of the farmhouse are filled with mint.

In an unusually early attack on English immigrants, Graves deplores the behaviour of the governor, admiral, general and archbishop who have recently settled in the Golden Vale; together with the resident attorney and doctor, they indulge in 'licentious mirth and jocularity', setting a bad example to the local people. One newcomer, however, is a man of different calibre. Mr Hamilton, Graves's idealized industrialist, is deplored by his neighbours because he is said to encourage poaching, though he points out that by giving employment to two notorious poachers, he has ensured that the men are now sober and industrious and their families no longer in want. This notion, that poor men without work ought to be provided with employment, is the essential argument put forward in this novel in order to justify what in a later century would be described as the 'rape of the fair country' – though it is not the mineral wealth of north Wales but its textiles that Mr Hamilton eventually utilizes for the benefit of his workers.

The revolution that Mr Hamilton brings about in the Golden Vale is far more radical than the development of 'factory parishes', the farm-based production of textiles which, according to Gwyn A. Williams, was at this period 'turning the country people of a great tranche of Wales, running from Machynlleth on the west coast, in a broad arc through Merioneth and Montgomeryshire in the north and north-centre to Denbighshire and the English borderlands, into a population of rural industrial workers with demographic and life-chance rhythms radically different from those of "traditional peasants"'.[8] While there is no evidence that Richard Graves had any personal knowledge of the textile industry in north Wales, his account of the factories built by Mr Hamilton in the Golden Vale certainly reflects industrial developments elsewhere in north Wales, notably the 'manufactory' of the Cotton

Twist Company, founded in 1783, two years before the publication of *Eugenius,* virtually in Thomas Pennant's own backyard. Pennant did not publish his account of the mill until 1796, but it is symptomatic of the optimism and moral blindness of the times that he was prepared to quote verbatim Christopher Smalley's glowing account of the arrangements for child workers at the factory (between three and four hundred of them) in the 'commodious houses' they occupied between shifts.[9] In contrast, John Jones of Llanasa would recall the 'foul Prestonian tyrrany' of Smalley's regime:

> Well I remember, how in early years,
> I toil'd therein, with unavailing tears . . .
> No bondage state – no inquisition cell,
> Nor scenes yet dearer to the Prince of Hell,
> Could greater acts of cruelty display
> Than yon tall factories on a former day;
> E'en neighbouring forests frowned with angry nods,
> To see, Oppression! Thy demand for rods!
> Rods doom'd to bruise in barb'rous dens of noise
> The tender forms of orphan girls and boys!
> Whose cries – which mercy in no instance found,
> Were in the din of whirling engines drown'd.[10]

Like Pennant, Graves was either ignorant of or chose to ignore the human misery associated with the factory system. Although the children of the Golden Vale attend an early version of an Industrial School[11] (patronized by the Hamilton ladies), where the boys are taught to labour and the girls to knit and spin and improve their needlework, thus qualifying either as servants or as workers in the woollen factory, there is no suggestion that they are employed in the mills at a tender age. Indeed, at one point in the novel a group of local children add a picturesque touch at Louisa Hamilton's birthday celebrations when, 'set in motion by a Welch harp, with a tabor and pipe', they perform '*Of a noble race was Shenkin, Nancy Dawson,* and one or two easy dances more, in very true time' (II, pp.14–15).

When Eugenius returns to Wales four years after his first visit, he has mixed feelings about the changes that have come about as a direct result of the industrialization of the Golden Vale. He notes that the roads have improved and that where there were few travellers, he now meets 'two or three [*sic*]' busy people going to and from the vale.

Several new cottages and other buildings give an appearance of cheerfulness and industry. Yet he admits that these add little to the prospect and on visiting the Hamiltons he would have 'inveighed against the encroachments of arts on the prerogative of nature' (I, p.101) had he not been warned that Mr Hamilton himself

> had partly projected, and greatly encouraged, a manufactory of woollen stuffs, which were common in other parts of Wales; and which employed the poor, raised the value of their lands, and increased population, by finding a subsistence for several industrious families, who had by degrees settled in, or in the neighbourhood of, the valley. (I, pp.101–2)

Unlike Arthur Young, who, in the same year that *Eugenius* was published, described the factories of Coalbrookdale as too sublime to fit in with the gentle beauty of their surroundings,[12] the fictitious Mr Hamilton acknowledges 'the uncouth and artificial appearance of those structures, to which he was as great an enemy as I could be' (I, p.102). For all his apparent enthusiasm for industrialization, Graves never portrays the woollen mills of the Golden Vale as Joseph Wright of Derby painted the mill in *Joseph Arkwright's Mill* (1783), in which 'The Georgian domestic architecture . . . intrudes on the scene no more than might a brightly lit country house'.[13] In justifying his enterprise, Mr Hamilton firmly rejects the aesthetic dimension: 'matters of taste should be only of secondary consideration, and must frequently give way to convenience and utility' (I, p.102).

Just as Eugenius had first visited the Golden Vale as an admirer of romantic scenery, Mr Hamilton admits that he originally bought his house, South Rock, for its picturesque situation. It was a house to attract the admiration of a romantic youth:

> At the very extremity of the valley an old mansion house had attracted my notice, which was situated on the side of the hill, and appeared rising out of a group of trees on a ridge of rocks; to which a modern building, with a bow-window, had been added; and which discovered a taste superior to any thing I had seen in the neighbourhood. (I, pp.64–5)

However, Mr Hamilton also saw that the Golden Vale, like the neighbouring valleys, was peopled by a set of wretched, idle, unemployed and thievish inhabitants, rendered even more dissolute by the gentlemen who had recently come to live there; he realized that the poor people might be easily civilized and converted into useful members of society. As he explains to Eugenius, he proposed a scheme for a manufactory to Mr Jackson, an enterprising young man in a neighbouring county: 'In short, these poor creatures, who were before idle and dirty, and starving amidst these fruitful vales, are now well fed and well clothed, and live in health and plenty; and what is more, are brought to and habit of sobriety and honesty' (I, p.145).

Graves does not entirely triumph over the more romantic aspirations of his age: some remnants of the rural idyll remain even in this industrialized valley. Not only do the children dance to the 'Welch' harp on Louisa Hamilton's birthday, but the spirit of Rousseau still haunts the vale as one of the Williams girls, now Mrs Owen, makes a pleasing picture in the style of 'Berghem':[14]

> The maid was milking the cows under the shade of an old elm, where the patient animals were assembled, gently ruminating, and waiting in their turns to be eased of their salubrious burthen: – a little boy and girl were feeding the poultry; and in the chair at the door Mrs. Owen was sitting, with a Madonna air, hanging over and suckling her child. (I, p.126)

At a stroke, the industrialized Welsh landscape is metamorphosed into a Dutch pastoral landscape in the Italianate style while Rousseau's recommendation in *Émile* that mothers should feed their children themselves instead of employing wet nurses is silently invoked. (There is a certain irony in the fact that Graves dedicates *Eugenius*, the first Welsh industrial novel, to the 'Fair Reader' – not to one of profound erudition and universal reading, but to one who nurses her own children, plays Pope Joan with the curate's wife and sometimes reads a novel.) At this stage of the Industrial Revolution it seemed possible to have one's cake and eat it – woollen mills and new roads on the one hand, traditional dancing and breast feeding 'under the shade of an old elm' on the other. Similarly, while the entrepreneur, Mr Hamilton, continues to live at South Rock after the industrialization of the Golden Vale, there is always the possibility of escape. The Hamiltons enjoy 'health and ease, innocence and cheerfulness' in the country, but Shrewsbury and London beckon from time to time:

> In the depth of winter (especially if it proved very severe) they sometimes spent a month in lodgings in Shrewsbury, which abounds with as many genteel families, and gentlemen of liberal education, as most

provincial towns in England. And as Mr. Hamilton had relations in the neighbourhood of London – where he himself had lived before he came into . . ., and where a considerable part of his property lay – he generally took one or two of the young ladies with him, in their turns, for a month; which furnished the family with sufficient knowledge of the polite world, and with the prevailing topics and transactions of fashionable life. (II, pp.42–3)

Most of the second volume of the novel is devoted to Eugenius's courtship of Flora Williams in London, but they return to the Golden Vale to be married, when Mrs Hamilton's female scholars meet them at the churchyard gate and strew flowers along the path to the church door. After his marriage, Eugenius sets out to emulate Mr Hamilton and Mr Jackson, who now employ four hundred people in different branches of manufacture, 'so that we have hardly an idle or vicious, and of course hardly a poor person, within some miles of the Golden Vale' (II, p.187). But even the budding entrepreneur requires a home fit for a late eighteenth-century gentleman: Eugenius buys the admiral's farm and mansion house and makes alterations which give him a fine sloping lawn down to the river and a view of the hanging woods and hills which rise above its banks.

Although Eugenius is thus spared a view of the factories from his windows, Richard Graves has little time in his fiction for romantic self-indulgence. Just as he had earlier rejected Methodistic enthusiasm in *The Spiritual Quixote* and Shenstone's brand of self-centred rustic retirement in *Columella*, Graves's endorsement of industrial development in the Golden Vale demonstrates his capacity to reject the pieties of early Romanticism in favour of an active, quintessentially modern way of life. Unlikely though it may seem, the eccentric and elderly incumbent of Claverton produced in *Eugenius* a novel which has some claims to be described as the first 'Welsh' industrial novel – a work of remorseless optimism and (one guesses) invincible ignorance, but immaculately predicated on a concern for the economic welfare of a people without work.

9

'The venerable name of religion'

DRUIDISM IN *IMOGEN* BY WILLIAM GODWIN

Born into a dissenting family, William Godwin (1756–1836) has himself described 'the puritanical strictness' of his education, the sabbatarian rigour of his upbringing (he was once reprimanded for levity when he picked up the cat on a Sunday) and the 'religious enthusiasm and bigotry' that was instilled into his infant mind.[1] His father, John Godwin, was minister successively at Wisbech in Cambridgeshire, Debenham in Suffolk and Guestwick in Norfolk. His grandfather, Edwin Godwin, was for forty years the minister at Bishopsgate Street, London. His grandmother, Judith Weaver, a Welshwoman from Knighton in Radnorshire, was the widow of Dr Samuel Jones, head of a dissenting academy in Tewkesbury and son of the Revd Malachi Jones, a minister of the gospel in Pennsylvania. His uncle, Edward Godwin, was 'a distinguished preacher in the Methodist connection, and an eager publisher of experiences, devout allegories, and hymns'.[2] As he grew up, Godwin's sole ambition was to follow in the family footsteps and enter the ministry himself. Under the brutal tutelage of Samuel Newton, he embraced Sandemanianism, a form of Calvinism even more repressive than the creed in which he had been brought up at Guestwick.[3] From 1773 to 1778 he attended the Hoxton dissenting academy in London where he devoted himself to the search for truth:

> I was perpetually prompting myself with the principle, *Sequar veritatem* – I read all the authors of the greatest repute for and against the trinity, original sin, and the most disputed doctrines – but I was not yet of an understanding, sufficiently ripe for impartial decision, and all my enquiries terminated in Calvinism . . . I formed during this period, from reading on all sides, a creed upon materialism and immaterialism, liberty and necessity, in which no subsequent improvement of my understanding has been able to produce any variation – I was remarked by

my fellow collegians for the intrepidity of my opinions, and the tranquil fearlessness of my temper.[4]

In debates with his fellow students he was willing to take 'the negative side' in discussing the being of God, but he did not yet have the courage to persist in his objections 'and finally took refuge in the argument *a priori*, as outlined in Dr. Samuel Clark's Discourse on the Attributes'.[5] In 1778 he became minister at Ware in Hertfordshire, moving to Stowmarket in Suffolk in 1779. He records that during this period 'my orthodoxy was insensibly declining; I rejected the doctrine of eternal damnation, and my notions respecting the trinity acquired a taint of heresy'.[6] In 1781 he read Holbach's *Système de la Nature* and became a deist:[7] 'My opinions fluctuated however, and shortly after I subsided into Socinianism.[8] This continued to be my [faith] creed till 1788, when I took my last farewell of the Christian faith.'[9] In June 1783 Godwin resigned from his post at Beaconsfield where he had been minister for the previous six months. Within a year he had produced three short novels, *Damon and Delia*, *Italian Letters* and *Imogen*, and, if it would be invidious to search for direct references to the spiritual crisis that had brought about his departure from the ministry, it is certainly possible to find in *Imogen*, written between January and May 1784, some traces of the 'fluctuating' religious ideas embraced by Godwin before he took his 'last farewell' of Christianity.

Imogen: A Pastoral Romance From The Ancient British (1784) was first published anonymously by William Lane, Leadenhall-street, in two volumes. For many years it was thought to be lost to the world, but by 1963 two copies of the first edition had been tracked down, a complete text in the Salisbury Library in Cardiff, and another, lacking two pages, now in the Berg Collection of the New York Public Library. In his Introduction to the reprinted novel,[10] Jack W. Marken notes that its setting in north Wales at the time of the Druids focuses on the eighteenth-century revival of interest in native sources of myth and suggests that Godwin could have looked at works by John Toland, William Cooke, John Smith and Hugh Blair:[11]

> In any event, Godwin's novel is full of druidical mythology. The sacrifice to the gods, the veneration of the bards, and the sacredness of the oak and the teachings of the prophets are all incorporated. Godwin's originality in the novel lies in the association of this lore and contemporary moral didacticism with the *Comus* plot.[12]

Marken describes Godwin's creation in *Imogen* of an ideal Druidic society, an idea which is further explored in the 'critical discussion' appended to the text. Thus Martha Winburn England suggests that 'The choice of pastoral form, with its convention of an Age of Gold in ancient Britain, had a validity that can be felt in the opening scenes with their recognizable Welsh locale.'[13] In his assessment of Godwin's debt to Rousseau, Burton R. Pollin makes a similar point: 'It is clear, in this vista of ancient Wales, that Godwin is favoring a golden age preceding culture, as constituting the acme of felicity' – a golden age devoid of such excesses as intemperance, cruelty and insincerity.[14] Irwin Primer follows the same line when he suggests that, in the bardic song recited by Llewelyn, 'Godwin may well be offering the pure, natural religion of the Druids as the preferable alternative to modern Christianity, a view suggested or implied in Toland's writings on the Druids'.[15] According to Primer, Godwin seems to reveal in *Imogen* a sympathetic and partisan attitude to deistic natural religion, thus providing further evidence of the progressive deterioration of his religious faith in the 1780s. The notion here is that Godwin creates a golden age in which the Druids practise a pure natural religion as a viable alternative to Christianity.

However, a careful reading of the novel, together with a survey of the sources available to Godwin, suggests that his view of the Druids – like his own espousal of deism and 'the progressive deterioration of his religious faith' – was almost certainly a more complex business than Pollin and Primer allow. Godwin and his contemporaries inherited a considerable body of literature which conveyed diverse and often unflattering interpretations of the Druids and their culture. This literature included a group of early texts dating from 200 BC to 400 AD and an assortment of later material in Latin and English, much of it, as A. L. Owen records, 'a literature of single pages and paragraphs'.[16] Owen demonstrates that 'English literature on the Druids stems from a few passages in classical and patristic literature which, brief as they are, have possibly never yielded two identical interpretations'.[17] In one of the earliest references in English, Alexander Barclay's *The Shyp of Folys of the Worlde* (1509), the Druids figure (unflatteringly) as intoxicated dancers, 'Makynge theyr sacrafyce with furour noyse and shout / Whan theyr madnes settyth theyr wyt asyde'.[18] Nearly three centuries later, after a stream of references to Druidism in Renaissance histories, religious polemic and antiquarian studies, as well as a number of guest appearances by Druidism in poetry and drama, the Revd Edward

Ledwick was moved to acid comment: 'On no subject has fancy roamed . . . with more licentious indulgence than on that of the Druids and their institutions.'[19] Ledwick was writing in 1784, the year when Godwin's fancy roamed in *Imogen*. Owen points out that, with the distinguished exception of John Aubrey (whose scholarly and influential work on Stonehenge was never published),[20] 'Nearly every one who has written of them at any length has written of Druids of his own making'.[21] By the end of the century, 'licentious indulgence' had led Iolo Morganwg to the Primrose Hill Gorsedd in 1792 and the forged poems of *The Myvyrian Archaiology of Wales* (1801–7),[22] in which he 'smuggled his "Aboriginal" and baptized Druids into early Welsh literature'.[23] Such developments lie beyond the scope of this chapter, though it is proper to note that in *Imogen*, in what may appear to be a bizarre exercise in prose fiction, Godwin is in fact engaging with some of the material whose 'pompous Shews and Appearances', as Henry Rowlands phrased it,[24] would permanently alter, not to say disfigure, the cultural face of Wales.

Pollin and Primer are not alone in failing to recognize the 'madnes [*sic*]' of the Druids. While denying that Godwin is concerned with a golden age of the past ('he rewrites Milton's exemplary theme of virtue in distress as a paradigm of revolutionary experience, highlighting the power of private judgement to dethrone hereditary vice'),[25] even Patricia Clemit accepts that the use of Druidic material in *Imogen* is consistent with radical political thought:

> Godwin is not concerned with an idealized past but with a secular myth of a future state, as he builds on the association of the Druids with independence and political liberty shared by Milton's 'Lycidas' and the work of eighteenth-century patriot poets such as James Thomson and Thomas Gray.[26]

Clemit's case for *Imogen* as a representation of 'revolutionary' thought is persuasive, but she ignores the fact that Godwin's references to Druidism by no means point exclusively to ideas of 'independence and political liberty'. Far from creating merely a 'secular myth', Godwin offers in *Imogen* fragments of a theology which cannot be described as a simple essay in deism but rather as a complex expression of spiritual angst.

Despite the facetious tone of the Preface, in which he discusses the likely authorship of the manuscript (he decides that his ancestor, Rice ap Thomas, who flourished in the reign of King William III, is a more likely candidate than the bard Cadwallo, 'who probably lived at least one hundred years before the commencement of our common aera'), Godwin is at pains to establish the theological framework of his novel from the outset:

> It is impossible to discover in any part of it [the manuscript] the slightest trace of Christianity. And we believe it will not be disputed, that in a country so pious as that of Wales, it would have been next to impossible for the poet, though ever so much upon his guard, to avoid all allusion to the system of revelation. On the contrary, every thing is Pagan, and in perfect conformity with the theology we are taught to believe prevailed at that time. (p.21)

The reference to Welsh piety may well be ironic, like the disingenuous reference to 'the theology we are taught to believe prevailed at that time'. Owen points out that after much disputation, the seventeenth century had ultimately 'produced a Druid who was as near being a Christian as makes no difference',[27] a notion ridiculed by the deist, John Toland, when he claimed with barbed irony in his *History of the Druids* (1720) 'that no heathen priesthood ever came up to the perfection of the Druidical . . . as having been much better calculated to beget ignorance, and an implicit disposition in the people, no less than to procure power and profit to the priests'.[28] The Christian version of Druidism was defended by William Stukeley who demonstrated in his prospectus to *Stonehenge A Temple Restor'd to the British Druids* (1740) 'that the first religion was no other than Christianity, the Mosaic dispensation, as a veil, intervening'; he claimed that the Druids had brought the patriarchal religion to Britain together with '*the notion and expectation of the Messiah, and of the time of the year when he was to be born, of his office and death*'.[29] As Owen remarks,

> In order to follow Stukeley it is helpful to know that he was not only discussing the Druids but skirmishing with a '*fashionable and audacious*' enemy, deism. Toland was the original pest who provoked him, and in *Stonehenge* the foes of the priesthood were having their own arguments turned against them. The deists claimed that if the tenets of Holy Writ were wholly and self-sufficiently reasonable, and that if the unaided efforts of reason could efficiently demonstrate the truth of religion, the conception of revelation was redundant . . . [Toland] covertly assailed

the Church of England by attacking the Druids. Stukeley, for his part, counter-attacked by replying that the Druids believed in revelation and in the Trinity, and that they were quite capable of the subtlest ratiocination, and that the Church of England still preserved their teachings.[30]

By claiming that 'every thing is Pagan' in the extensive valley of the Clwyd, Godwin implictly rejects Stukeley and the long-established tradition of christening the Druids. By his own account, he had espoused deism for a time, and it seems quite likely that in *Imogen* he is supporting the views of Toland. But, in doing so, he is very far from suggesting that the Druids practise a 'pure, natural religion' (as Primer contends): on the contrary, Toland's Druidical priesthood – and perhaps Godwin's too – is bent on procuring 'power and profit' at the expense of 'the people'.

It had long been a subject of debate as to whether the Druids practised monotheism or polytheism.[31] In *Imogen* Godwin for the most part adopts a pagan polytheism: the immortal Gods are much in evidence, regarded with fear and gratitude, approached with prayer and 'fervour of devotion' and apt to help, bless and pity mortals by protecting the virtuous. Thus the heroine is defended from the wicked Modred by a Mercury-like figure when the Gods send down 'their swift and winged messenger to shield her virtue' (p.31). In Godwin's theocracy, the Druids operate as a priesthood; as in many classical accounts of the order, they are experienced in the nature of the divine; they teach the immortality of the soul; they live in groves in the forest and venerate the mistletoe and the oak; they are honoured by the communities in which they live; most tellingly, they practise human sacrifice. Godwin ignores the Vates who, according to Caesar, formed with the Druids and the bards the highest caste of society, but he includes some later additions to Druidic lore, notably the idea propounded by Aubrey, Toland, Stukeley and others, that their religious practices were associated with Stonehenge and other stone circles. (It is not without interest that, at the time of writing *Imogen*, Godwin was recording the measurements of Stonehenge.[32]) Hence the description at the beginning of the novel, where Imogen and Edwin attend 'an anniversary of religious mirth' near the village of Ruthyn: 'The sun shone with unusual splendour; the Druidical temples, composed of immense and shapeless stones, heaped upon each other by a power stupendous and incomprehensible, reflected back his radiant beams' (p.29). (Rather surprisingly, Godwin transfers most of the action of the novel from Anglesey, the historical site of British Druidism, to the Clwyd valley, though, by suggesting that his Druids occupy 'secret cells' on Mona, he provides a covert reminder of their eventual massacre, as described by Tacitus.[33])

It would be probably be a mistake, however, to take Godwin's word for the fact that in this novel 'every thing is Pagan'. By his own account, he was a Socinian at the time of writing *Imogen* and, therefore, still nominally a Christian. Shortly after resigning from the ministry in June 1783, and only a few months before publishing his first attempts at fiction, he had brought out a volume of six sermons, *Sketches of History* (1783), 'notable for its evangelical praise of Christ and his lessons for the world'.[34] Preoccupied as he was in four of these sermons with the arraignment, crucifixion, resurrection and character of Jesus, Godwin's scepticism and radical ideas about individual liberty were already evident in his view that the rights of the Creator do not extend to making an innocent being miserable ('God himself has not the right to be a tyrant').[35] Conversely, although Godwin eventually became an atheist, his earlier conviction that the Christian life is a scene of trial, involving pain and suffering as well as temptation and sin and the possibility of forgiveness, remained ingrained in his thought processes.[36] Thus, although there may be no direct allusion to the person of Christ in *Imogen*, Chapter I begins with a bardic version of the Christian life, complete with a reference to the one God ('the Most High') and 'the crown' of eternal life:

> LISTEN, O man! To the voice of wisdom. The world thou inhabitest was not intended for a theatre of fruition, nor destined for a scene of repose. False and treacherous is that happiness, which has been preceded by no trial, and is connected with no desert. It is like a gilded poison that undermines the human frame. It is like the hoarse murmur of the winds that announces the brewing tempest. Virtue, for such is the decree of the Most High, is evermore obliged to pass through the ordeal of temptation, and the thorny path of adversity. If, in this day of her trial, no foul blot obscure her lustre, no irresolution and instability tarnish the clearness of her spirit, then may she rejoice in the view of her approaching reward, and receive with an open heart the crown that shall be bestowed upon her. (p.25)

What is clearly conceded here, in terms perfectly compatible with Christian discourse, is the notion that temptation and adversity are decreed by 'the most High', an idea that Godwin had already attacked in his sermons: God himself does not have the right to make an innocent being miserable.

B. S. Tysdahl argues that in *Imogen* Godwin's 'moral geography' is forced.[37] Certainly the evocation of a primeval golden age in a remote valley in north Wales sits oddly with bardic warnings of the necessity of 'the ordeal of temptation, and the thorny path of adversity'.

> The extensive valley of the Clwyd once boasted a considerable number of inhabitants, distinguished for primeval innocence and pastoral simplicity. Nature seemed to have prepared it for their reception with all that luxuriant bounty, which characterises her most favored spots. The inclosure by which it was bounded, of ragged rocks and snow-topt mountains, served but for a foil to the richness and fertility of this happy plain. It was seated in the bosom of North Wales, the whole face of which, with this one exception, was rugged and hilly. As far as the eye could reach, you might see promontory rise above promontory. The crags of Penmaenmawr were visible to the northwest, and the unequalled steep of Snowden terminated the prospect to the south. In its farthest extent the valley reached almost to the sea, and it was intersected, from one end to the other, by the beautiful and translucent waters of the river from which it receives its name. (p.25)

There is certainly a curious moral ambivalence in the presentation of this happy valley. Ostensibly, 'all was rectitude and guileless truth': it had never been disturbed by warfare, crime and 'the iron hand of tyranny' were unknown, and the inhabitants were strangers to riches, 'for they all lived in a happy equality'. Even so, the inhabitants are not immune from the powers of evil. Rodogune, the mother of Roderic, is said to have entered ('within the memory of the elder of shepherds') a 'dark and criminal alliance with invisible powers' and corrupted some of those inhabitants of the Clwyd valley distinguished for 'primeval innocence and pastoral simplicity': like Comus, she has held in her enchanted castle in the mountains 'crouds of degenerate shepherds, groveling through the omnipotence of her incantations in every brutal form' (p.46). Similarly, the arch-villain of the piece, Roderic himself, is allowed to enter the valley and forcibly abduct Imogen in his 'car'. The spiritual anguish that occasionally appears to explode through what may appear to be a mere pastiche of *Comus* is the idea – already touched on in the sermons – that human suffering is tolerated, even instigated, by the deity. When an 'inimical goblin' bursts through a condensed cloud and arraigns Roderick with 'bitter sarcasms', he makes the complicity of the gods with evil acceptable by making their victim a wealthy man:

> The Gods, when the Gods are willing to perfect a character of deparavity, in order to make vice consummately detestable, or to administer an exemplary punishment to distinguished wickedness, bestow upon that man, as the last of curses, and the most refined of tortures, extensive possessions and unbounded riches. (p.74)

Here Godwin parades a familiar argument of eighteenth-century moral philosophy: that individual wickedness is hateful and, therefore, a deterrent to the rest of mankind; in so doing, he displays his radical opinions by making his villain an aristocrat ('distinguished wickedness'), to be punished as an example to others of the same caste.

Elsewhere in the novel, however, notably in the three bardic songs performed at the 'festival of religious mirth' at the beginning of the novel, Godwin conveys a much more troubled apprehension of the nature of the deity. After a rural feast and a variety of activities including sports, dancing, wrestling, and hide-and-seek, the peasants of the Clwyd valley are summoned by the sound of harp, rebec and pipe, and gather round 'the honoured troop of the bards, crowned with laurel and sacred mistletoe' (p.31). In the first song, a young bard sings of Modred's pursuit of the chaste daughter of Cadwallo, providing a kind of preview of Imogen's coming ordeal when she falls into the clutches of Roderick. Probably the most significant moment in this song (in which the bard 'out-Ovids Ovid'[38]) occurs at the point in the chase where Cadwallo's daughter is transformed from a trembling hare into a ravening beast:

> on a sudden there burst from a cave a hungry and savage wolf; it was the daughter of Cadwallo. Modred started with horror, and in his turn fled away swifter than the winds. The fierce and ravenous animal pursued; fire flashed from the eye, and rage and fury sat upon the crest. Mild and gentle was the daughter of Cadwallo; her heart relented; her soft and tender spirit, belied the savage form. They approached the far famed stream of Conway. Modred cast behind him a timid and uncertain eye; the virgin passed along, no longer terrible, a fair and milk white hind. (p.31)

In context, this reads not so much as a feminist reaction to the threat of rape as a sudden eruption of anger on the part of the author – on behalf of the victim maybe, but more convincingly as a burst of impatience which subverts the Miltonic 'moral' of the story, that unprotected virtue, however gentle, however passive, is at all times under divine protection. As England justly observes of Imogen's escape from her own pursuer, Roderick, this idea is not backed by any belief in Godwin's mind: 'He never presented with conviction any character whose innocence saved him.'[39] For a moment or two, between her appearances as a trembling hare and a white hind, Cadwallo's daughter is herself a 'fierce and ravenous animal', as if to demonstrate, perhaps with deliberate irony, that it is only in such manifestations that the power of evil represented by Modred can be literally put to flight.

In the second bardic performance, irony is employed much more savagely, as Godwin focuses on the Druidical practice of human sacrifice. Caesar had described the 'wicker man', a gigantic effigy made of twigs which was stuffed with victims for the sacrificial fire.[40] There had been a number of ingenious attempts to defend the practice, though William Richards had included a satirical description of 'one Goodman *Druis*' in *Wallography* (1682), his scurrilous account of the Welsh: 'He was dextrous at a Fortune, and *Old-Dog* at Augury; and the only thing we dislike in him, is, he sacrific'd Men, and so divin'd by Butchery.'[41] More recently, the sacrifices of the Druids had been described with a certain ghoulish relish by the Revd James Foot in *Penseroso* (1771):

> Although some useful truths charm'd in the song
> Of Druid wisdom, and with awe their groves
> Beheld the natural light through thickest shades
> Oft' shew her radiant presence, yet the pomp
> Of bloody Altars, knives and death prepar'd
> For human victims, where by force compell'd
> They shed their blood bewailing, made their groves
> The bloody shambles of misguided zeal,
> And the vile Priests the butch'ring tools of Heav'n.[42]

In describing the sacrifice of the young shepherd, Arthur, Godwin's second bard also dwells on the gory details of the scene, an emphasis which seems strangely inappropriate for a poet who is said to be 'full of gentleness and sensibility':

He had ever been distinguished by an attachment to solitude, and a love for those grand and tremendous objects of uncultivated nature with which his country abounded. His were the hanging precipice, and the foaming cataract. His ear drank in the voice of the tempest; he was rapt in attention to the roaring thunder. When the contention of the elements seemed to threaten the destruction of the universe, when Snowdon bowed to its deepest base, it was then that his mind was most filled with sublime meditation. His lofty soul soared above the little war of terrestrial objects, and rode expanded upon the wings of the winds. Yet was the bard full of gentleness and sensibility; no breast was more susceptible to the emotions of pity, no tongue was better skilled in the soft and passionate touches of the melting and pathetic. He possessed a key to unlock all the avenues of the heart. (pp.32–3)

Despite his 'lofty soul', there is little sublimity evident in his song and any pathos he achieves is chilling. Indeed, he strikes a note at the beginning that sounds very much like authorial sarcasm as he tells of a dreadful famine that laid waste the shores of the Menai: 'Heaven, not to punish the shepherds, for, alas, what had these innocent shepherds done? but in the mysterious wisdom of its ways, had denied the refreshing shower, and the soft-descending dew' (p.33). Godwin, through his bardic mouthpiece, unmistakably calls into question the 'mysterious wisdom' of a divinity that inflicts such suffering on innocent humanity. There is also grotesque irony in the fact that, though Arthur's prayer to the 'all-merciful divinity' is indeed answered, the benign influence of rustling showers and pearly, orient dew is achieved at the expense of his own life ('the awful voice of the Druid proclaimed the decree of heaven!'). If at one level his sacrifice is presented as an act of heroism and patriotism, Evelina's reaction allows the bard (and Godwin too, perhaps) to shriek impotently against the barbarity of such a divinity. When the altar is made ready, the fillets brought forth and the sacred knife glitters in the hand of the chief of the Druids, the bards sing their song of death to the accompaniment of the harp. Arthur's eyes gleam with immortal fire, but Evelina in her distress is wild and ungovernable, like a wild beast robbed of its young:

> For an instant the venerable name of religion awed her into mute submission. But when the fatal moment approached, not the Gods, if the Gods had descended in all their radiant brightness, could have restrained her any longer. The air was rent with her piercing cries. She

spoke not. Her eyes in silence turned towards heaven, distilled a plenteous shower. At last, swifter than the winged hawk, she flew towards the spot, and seized the sacred and inviolable arm of the holy Druid, which was lifted up to strike the final blow. 'Barbarous and inhuman priest,' she cried, 'cease your vile and impious mummery! No longer insult us with the name of Gods. If there be Gods, they are merciful; but thou art a savage and unrelenting monster. Or if some victim must expire, strike here, and I will thank thee. Strike, and my bosom shall heave to meet the welcome blow. Do any thing. But oh, spare me the killing, killing spectacle!' (p.34)

Like the metamorphosis of Cadwallo's daughter into a wolf, Evelina is compared with a hawk as she flies at the 'holy' Druid (the irony is palpable). She attacks the priest physically and verbally, accusing him of 'mummery', a word with time-honoured connotations of popish ritual but possibly referring here to Godwin's recent reading of Holbach, who ascribes the origin of religion to the primeval fear of Nature and the need to conciliate its unknown powers: 'Some irascible and placable divinity was always at the bottom of it, and it was on this puerile and absurd notion that the priesthood founded its rights, its temples, its altars, its wealth, its authority and its dogmas.'[43] On such crude foundations, Holbach continues, rest all the religious systems of the world: 'invented originally by savages, they still have the power to control the fate of most civilized nations.'[44] Evelina rejects Arthur's sacrifice as a means of placating the mysterious power that has brought famine to the shores of the Menai, although 'at times like this the blood of a human victim was accustomed to be shed upon the altars of heaven' (p.33); like Holbach, she questions the very existence of such a deity ('No longer insult us with the name of Gods'). When the bard directs his listeners to behold the lovely youth 'sunk on the ground, and weltering in his blood', he gives reassurances that Arthur will possess immortality and that his precious memory will be embalmed in song – but he also admits that he is unable to soothe the 'unexhausted grief' of Evelina.

The transition to the third bardic song, sung by 'the reverend Llewelyn', appears to represent a disorientating shift from angry scepticism to a hymn of praise and gratitude to heaven. The pagan gods are replaced by a Creator, the almighty word who spoke 'the rude and shapeless chaos' into form, in an account which follows closely the story of the creation in Genesis. In tune with other eighteenth-century physico-theological paeans of praise,[45] the bard calls upon the whole creation to praise its maker, reminding mankind that 'ye favoured sons of the eternal father, be it yours in articulate expressions of gratitude to interpret for the mute creation, and to speak a sublimer and more rational homage' (p.36). The subject matter of Llewelyn's song is perfectly commensurate with both Christianity and the tenets of eighteenth-century deism. But, if the reference to 'more rational homage' suggests that Evelina's anger against the gods has been quickly transposed into an intellectually respectable worship of the Creator, Llewelyn's song continues, ludicrously enough, with a reminder to the sinful that after death they will assume the shapes of wolves, horses, goats and boars – whatever form is congenial to their vices – while, on the other hand, 'Upon the upright and the good, attendant angels wait' (p.37). Llewelyn makes no direct reference to the parable of the sheep and the goats, but he certainly reminds his listeners of the final destruction of the earth by fire, thus ending his song with images and ideas that derive from orthodox Christianity (polytheism and laurel crowns notwithstanding) rather than Holbach's variety of deism: 'And when all the objects that you now behold shall be involved in universal conflagration, and time shall be no more; ye shall mix with Gods, ye shall partake their thrones, and be crowned like them with never-fading laurel' (p.37).

Clearly, such a passage calls into question England's view that Godwin's choice of the Druidic age 'allowed him to deal with a society that stood in no necessary moral relation to the Christian era, that had no need to argue oppressive questions of original sin and predestination'.[46] A close reading of the bardic songs in *Imogen* suggests some glaring inconsistencies in the religious ideas propounded there, and, without resorting to a crude equation with Godwin's own state of mind while he was writing the novel ('My opinions fluctuated'), it does seem possible to find internal evidence of an uneasy deism whose rationality is threatened by both the remnants of Christian faith and the eruption of disbelief ('No longer insult us with the name of Gods'). In a critique of *Political Justice*, Godwin picked out Sandemanianism as one of its principal errors, 'an inattention to the principle, that feeling, and not judgment, is the source of human actions'.[47] In a study of Godwin that focuses on his writing as 'a fantasy of reason', Don Locke argues that the official Godwin, reared in a severe, unrelenting Calvinism, became the dispassionate intellectual who judged all things in the light of eternal and impartial truth – while behind this façade of pure reason lay a tangle of repressed doubts and fears, so that his novels would 'seethe' with anxiety, despair and loneliness.[48] In discussing the diction of *Caleb Williams*, England uses the same term when she notes that 'the flatness is seething' and that 'When at last . . . a Biblical imprecation erupts into the text, it comes with the voice of despair and in the words used by the priests of Baal to call upon their non-existent god'.[49] In *Imogen*, in such images as Cadwallo's daughter as a wolf and Evelina as a hawk, religious feeling erupts through Godwin's Druidic version of *Comus* to pursue with 'rage and fury' the bland assurances and cruel impositions of a theocracy which calls forth the reverence and devotion of 'the people' ('They called together their innocent thoughts for the worship of heaven' (p.35)) but which is also, in Foot's inspired phrase, a 'bloody shambles'.

After Arthur has weltered in his own blood, his Druidic murderers revert to being the respectable servants of the gods. The Druid Madoc who lives on the shores of Lake Elwy, guarding 'that huge pile of stones . . . which had been reared ages since, by the holy Druids' (p.43), is a benevolent cross between Friar Lawrence and Goldsmith's hermit in 'Edwin and Angelina',[50] as he gives the young hero (another Edwin) shelter in his cell and presents him with a beauteous flower whose root, in Miltonic tradition, is a sovereign antidote against all blasts, enchantments, witchcraft and magic. Subsequent references in the novel to the Druids and the gods they serve are respectful, though there is one curious episode near the end of the story which seems to convey elliptically another angry comment on the godhead. When Imogen's abductor, Roderick, offers Edwin a cup of vice, he is shown to be godlike:

> The beauty of his person was worthy of the synod of the Gods . . . his garb, his step, his gesture had something in them of the angelic and celestial without the blaze of divinity, and without the awfulness that surrounds the godlike existencies, that sometimes condescend to visit this sublunary scene. (p.103)

When Edwin spills the liquid and hurls the cup to the ground, Roderic lifts his wand:

> It was the fiery ordeal that summons human character to the severest trial. It was the *judgment of God* in which the lots are devoutly committed to the disposal of heaven, and the enthroned Divinity, guided by

his omniscience of the innocence of the brave, or the guilt of the presumptuous, points the barbed spear, and gives a triple edge to the shining steel. If the shepherd had one base and earth-born particle in his frame, if his soul confessed one sordid and sensual desire, now was the time in which for his prospects to be annihilated and his reputation blotted for ever, and the state and empire of his rival to be fixed beyond the power of human machinations to shake or subvert it. (p.104)

In her comment on this passage ('one of those "faults" which make the work into something much more than a piece of sterile eclecticism'),[51] England relates Roderic's wand to Ithuriel's spear and Michael's shining sword, and suggests that here Evil is armed with a weapon usually placed on the side of the good: 'this ambiguity of associations may not be admirable, but the passage speaks in the true voice of a man getting ready to denounce the law as the greatest social evil.'[52] It should be added that the law is specifically defined, in italics, as 'the *judgment of God*': Godwin eschews simile – Roderic, already given the features of Milton's Satan, is here identified with God Himself as he holds Edwin at the bar of justice. If Godwin is indeed getting ready to denounce the law as the greatest social evil (in *Political Justice*), he is also implicitly denouncing the godhead as the source of that evil. When Edwin has seized and broken Roderic's wand and thereby made his evil mansion in Snowdonia vanish into thin air, Imogen herself may approve 'the justice of the Gods in the banishment of Roderic'. By this stage, however, Godwin's text has already demonized God the Lawgiver.

It would be misguided to read *Imogen* as if it offered a clearly argued account of Godwin's religious ideas at the time of writing. Even in his philosophical and political work, his method of composition was exploratory: 'When a man writes a book of methodical investigation, he does not write because he understands the subject, but he understands the subject because he has written.'[53] His daughter, Mary Shelley, described his painstaking method of revising his work, correcting a paragraph up to eight times and on one occasion needing to consult a doctor after 'a sense of confusion of the brain came over him' after exerting his intellectual faculties to the limit.[54] Even so, Locke finds evidence in *Political Justice* that Godwin changed his mind as he wrote or became so immersed in his chain of reasoning that he followed arguments wherever they led, however implausible.[55] It would take a bold commentator to claim to have discovered in *Imogen* precisely where Godwin 'stood' in relation to Calvinism, Sandemanianism, deism, Socinianism or atheism, though the text is clearly marked by the contradictions, perhaps even the turmoil, of the author's religious thinking. It is perhaps not too bold to claim, however, that far from inhabiting a golden age of 'primeval innocence and pastoral simplicity' – as the author claims – the young people who defy and triumph over Roderic in *Imogen* are in fact poised between the tyranny of the aristocracy (in Clemit's reading) and the tyranny of religion, glimpsed in the indelible image of the sacred knife that 'glittered in the hand of the chief of the Druids'.

10

Proud Cambrians and mantua makers

✍

ANNA, OR, MEMOIRS OF A WELCH HEIRESS
BY ANNA MARIA BENNETT

Anna Maria Bennett has achieved a certain status as a 'Welsh' writer in recent years,[1] though there is very little reliable biographical evidence available at present to suggest that she was born and brought up in Wales. The few facts known about her early life mostly derive from the entertaining but spiteful account given by Charles Lee Lewes in his *Memoirs*, in which he claims she was 'the daughter of Mr. Evans, a grocer on the Back, Bristol, (who was a native of Merthertidwell, in Glamorganshire,) where this lady was born'.[2] If she was indeed born on or near Welsh Back in Bristol, she must have begun life within earshot of a cacophony of Welsh voices ('Quick broken Tones in gutt'ral Words express') as supplies from 'the *Wallian* Fleets' were unloaded on the quay opposite the great church of St Mary Redcliffe, tolling its bell across the harbour:

> Hark! when the heavy *Tenor*'s sullen Sound
> Calls Mortal Man to earthly Parent Ground;
> The noisy Cymbal casts a dreadful Roar
> Along the busy Bank of th'adverse Shore.
> Where shriller Sounds from vocal Clappers fly,
> And cackling Dames with feather'd *Cacklers* try.
> For here the *Wallian* Fleets, like, *Noah*'s Ark,
> With Couplets stuff'd, a Medley-Stock debark;
> O'er which the chatt'ring Tribe in dapper Dress,
> Quick broken Tones in gutt'ral Words express.[3]

However, there is no record of her birth in the parish register of St Nicholas, Bristol – and she was certainly not the daughter of the Bristol grocer, David Evans, as J. F. Fuller has claimed.[4] In view of the ambiguity of Lewes's punctuation, it should be added that there is no trace of either Anna Maria Evans or her father, John Evans,[5] in the parish records for Merthyr Tydfil. Although internal evidence in *Anna, or, Memoirs of a Welch Heiress* suggests that she may have known this part of Wales, this is not substantiated by any documentary evidence currently available. Lewes goes on to claim that she married 'one Bennet, a tanner at Brecknock', but, if this was so, the tanner was later metamorphosed – like the Bristol grocer – into a customs house officer.[6]

According to Lewes, Anna Maria had been a 'slop-seller' – otherwise a dealer in cheap clothes – in Wych-street, St Clement's, and was working in a chandler's shop in the borough when she was first noticed by Thomas Pye[7] and elevated to the post of his housekeeper at Tooting. Lewes adds that she had also 'for a long time been mistress of a workhouse, but latterly held it by deputy',[8] a puzzling claim in view of the fact that her liaison with Pye probably lasted for a quarter of a century, almost certainly beginning before the death of his wife in 1762 and ending, according to Lewes, in bizarre circumstances only a few months before the Admiral's death in 1785.[9] In his will, Pye gives his name to five of Anna Maria Bennett's children: Thomas (born about 1761),[10] Harriet (born about 1765),[11] Caroline Sophia, Polly and Nancy.[12]

Anna Maria Bennett brought out her first novel during the year of Pye's death and at least five more were published between 1786 and 1806.[13] By 1792, her daughter, the actress Harriet Esten, had become the mistress of the Duke of Hamilton and obtained through his interest the lease of the Theatre Royal, Edinburgh. Lewes comments caustically on Mrs Bennett's disastrous attempt to manage the theatre on her daughter's behalf ('the practice of uncontrouled severity in the mistress of a workhouse over parish paupers, was not the rule of conduct to be exercised over the sons and daughters of the sock and the buskin').[14] Mrs Bennett is glimpsed a year or two later moving from lodgings in Nassau Street to share Harriet's 'magnificent elevation' in Half Moon Street, Piccadilly.[15] She died at Brighton on 12 February 1808, her funeral taking place nine days later: 'The solemn procession arrived from Brighton at the Horns [Inn], on Kennington Common, about twelve o'clock, where it was joined by a numerous and most respectable train of friends, who attended her remains to the grave.'[16] It is not yet known where she was buried.

Of the six novels known to be written by Anna Maria Bennett, two are set partly in Wales: *Anna, or, Memoirs of a Welch Heiress* (1785) and

Ellen, Countess of Castle Howel (1794). Some of the themes dealt with in these novels have been explored by feminist critics whose aim it is to restore Bennett 'to the canon of Welsh women writers'.[17] Francesca Rhydderch discovers in Bennett's fiction politically potent symbols of Welsh decline in relation to developing Britishness in the eighteenth century, and identifies indicators of a process of erosion of its indigenous culture 'suggesting that Wales is undergoing a general appropriation like that of the more exotic colonies of the British Empire'.[18] The present chapter focuses on Bennett's first Welsh novel and is principally concerned with charting the ways in which the heroine's need to earn her own bread is uneasily related to the theme of aristocratic pride of blood and the Welsh obsession with genealogy: even in this novel of 1785, one detects, perhaps, the first stirrings of that great surge of radical thought and feeling that would find expression in the revolutionary fiction of the following decade. The subtitle of the novel, *Memoirs of a Welch Heiress*, possibly taps memories of the two great heiresses of eighteenth-century Wales, Elizabeth Lewis[19] and Charlotte Herbert,[20] as well as the glut of lesser heiresses that occurred during the early part of the century as the male lines of many Welsh families died out.[21] The family names in the novel – Edwin, Herbert, Mansel, Turbville [*sic*] – are those of the gentry in eighteenth-century Glamorgan,[22] while Anna's ancestral estate, Trevannion, brings to mind the great estate of Y Fan, popularly 'the Van',[23] inherited by the Countess of Plymouth, formerly Elizabeth Lewis, in 1734. It is to these echelons of society that Anna belongs by birth, but Bennett adapts the male territory of the mid-eighteenth-century picaresque novel by replacing the young hero, carelessly venturing forth to sow his wild oats, with a heroine whose progress from poverty and insecurity to wealth and power as the Countess of Trevannion is fraught with physical and moral danger. Orphaned as a young child, Anna is abandoned to the tender mercies of the rapacious Daltons. Turned out of doors by her adoptive mother, Mrs Melmoth, after the propositions of Colonel Gorget, she takes refuge with the Revd and Mrs Mansel in Wales and becomes acquainted with the Herberts of Llandore Castle and their relations, the Edwins. Forced to work for her living after the death of Mrs Mansel, she fights off the advances of Hugh Edwin, eludes the snares set for her by Gorget and suffers poverty and illness before being restored to her rightful position as Lady Ann Trevannion. The 'rags to riches' plot is patently absurd, but there is no denying the powerful message conveyed throughout in its depiction of the vulnerability of a penniless young woman in eighteenth-century society, and no avoiding the questions Bennett raises about the value of female labour and (female) aristocratic pride.

There are a number of features in *Anna* that suggest a strong identification between the author and her heroine. Rhydderch has already pointed out the importance of naming in this novel,[24] but it is also worth noting that, when Anna's father dies and leaves his small daughter friendless and destitute in a London lodging-house, the child can remember nothing except her first name – which happens to be that of the author herself:

> by degrees, all memory of the past was lost, nor could they, by any exertion in their power, draw from her the surname of her parents; her own, she told them, was Anna; if she wanted any thing, it was 'give it Anna,' or 'let Anna have it;' but, her ideas were so infantine, they could learn nothing from her innocent talk that could lead to any discovery of where she came from, or whom she belonged to. (I, pp.9–10)[25]

The identification of author and character is perhaps hinted at elsewhere in the novel, in the odd fact that although the fictitious Anna's father was son and heir to the Earl of Trevannion, her mother was the daughter 'of a tradesman who dealt in butter and oats, the produce of that country [south Wales]' (III, p.238), recalling Lewes's claim that Anna Maria Evans was the daughter of a Welsh grocer. There is also the possibility that the author bases her description of Llandore, where Anna spends four years of her life, on 'Merthertidwell'. But the experience which the two Annas principally share is the necessity to earn their own living. The fictitious Anna is obliged 'to get her bread' by sewing, as an alternative to prostitution, just as her author is said to have earned her living as a 'slop-seller' (Lewes does not record whether she made the cheap clothes she sold in her shop) and becoming a 'housekeeper'. Yet, reflecting contemporary attitudes to gender and class, the author's representation of this female experience of work is highly ambivalent. On the periphery of the novel, there are no fewer than three young women who serve apprenticeships as needlewomen, one as a milliner and two as mantua makers, the latter funded by the 'annual bounty'.[26] When Anna is first taught to sew during her stay with the Melmoths in Wiltshire, her governess, aiming to make her 'an useful member of society', takes care that domestic needlework is blended with the ornamental:

Anna conquered every thing; she soon put Mrs. Melmoth out of conceit with her millener. No cap or hat pleased but those of Anna's making; the family needle-work went all through her hands, and she became, to the great pleasure of Mrs. Barlow, and the gratification of her own pride, of real use to her benefactress. (I, p.67)

However, Anna's 'pride' is constantly referred to during the course of the 'needlework narrative'[27] embedded in the structure of Bennett's novel – a latent aristocratic pride which finds humiliation in plain sewing. Once she leaves Melmoth Lodge, the future Countess of Trevannion is rarely allowed to dabble in anything but 'ornamental' needlework.

After being turned out of home by Mrs Melmoth at the age of fifteen, Anna takes refuge with her former governess (and needlework teacher), who has married a Welsh parson and is now Mrs Mansel. The four years Anna spends in Llandore – the only part of the novel to be actually set in Wales – are important in the novel not only in establishing her relationship with Lady Cecilia Edwin by way of a symbolic piece of fine embroidery, but also in conveying what might be described as a brief vision of an ideal society against which to measure Anna's later experiences as a poor working woman and 'Welch heiress'. Whether or not Anna Maria Bennett had any personal knowledge of 'Merthertidwell', her description of Llandore may well represent the remote village of Merthyr Tydfil some years before it became the first boom town in industrial Wales. Like Merthyr, Llandore is eighteen miles from Brecknock (or Brecon) via a dangerous mountain road and is situated on the River Tave (or Taff); like eighteenth-century Merthyr, Llandore has some large iron works managed by a Mr Wilkinson.[28] Anna's journey to Wales impresses on the reader the remoteness and otherness of her destination. In the care of a clergyman's widow, Mrs Bowen, who has been arranging her daughter's apprenticeship as a milliner, Anna sets out from London on the Brecknock stage which leaves Lad-lane twice a week.[29] From Brecknock, the journey continues on horseback, Anna riding pillion behind Mrs Bowen's son,

> and the craggy narrow roads, sometimes ascending nearly perpendicular, at others frightening her with their sudden declivity, and the almost barren mountains, which bore no traits of inhabitants, except the numerous flock of sheep, contributed not a little to the tediousness of

the journey; more especially as her conductor understood not her language. (I, pp.201–2)

Since Anna arrives at Llandore after dark, her first view the next morning of 'the most beautiful valley Nature ever formed' is extraordinarily luminous, the only sustained description of place in the entire novel:

> The situation of the village of Llandore is beautifully picturesque and romantic; it stands in a fertile valley, through which runs the river Tave, whose frequent, but harmless overflowings, give a richness and verdure more captivating to the eye, from the wild mountains which form, to appearance, an inaccessible chain on each side of the vale, irregularly interspersed with various old ruins, the sad memento of the faded glory and sunken dignity of the ancient inhabitants of Cambria. In the middle of a large green church-yard, stood the church, and round it, in two semi-circles, on the outside of the wall, were the white-washed neat dwellings of the inhabitants, with here and there a break for a better house than common, such as the parsonage, the doctor's, lawyer's, exciseman's, and presbyterian parson's. The river was so divided above the village, for the conveniency of working two mills at the other extremity, that a stream of clear water ran at each side at the back of the houses, and joined a mile farther; the green of their little orchards and gardens were beautifully contrasted by the snow-white appearance of the walls which surrounded them. Lime was so very cheap, and cleanliness in such high estimation at Llandore, that the meanest but vied in hue with the best house there, which was the parsonage. (I, pp.205–6)

The author first achieves an effect familiar in the work of contemporary artists, a 'picturesque and romantic' Wales, in which the 'wild mountains' become positively alpine in gradient and dense with monuments to vanished glory. But the switch from present to past tense, as the description of the ancient landscape is followed by a carefully observed sketch of the village, signals a change from the conventional pictorial language of early Romanticism to a precise evocation of a remembered scene, the circular shape of the village, the clear running water and the snowy white walls suggesting something like a vision of paradise. The vision fades very quickly, however. The inhabitants of those 'better . . . than common' snow-white houses – the lawyer, the dissenting teacher, the doctor and the exciseman –

occupy precisely the level of society to which the author herself belonged, at least at the time of writing her novel (her husband and father were customs officers, her brother was a lawyer);[30] the fictitious Anna belongs to the same bourgeois circle – the Mansels occupy the parsonage, the best house in the village. Yet the wives of the lawyer, doctor and the rest are rejected as 'too rude and uncultivated to give or receive, that delicate pleasure arising from the intercourse of refined sentiments and polite manners' (I, p.212) (though it is acknowledged that they do at least speak English). Anna's preferred social contacts are made not with these middling folk but with their aristocratic neighbours up at Llandore Castle, while the poorer classes of the village merely provide an occasion for the charitable impulses essential in an eighteenth-century heroine: 'Anna became the chearful dispenser of charity; her youth and vivacity made the learning the Welch language easy and useful; she soon became the interpreter of the poor to her maternal friend' (I, pp.211–12). As a learner of Welsh, Anna is a rare spirit in eighteenth-century fiction but, in context, her acquisition of the language is inseparable from a patronizing sense of the inferiority and essential foreignness ('the interpreter of the poor') of the common people. She has yet to experience true poverty and the necessity of labouring in order to eat. She has yet to meet Mr Bently who never sets foot in Llandore but, importantly, stands 'in the medium' between the rich and the poor.

When Anna later recalls her four years in Llandore, it is with that longing for the remembered past that might be described as *hiraeth*. Significantly, it is 'the humble style' of her life with the Mansels for which she yearns. Thus, when Anna is walking in Kensington Gardens, believing she has lost Charles Herbert, the love of her life, whom she first met at Llandore, she meditates with an aching sense of loss on those happy years in Wales:

> Here the still breeze that ushered in the finest spring morning ever seen, the dead silence, the solitude of those delightful shades, brought to her recollection the past, the never to be recalled happiness she had known at dear Llandore; the innocent recreations, the rural pastimes, the morning walk, the evening ramble; 'Oh,' said she, 'that they had never been!' (IV, pp.138–9)

Similarly, when she is riding with the Revd Mr Mansel across the down from Bath to Bristol and he points out 'the Welch hills, in the way to Llandore' and fondly refers to his late wife, his 'departed saint', his companion begs him not to mention that blessed woman:

> no more retrace that spot, those scenes! which are closed on me for ever; misery and despair are the only reliques of the peaceful serenity of four happy years spent at dear Llandore . . . Your village, your house, the white chimnies of Llandore, are this moment in my sight: there you sit in your morning gown, reading; here is my more than mother, trying on a pair of spectacles, laughing at her own figure in them: between you stands the happiest of orphans, just equipt to go with dear Miss Herbert to the castle, detained only to receive a charge, delivered in the voice of kindness, not to be out late; not to venture through farmer Jones's field, and not to overheat myself by walking. Oh, that all my life had been passed in that humble style! (IV, pp.211–12)

Anna's life in Wales is not, however, spent entirely in 'humble style'. On one occasion, she is invited to accompany her friend, Patty Herbert of Llandore Castle, on a visit to the Edwins at Dennis Place. Anna is a nobody, living on the charity of the Revd and Mrs Mansel, but Patty's aunt, the formidable Lady Cecilia Edwin, daughter of the Earl of Trevannion, takes an interest in the girl, and it is at this point that Bennett resumes the needlework narrative:

> In one of the frequent airings, when Anna was honoured with a seat in Lady Edwin's cabriole, her noble conductress pointed out to her the beauty of the shrubs and flowers that grew in profusion on the wild mountain tops; adding, she would give the world to have the coat and train of a birth-day suit worked from them.
>
> Embroidering was the forte of our heroine: Mrs. Mansel was one of the finest work-women in England [*sic*], and being fond of the occupation, had rendered her pupil equal to herself. Eager to cultivate the farther good will of Lady Cecilia, Anna instantly offered to finish one by the Queen's birth-day, when Miss Edwin was to be presented.
>
> Lady Edwin smiled at her eagerness to undertake a task which she did not believe could be accomplished, till she beheld the pencil of her young companion tracing from life, in a very masterly manner, the shrubs she admired.
>
> A piece of rich white sattin was directly written for, and from a temple, on top of an adjacent hill, which served as a point of view from Dennis Place, the pattern was drawn and coloured with such taste, that

the fair artist began to be spoken of as a prodigy at Dennis Place, while she was toasted by all the male visitors round the country, as the loveliest creature in it. (II, pp.4–5)

It has not been disclosed at this stage in the novel that Lady Cecilia is in fact Anna's aunt but symbolically, perhaps, the motif for Anna's embroidery, a pattern based on the wild flowers that grow 'in profusion on the wild mountain tops', signifies the hidden bond between them as they are *both* heiresses to estates in wild Wales – Lady Cecilia has inherited Dennis Place from her mother, while Anna is eventually revealed as the heiress of Trevannion (ousting her aunt from the succession).

The natural affinity between aunt and niece, the aristocratic woman and the penniless girl, is further established when it is stressed that Anna's 'great share of pride' often renders the sense of her dependent situation on the charity of strangers insupportable, 'and that pride first pointed out the necessity of employing those talents to advantage which God had blessed her with' (II, p.8). Her talent is for sewing and, having been advised by Mrs Mansel on 'arranging the foil, and shading the flowers', she eventually removes the embroidered white satin from the frame and sends it to London. The encomiums bestowed on her work by the best judges are 'flattering to her pride', and, although she is paid for her work, the commercial nature of the transaction is carefully concealed. When Lady Cecilia sends her twenty pounds for the first breadth, the author (interpolating her own comment in italics) presents a tableau of Anna kneeling at the feet of the Mansels, the purse in her offering hands:

> If the reader has ever feasted on the sensibility of generous minds, he [*sic*] will, perhaps, have some idea of the returns made by our Welsh parson and his wife, to the grateful overflowings of an uncorrupted heart; if he has not, description will do nothing for him; Mrs. Mansel slept not till she had sent for linen, a new riding habit, and other articles of rural finery, for our heroine (*all this any body may understand*) to the full amount of twenty the pounds. (II, p.9)

When the job is finished, the payment of fifty pounds is carefully described as a 'present' from Lady Cecilia.

After Mrs Mansel's death, the necessity for Anna to earn her own bread and pay for her keep is no longer concealed under euphemisms such as 'cultivating the good-will of Lady Cecilia', or offering the Mansels 'the uncorrupted overflowings of a grateful heart'. Mr Mansel's sister hints that 'She hated to see those who are able, and having nothing of their own, unwilling to work, loitering about at if their whole business in the world was to be maintained at other people's expence' (II, p.75). When Anna returns to the Daltons in Middlesex, she is told with very little ceremony that 'it was time for her to think of some mode of living, without being a hanger on from one to the other' (II, p.83). When she is unfairly sacked from her first job, as companion to Lady Cecilia, Dalton again tells her 'it is time "she knew how to get her bread"' (II, p.153). Although Anna is hurt by Dalton's harsh expressions, 'yet she could not in justice disapprove of them; she saw his large family, all of whom were now getting their own livelihood by the laudable exertions of industry' (II, p.159). If hard work is praiseworthy, however, the idea of assisting Peggy Dalton, who has completed her apprenticeship as a mantua maker and set up her own business, fills Anna with shame: 'Spite of herself, some latent hopes would arise that she might one day be united to Charles, and in that case, would the proud Cambrians of his family ever acknowledge a mantua-maker or a milliner?' (II, p.153). As Kathryn R. King observes of the sub-plot of Charlotte Smith's *The Old Manor House* (1794), the needlework imposed on Monimia belongs to the novel's critique of class as well as gender oppression.[31] Unlike Smith's seamstress-heroine, Anna is required to do very little plain sewing, yet her latent aristocratic pride is outraged by her situation:

> Peggy, the eldest, lived with them [the Daltons], and contributed to their general support; she had a great deal of work about the village, and it being now summer, when most young folks, in the middle line of life, have what new cloaths they can afford, was very full of business – the assistance of our heroine was therefore no less timely than acceptable, and her natural taste being good, she very soon took all the trimming and ornamental part on herself; added to this, her late residence in the great world, enabled her to instruct Miss Dalton in the fashions most in vogue, whose fame in consequence became so great, that the ladies, that is to say, the tradesmen's wives, who, either by the success of industry, or a spirit of prodigality, had country houses, began to employ and recommend her to each other, so that business came in very fast, and Dalton, consequently grew more civil.
> But the latent disease of the mind depends not on either success or

disappointment in the common occurrences of life; and pride had too great a share in Anna's composition to render her easy in such a situation. (II, pp.159–60)

Even so, Anna only narrowly avoids being bound apprentice to Peggy. As she reminds her aunt towards the end of the novel, 'how near was I being apprenticed to a mantua-maker?' (IV, p.117). The reader senses her frisson of horror.

The final episode in Bennett's 'needlework narrative' occurs when Anna is recovering from smallpox and once again needs to support herself. Characteristically, her decision to embroider as an outworker for the Desmoulins of Pall Mall is 'more flattering to her pride than going into service'. Having acquired a second-hand frame, she handles the most exquisite garments ('It was elegantly fancied, and variegated in the most beautiful taste, with embroidery, foil, spangles, and crape' (III, p.210)). However, Bennett also allows the reader a glimpse of Anna's working conditions when Mr Bently, the philanthropist who 'preferred the society of uncultivated poverty, to that of unfeeling affluence', happens to see Anna 'remove a blind from the window, which, as the day was shutting in, obstructed the light, and sit down at her frame to work' (III, p.255). He overhears a woman in the snuff shop opposite remarking 'how industrious that poor sick young woman was. "She is now," added she, "poring between the lights, – no wonder she looks so ill; – poor thing, I am sure she does not eat the bread of idleness"' (III, p.255). Significantly, in view of the stark choices open to a destitute young woman, Bently has tracked her down to find out whether or not she is being kept as Hugh Edwin's mistress. He takes lodgings over the snuff shop and 'watched our heroine, till he was convinced her own labour supported her, as he overlooked her whenever he pleased' (III, p.256). The fictitious Anna (unlike the other Anna, her author) has avoided both prostitution and plain sewing: she is worthy of her proud Trevannion blood.

Anna, a skilled needlewoman who avoids being 'bound' by a hair's breadth, is crucially not merely an heiress in disguise but specifically a '*Welch*' heiress and, in crowding the fictional canvas of *Anna* with a large number of her heroine's compatriots, Bennett does not scruple to make use of national stereotypes. As a Methodist preacher of humble origins, for instance, the Revd John Dalton is represented as a chapbook Welshman: he is both reviled for his poverty (as the clever son of a carpenter in a large town in south Wales, he was given a place in the free grammar school for the double purpose of cleaning the preceptor's shoes and sweeping the schoolroom) and revealed as a thief (this Taffy slyly agrees to foster Anna at the beginning of the novel entirely because he realizes that the child's trunk contains a sum of fourteen hundred guineas, which he duly appropriates). Bennett's handling of another national stereotype, the Welsh obsession with genealogy, is more subtle but betrays an ambivalence at the heart of the novel: uncertainty about the value to be placed on Welsh ideas about class and caste coexists in the text with unease about the true value to be placed on female labour – anxieties which radically affect the ways in which we are asked to 'read' Anna's fairy-tale metamorphosis from needlewoman to 'Welch heiress'. The significance of what Bennett refers to as 'the Cambrian stream in her veins', is principally explored through the character of Lady Cecilia Edwin, born Trevannion, Anna's alter ego and the person (it is implied) she could become, in time. Lady Cecilia is the daughter of the old Earl of Trevannion (Anna's grandfather), who was

> so strictly attached to his country, that he never but once in his life left it, to visit the court of London, and that was on the marriage of the then Prince of Wales – He was descended in a regular line from Llewellin, Prince of South Wales, and every marriage and intermarriage in his line of ancestry, were among the descendants of some or other of the ancient Cambrian heroes – This family pride descended to his daughter. (I, p.229)

Like an earlier incarnation of Lady Llanover, Lady Cecilia insists that at Dennis Place, 'her servants, her tradesmen, even her cattle must be Welch; nay, so attached was she to the Cambrian stream in her veins, she would, as she often declared, rather have chosen to marry her children to the peasant of her own wild hills, than to nobles of any other country' (I, p.231). Her son is married off to Miss Turbville, heiress of an estate that marches with Sir William Edwin's, while her daughter is rescued from an unfortunate marriage with the villainous Gorget: 'Welch obstinacy was not to be subdued by Irish fraud; for, though . . . he had the princely Llewellins, the heroic Tudors, and the valiant Hughs of her race, at his finger's end; it would not clear, from his own genealogy, the blot of Gorget' (III, pp.53–4).

Predictably enough, such fanaticism is open to ridicule: despite the fact that she is said to have a firm undaunted mind, a benevolent spirit, a soul that scorned an act of meanness, and so forth, at one level the portrayal of Lady Cecilia borders on farce. At Dennis Place she is aided and abetted by her sister-in-law, Miss Winifred Edwin, who 'could tell off hand every blot on the ancestry of all the old families in the principality, holding in infinite contempt, as upstarts, those who she could trace their parentage no farther than three or four hundred years' (I, p.236). When 'an artful beggar' pretends to be a distant relative and 'the roll was fetched', his lame account of himself and his failure to speak 'the language of the country' puts him in danger of being given over to 'the discipline of the servants'; however, Lady Cecilia decides that his name is his protection, and he is allowed to go. Such incidents may be a matter of historical record, but Lady Cecilia's young guests are amused by their hostess's obsessions ('family mad' as Patty Herbert puts it) and withdraw 'to laugh over the prejudices of high blood' (I, p.228).

Importantly, fanaticism of this kind is also seen as pernicious. In adapting the time-honoured joke of the Welsh obsession with genealogy to her own purposes, the author moves on to the territory that Jane Austen would make her own in *Pride and Prejudice*. The author makes no bones of the fact that 'The weak side of Lady Edwin was family pride' (III, p.53), which specifically counterbalances her many virtues and actually prompts a comparison with the villain, Gorget, though Bennett is at pains to point out that Lady Cecilia's pride 'was founded on a real grandeur of soul, that valued the virtues as much as the honour of her ancestors; and she piqued herself on equally supporting both: his was the poor boast of riches accumulated with disgrace, and wickedness crowned with success' (III, pp.54–5). When her son, Hugh Edwin, turns out badly and is eventually killed in a duel, her mourning is tempered by relief that he will no longer be a disgrace to the family: 'constitutionally attached to the dignity of her family, she considered his early fate, though it wrung all the mother in her soul, as a period to the immorality and extravagance of his actions; such a life reflected disgrace on the blood of the Trevannions' (IV, p.102). When Cecilia Edwin brings further disgrace on the family by eloping (with a Scot), her letter to her mother focuses inevitably on the issue of their 'blood': 'the truth is, our blood has from generation to generation, by flowing in the same regular channel, at last wearied itself by its own sameness, and Mr. Dunbar assures me, *his* is no less respectable; so that a little change will be an advantage to both' (IV, p.256). Lady Cecilia consoles herself for the loss of both her children by writing to Anna, in whom 'the virtue, as well as honour, of our house is united' (IV, p.251); she begs her to take the only step that will enable her aunt to meet the eyes of her countrymen: 'You must bring to Trevannion House a chief worthy of such vassals' (IV, p.255). Anna reflects that her aunt has only one fault, 'if her bigoted regard to the honour of her family could be so called'; she had thought that the blood of Trevannion would protect her children from vice, forgetting that, in the great world beyond the family mansion, 'example from the multitude was far more prevalent on the minds of prosperous youth, than the dry precepts of individuals' (IV, p.257). The reader is left in no doubt that, like her aunt, Anna has 'a grandeur of soul' appropriate to her exalted rank. But during the course of the novel there have also been numerous references to her own pride, described ominously as 'the latent disease of the mind' when she is facing the humiliating prospect of being employed by one of the Dalton girls as a dressmaker. Having inherited that pernicious 'pride of high blood' from the Trevannions, Anna (it is hinted) has at least the potential to share her aunt's obsessions.

The myth of Welsh family pride is thus debunked and queried and, more radically, the whole toppling edifice of eighteenth-century aristocratic superiority is called into question. To do so in a 'rags to riches' plot may reflect a certain cynicism on the author's part about the social order in which her heroine eventually takes her rightful place; at the very least, the contradictions in the text imply a fundamental anxiety about the structure of society in which the fantasy of Anna's transformation from penniless orphan to 'Welch heiress' is enacted. In the fictitious society created by Bennett's first novel, women's labour is both admired as 'the laudable exertions of industry' and deplored as shameful and demeaning; at the other end of the social spectrum, an aristocratic position in society is shown to be the source of both 'grandeur of soul' and overweening pride (as well as gross immorality). It is perhaps the philanthropic Mr Bently, a minor character whose curious and in some ways superfluous presence in the novel is otherwise difficult to explain, who provides a key comment on these ambiguities in the text. When he takes Hugh Edwin to court for knocking him down in the street, Bently makes an eloquent speech to the magistrate on the overbearing behaviour of the rich: 'poh, says the great man, *you* shall not tread the same ground, breathe the same air, look erect, or wear your beard like me . . . not because I am better, older or wiser, but because I am *richer* than you' (II, p.196). By his own account, Mr Bently positively relishes the opportunity 'to stand in the medium between the overbearance of the rich, and the rights of the poor' (II, p.197). Significantly, this representative of the middling sort – that level of society briefly transfigured in Anna's visionary glimpse of Llandore – clearly champions 'the rights of the poor' against 'the overbearance of the rich', thus heralding modestly but unmistakably the great surge of radicalism that would come to a head in the following decade, heralded by Tom Paine's *The Rights of Man*.

When the heroine is eventually transformed from rags to riches, one notes that amid the general celebrations, the narrator's rhetorical question sounds curiously grudging: 'THE time was now arrived, when Anna was to be introduced into what is called life; sensible, accomplished, beautiful, rich, and nobly born, were it possible she could be less than the rage?' (IV, p.55). At the end of the novel, Anna at last returns to Wales: 'the real heiress of Trevannion was met by the tenants and vassals of her estate, and followed through two counties by the acclamations and unfeigned joy of the honest, unconquered, though uncultivated, Cambrians' (IV, p.259). Under the circumstances, the reader (especially if she is an unconquered, uncultivated Cambrian) is likely to respond with a certain scepticism, a grudging 'Oh, yes?'

11
'In the airy Regions of Fancy'
✣
ELLEN, COUNTESS OF CASTLE HOWEL BY ANNA MARIA BENNETT

By the time Anna Maria Bennett brought out her fourth novel, *Ellen, Countess of Castle Howel* (1794), her daughter Harriet, 'the celebrated actress, Mrs. Esten',[1] was already enjoying considerable success on the stage. Launched on her theatrical career by her mother, Esten made her debut as Jane Shore in Bristol in June 1786, then worked in Ireland and Scotland before being engaged for the first of four consecutive seasons in London.[2] Boaden greatly admired her: 'THE first event of any theatrical importance in the winter season of 1790–1, was an acquisition of an enchanting woman and most interesting actress to the boards of Covent Garden.'[3] He ranked her as second only to the great Mrs Siddons in tragedy and to Miss Farren in comedy, describing her as delicately and gracefully built, with particularly expressive eyes and 'mental accomplishments' inherited from her mother:

> Mrs. Esten's mother was the once celebrated Mrs. Bennett, upon whose novels our ladies depended for all the interesting romance of upper life, and looked not always in vain for a charm against the morning's ennui. No man need be ashamed of such reading as could amuse our greatest statesman; and I am inclined to attribute greater merit to such inventions, than to productions of a graver character, but so constructed, as to be useless to the wise and repulsive to the unlearned. From this mother Mrs. Esten received her mental accomplishments – perhaps something of the *novel* adhered to her through life.[4]

When Harriet's marriage to Lieutenant James Esten foundered, Mrs Bennett cleared her son-in-law's debts, on condition that he severed all connections with his wife and children, and left the country. In the

Dedication of her third novel, *Agnes de Courci* (1789), published the same year in which Harriet obtained a deed of separation from her husband,[5] Mrs Bennett made fulsome reference to her daughter's friendship with Colonel Hunter.[6] (The Colonel's name was duly bestowed on one of Harriet's children.[7]) By the summer of 1792, she had become the mistress of Douglass, 8th Duke of Hamilton,[8] and had won the lease of the Edinburgh Theatre Royal, in partnership with Stephen Kemble. When Hamilton was appointed a patentee of the theatre Kemble was ousted, but during the period of litigation that followed, Harriet moved back to London for her third season at Covent Garden, leaving the management of the Theatre Royal to her mother.[9] The play went on – Kemble notwithstanding, even the Whitlocks duly trod the boards at Edinburgh during the 1792–3 season.[10] But for Anna Maria Bennett it was a time of great strain and stress: by her own account, she avoided a nervous breakdown ('Mental Derangement') only by escaping into a world of fantasy ('the airy Regions of Fancy'). In short, she wrote *Ellen, Countess of Castle Howel*, which was published with a prefatory 'Apology' dated from London on 12 March 1794:

> Four Hundred Miles distant from Home, Family and Friends, a Stranger in a Country, where she was literally *taken in*, her Spirit broken, her Health impaired, her little Fortune sinking, the unoffending Victim of a Party, who forgot their Character and Manhood, to combine against the Laws they professed to Support, and the Sex they were born to protect, her Domestic Peace and *dearest pride* totally destroyed, what wonder Female Fortitude sunk under such accumulated Ills? and that as a Resource from Mental Derangement she sought, in the airy Regions of Fancy, any Subject which by diverting thought from 'Self,' might sometimes afford a temporary 'oblivion of Sorrow.'[11]

Four months after *Ellen* was published, Harriet bore the Duke a daughter, Ann Douglass Hamilton.[12] It is not recorded whether the child was named for her grandmother.

In *Ellen,* the orphaned heroine is brought up at Code Gwyn by her grandparents, Sir Arthur and Lady Meredith. Ellen repairs the family fortunes by marrying an old man, Lord Castle Howel, but, when she pays her first visit to London soon after the wedding, she succumbs to the temptations of city life, amassing gambling debts as well as being suspected of adultery. Repudiated by her husband, she takes flight to the north of England, accompanied by her maid, Winifred Griffiths; here she bears a child and is reconciled to her husband, but shortly afterwards he is killed in a hunting accident, leaving her free to marry her childhood sweetheart, Percival Evelyn. Francesca Rhydderch has studied *Ellen* as an 'an ambivalent narrative of Britishness';[13] the present chapter explores broadly similar territory, dealing mainly with the ways in which Bennett develops her twin themes of the demise of a feudal way of life and the corruption of the 'child of nature' – themes which seem to run strangely counter to one another as the novel proceeds. Indeed, in a number of puzzling ways, Bennett seems wantonly to undermine the credibility and moral integrity of her story, and, although one might account for these rifts in theme and plot as evidence of the author's carelessness and incompetence, it is also possible to see them as angry stabs at the creatures of her imagination, as a painter suffering from 'mental derangement' might slash at a canvas and deliberately deface the work in progress. To some extent, the acrimony that expresses itself in this text can be identified with the radical sentiment that had made the apotheosis of Anna, Countess of Trevannion, in Bennett's first novel, less than wholehearted; even in 'the airy Regions of Fancy', Bennett's portrait of Ellen, Countess of Castle Howel, is less than eulogistic, while there are some indicators that in her depiction of the upper classes and the power of wealth, she too rails against 'things as they are', at exactly the same point in history that Godwin produced in *Caleb Williams* his own epoch-making radical novel. Given the fact that Bennett's *cri de cœur* in her 'Apology' invites speculation about her state of mind when she wrote the novel, it is tempting to suggest that the bitterness that informs *Ellen* is a projection of the anger she was feeling both towards and on behalf of her daughter, whose 'magnificent elevation' as a kind of surrogate duchess scarcely disguises the sordid fact that, like her mother before her, she had fallen victim to a social system which allowed women few legitimate routes to money and social status. Anna, in Bennett's first novel, prefers the social degradation of working as a needlewoman to becoming a high-class courtesan. One of the central ironies of *Ellen*, however, is the fact that the heroine's marriage to Castle Howel is in effect a kind of prostitution – as degrading and money-grubbing in its way as Harriet's relationship with the Duke?

In *Anna*, the village of Llandore, which remains a source of *hiraeth* for the heroine long after she has returned to London, is set against a backdrop of 'wild mountains' which are interspersed with old ruins that provide a 'sad memento of the faded glory and sunken dignity of the ancient inhabitants of Cambria'. In *Ellen,* the focus moves to the wild mountains of north Wales and to the dilapidated fortified mansion of Code Gwyn which stands below the ruins of an ancient fort. Rhydderch has argued that, in her Welsh novels, Bennett deploys the imagery of castle and estate as a political metaphor: the decline of the politically independent constitution of Cambria since the 1536 Act of Union is indicated in her representation of the 'various old ruins' which Anna sees on her arrival in Wales, and in the 'faded glory' depicted in *Ellen* as the fortunes of the Meredith family estate sink almost into oblivion: 'Just as the condition of the Welsh estate deteriorates, so too, it is implied, do the heritage and identity of the country within the borders of which that estate is situated.'[14] If Bennett is indeed wielding a political metaphor in this way, she would seem to have an imperfect grasp of Welsh history. Code Gwyn is described as 'a large Gothic mansion, built at a time, when imperfect laws and civil discord obliged the chiefs of the country to consult safety, more than pleasure and convenience, in the construction and situation of their houses' (I, p.2). Beyond the mansion, 'at the end of one of front avenues ran a rapid and, now, discoloured torrent, over which was an antient stone bridge, the scene of many a bloody fray, when the gallant ancestors of the present family maintained their right against the inroads of the mountaineers' (I, p.3). While the exact period in history when these bloody frays occurred is not recorded, it is only too clear that the Merediths' 'gallant ancestors' were defending their domain against the indigenous Welsh – 'mountaineers' in the parlance of the day. Bennett may indeed be lamenting the 'faded glory' of Cambria, but, in her version of Welsh history, the 'ancient inhabitants' seem to have been none other than the Norman conquerors – or even the Edwardian castle-builders.

While Bennett's appropriation of what Katie Trumpener has defined as 'bardic nationalism' seems to be predicated on a limited understanding of Welsh history, the novel is to some extent a lament for the passing of the feudal nature of Code Gwyn, with its spacious hall ornamented with rusty swords, shields, helmets, trophies, banners and antlers, and its resident harpist. Although such a way of life had largely disappeared in Wales by the end of the eighteenth century, the hall at Code Gwyn is still the centre of the communal life of the household:

The hall appeared to be the bond of union between the heads of the family and the domestics – there the harper had his seat, and there the avocations and labours of the day constantly closed with a dance, in which all the younger part of the inmates mingled, without a frown on the brow of pride, or presumption in the bosom of poverty. (I, p.4)

It is, therefore, 'according to ancient custom' that the family at Code Gwyn has been dancing out the old year when guests arrive on an intensely cold, snowy New Year's Eve. The threat to the organic life of the household, which embraces the Merediths and their servants, is represented symbolically by the arrival of Lord Claverton whose first deed on arriving at Code Gwyn is to shoot Lion, Ellen's favourite dog. Significantly, though Sir Arthur himself as an inborn gentleman is not in any way 'abashed at the presence of a nobleman', the domestics are immediately hurried out of the parlour by the house-steward (no longer deemed worthy to share the same social space with their betters), while a tearful Ellen, her face and hands smeared with blood, drags in the carcass of poor Lion. While Claverton is certainly a danger to Ellen ('I'll have that girl'), the immediate threat to the survival of Code Gwyn itself comes from the son of a dissolute pauper, John Morgan Esq. ('the dæmon of avarice'), who was born locally, began his career as under-porter to a London-Welsh merchant, married the boss's daughter and eventually inherited both his father-in-law's business and his Code Gwyn estates. When Morgan calls in the mortgage on Code Gwyn, he precipitates in effect Ellen's marriage to Castle Howel and the train of events that follows. Although the threat of foreclosure is averted for a while when Castle Howel takes over the mortgage, the end of the Merediths' feudal rule seems imminent after his death in a hunting accident later in the novel. In another symbolic episode, the widowed Ellen returns to Wales and meets on the road to the village a sad procession of the entire household of Code Gwyn, including the harper, 'blind and lame, led by a grandson of the coachman's' (IV, p.41), with her grandfather, Sir Arthur, bringing up the rear in his wheelchair. Although convention demands that, by several unlikely twists of the plot, the Merediths are miraculously restored to their ancestral home at the end of the novel, decay, poverty and the inevitable ending of a way of life provide one of Bennett's dominant themes in this novel.

A simple reading of *Ellen* might suggest that it is essentially a dirge for lost innocence, lamenting not only the passing of the organic and harmonious lifestyle of what had once been a great feudal household at Code Gwyn, but also the corruption of its youngest representative, the 'child of nature' who succumbs to the vices of the metropolis. Yet Bennett runs into considerable difficulties in developing these interrelated themes, not least because she overtly champions the principle of 'female education' and there is, consequently, an inevitable mismatch between the idealized notion of Ellen as a 'child of nature' and her view of Ellen as a poorly educated Welsh hoyden.[15] In her fifteenth year, she may be beautiful and good (with the face of Venus and the form of Diana), virtuous and charming ('the constant practice of every virtue, even in her unpolished state of nature, rendered her artless conversation charming and entertaining' (I, p.52)), but her author nevertheless acknowledges that she appears 'rude and ignorant' on first acquaintance. She is certainly more disadvantaged, for instance, than Fanny Burney's 'innocent abroad' in *Evelina* (1778) ('*a young female, educated in the most secluded retirement, makes, at the age of seventeen, her first appearance on the great and busy stage of life*'): although Evelina has been brought up by her guardian in Dorset, she is a 'little rustic' only in '*her ignorance of the forms, and inexperience in the manners, of the world*'.[16] Not only has the 'rude and ignorant' Ellen been brought up in an altogether remoter and wilder part of the country, but she has also received a totally inadequate education, as Bennett makes abundantly clear. In north Wales, Ellen has learned reading from the rector (her uncle), writing from the parish clerk, dancing from 'old Griffiths' (a family retainer), music from the harper and riding from the bailiff; she can catch a horse, gallop without bridle or saddle and climb to find birds' nests; she is an excellent shot and follows the hounds – in short, she is 'the greatest romp in the world'. Later in the novel, Bennett comments caustically on the neglect of 'the other sex'. Despite the family's straitened circumstances, Sir Arthur's elder son has received a university education:

> a liberal establishment there, was certainly a reason, why, in Sir Arthur's opinion, that 'no woman need be a scholar,' was adopted in the family, for Lady Meredith, with an affluent fortune would have thought very different, – however, an established rule for his daughters could not be expected to give way in favor of an orphan grand daughter.

Like her aunts, Ellen has received no formal education – in direct contrast to Percival Evelyn, a penniless protégé of her uncle, who manages somehow to find the money to send his pupil to Oxford:

and thus, while the whole attention of the reverend Mr. Meredith was given to an Eleve [Percival], who had no natural claims on him, his own niece was suffered to run wild about his father's house, every body petting, and every body, while they doated on her infant beauty and vivacity, neglecting a mind that wanted nothing but instruction. (III, pp.73–4)

According to Bennett's bracing eighteenth-century rationalism, Ellen's 'unpolished state of nature' may indeed be charming – but is otherwise deplorable. Like her aunts, she has been poorly educated, and she has been 'suffered to run wild': she is fortunate indeed to be sent away to Mrs Forrest's school at Bath, at Lord Castle Howel's expense.

Bennett's ironic style precludes, however, a straightforward interpretation of Mrs Forrest's bid to eliminate Ellen's Welsh accent by separating her from her maid, Winifred Griffiths:

The truth is, that though Ellen approached as near perfection as most heroines of her age, yet she certainly had a welch accent, which, to the refined ears of Mrs. Forrest, and her ladies, sounded a little uncouth; and, as Winifred's was a barbarous jargon of neither Welch nor English, but a bad mixture of both, which she plainly saw would never be got rid of, she prudently conditioned for their entire separation. (I, pp.143–4)

It is not entirely clear whether Bennett's readers should applaud Mrs Forrest's view that Ellen sounds 'a little uncouth', or disapprove of an affected English schoolmistress with 'refined ears'. Rhydderch recognizes that 'Ellen's own awareness of the need to become refined and accomplished suggests an internalization of English values'[17] and there is some evidence in the novel (beyond the reference to Winifred's 'barbarous jargon') to suggest that Bennett expects her readers positively to rejoice at the elimination of Ellen's 'welch accent'. In her 'unpolished state of nature', Ellen may have thrilled Claverton by 'warbling a welch air' (I, p.68), but, less romantically, the maids at Code Gwyn 'set up a lamentation in their own harmonious language, which very much resembled the Hibernian howl' (I, pp.103–4). It is even tempting to speculate that in her portrait of Mrs Forrest as both schoolmistress and successful writer, Bennett may have intended a graceful compliment to her fellow novelist, Sophia Lee,[18] and that Ellen's accomplishments after two years at school are catalogued without irony, even though Mrs Forrest's establishment can scarcely be compared to the university education enjoyed by Meredith and Percival Evelyn (and falls woefully short of the radical ideas urged only a few years later by Mary Robinson, who argued that girls should be permitted to take part in sport and would have liked to build 'an UNIVERSITY FOR WOMEN'[19]). Under Mrs Forrest's regime, Ellen no longer takes robust exercise; her person becomes delicate and her air easy and elegant; her charmingly vivacious manners become soft and politely refined; her voice, trained under Ruzzina, is 'possessed of all those thrilling graces, which melt on the ear, and reaches the soul of harmony' (I, p.150). The reader is invited to approve of Ellen's transformation.

Yet it serves Bennett's purposes that Ellen should remain to all intents and purposes 'a little rustic', despite her expensive education. The country/city motif comes into play when she is summoned from school, is married off to Castle Howel, and is taken to London soon after her wedding. The new Countess is immediately assailed by the temptations of high society: 'how was it possible *she* could be so stupid, as to prefer any of the obsolete amusements, which had filled a long summer's day, and winter's evening, in the mountains of Wales?' (II, p.49). The conventions of the genre ensure that Ellen remains chaste; but she does succumb for a while to the lure of gaming for high stakes, and when her own gaucherie prompts a duel between two of her admirers, her reputation is in shreds: unable to take refuge at Code Gwyn lest she antagonize her husband (who pays the mortgage), she heads north, accompanied by her faithful maid, who seizes the opportunity of travelling incognito to change her name to Maria as Winifred 'had such a welchy vulgar sound' (II, p.210).

It is Bennett's portrait of Winifred – an apprentice piece for the much admired Betty Brown in *The Beggar Girl*[20] – that best exemplifies in this novel the author's ambivalent attitude to the Welsh. Win's role in the narrative is essentially to provide a comic caricature of her mistress; in order to set off Ellen's beauty, breeding and (eventually) impeccable English accent, Win is described as an ill-made girl 'with black hair, eyes, and eye-brows, short nose, wide mouth, strong white teeth, high cheek bones, and a very fresh colour, [who] spoke very bad English, and worse Welch' (I, p.70). Yet it can be argued that the idea of Ellen's ancestral home as a feudal Welsh household is sustained beyond the early chapters of the novel almost entirely through the unlikely agency of this raucous, garrulous maidservant whose journeys with Ellen to Bath, London and up the Great North Road to Durham are punctuated by oft-repeated praise of Code Gwyn. Indeed, it could be said that the heroine's melancholic *hiraeth* for Llandore in *Anna* is replaced in the later novel by Win's rather noisier 'longing' to return to Wales – which in turn mirrors Ellen's quieter moments of nostalgia for her home. Throughout Ellen's ordeal in London and the north of England, the author ensures that Code Gwyn remains in focus. Win is highly indignant when Castle Howel's sister refers to Ellen's '*old* hole at Code Gwyn' (II, pp.157–8) and is shocked beyond measure when she realizes that Ellen dares not go home in disgrace:

> Down dropped the bundle out of Winifred's hands, 'not co to Code Gwyn! why where in the name of Cot almighty shall we co, then? I am sure if we don't co there we shall be like the tove out of Noah's hark, wandering about without a pit of resting place to put our foots upon.' (II, p.201)

She feels nothing but distaste for the trees, fields and broad rivers she sees as they travel north; she thinks of 'our high brown mountains in Wales!' and utters the heartfelt prayer, 'Wou'd to Cot of his infinite mercy, we were there' (II, p.221). When she catches cold, she feels she would be happy even in a pigsty at Code Gwyn, and, when she returns to north Wales after Castle Howel's death, even the amazing sights she has seen on her travels cannot compare with the Merediths' old house: 'for as to Code Gwyn house, she had seen the palace, and a poor thing Cot knows it was to see; and the mansion-house, and petlam, and Cot knows none of them was comparable to Code Gwyn' (IV, p.51).

As well as the ambiguities in Bennett's treatment of these central themes of the novel – the passing of a feudal household and the loss of innocence of its youngest (and last) representative – there are more glaring infelicities in the fantasy dreamt up to divert her thoughts from 'self'. One of the major flaws in *Ellen* was pounced on by a contemporary reviewer (were it not for a rather laborious and starchy defence of the genre, it would be tempting to suggest that the female critic was possibly Fanny Burney herself).[21] The reviewer, clearly a 'fan' of Bennett's novels, had enjoyed this one too, up to a point:

> We have formerly acknowledged the pleasures which we received in perusing the works of Mrs. Bennet; and we have been much entertained with the first three volumes of the present production, as they

abound in many of the excellencies which we have enumerated: – but, as the *time is come* for us to grasp the wand of the censor more forcibly than we have hitherto attempted on similar occasions, we select this performance for the express purpose of pointing out a growing error in modern novels.

Claiming that too much weight is given to the passion of love ('Start not, young friends!'), the reviewer asks whether gratitude, honour, friendship and propriety are to be sacrificed at the altar of this fascinating divinity and draws attention to the point in the novel where the Earl dies suddenly and Percival Evelyn feels frantic joy now that Ellen is free to marry him: she 'must *blame*, and severely, what is not *new* in this species of literary invention, but what will ever be reprehended by us, when all situations, however rationally and even affectionately happy, are overset to make way for *former love*'. How can Percival, son of a profligate Lord, who has nearly ruined the Meredith family, be thought a fit husband for the widowed Countess, demands the reviewer: 'Is this a proper lesson for the youth of either sex? – Indeed we think there is an honorable delicacy in forbidding SUCH BANNS!' The sudden death of Lord Castle Howel is certainly morally indefensible as a mechanism of the plot, though a modern reader is unlikely to visit the sins of Percival's father upon his head (it is not his fault that Claverton is a 'profligate Lord' or indeed that his grandfather is the rapacious John Morgan Esq.) and it is anyway questionable whether in this novel Bennett displays much interest in 'the fascinating divinity': *Ellen* is not 'about' the heroine's love affair with her terminally insipid hero. It seems much more likely that Lord Castle Howel is exterminated as a gleeful act of authorial revenge on a nobleman rich enough to buy a young wife.

Rhydderch argues that Claverton's predatory relationship with Ellen symbolizes the appropriation of Wales by England, delineated in terms of aggressive colonization, while Castle Howel represents the internalization of English values and norms.[22] This may be so, but the key point is that in an age in which money flowed,[23] both men have the wealth, rank and easy self-confidence to acquire, as mistress or wife, the granddaughter of a poor Welsh squire of ancient lineage. Economics rather than politics is at work here. (The author had cause to know a great deal about a woman's current market value: by a Deed of Gift, Admiral Pye had made over to her his house in New Suffolk Street, Middlesex Hospital, and bequeathed to her most of 'the Household

Goods and ffurniture in the said House';[24] the Duke of Hamilton would shortly settle £2,000 per annum on Harriet Esten during the minority of their daughter, Ann Douglass Hamilton, and £1,500 per annum thereafter.[25]) Bennett makes a half-hearted attempt to persuade the reader that Castle Howel's interest in Ellen – in her fifteenth year – is 'disinterested'. But the same reader has already noted that Castle Howel has the reputation of being 'a cross, proud, reserved old man'; he is described as indolent and careless (and absorbed in botany), too lazy, in a word, to divorce his first wife, the former Miss Capus of Spital-Fields, who is still alive when Ellen comes on the scene. A month after the death of her predecessor, Ellen is summarily taken away from school and in her seventeenth year is browbeaten into forming a resolution 'as strong as heroic' to save her family from eviction by marrying Castle Howel. The nature of the bargain ('for the avowed purpose of propagating the species') is fully recognized by the gossips when the 'rustic' makes her first appearance as a married woman in London society. When Ellen is disgraced, she flees to the north in order to prevent the Castle Howel family seizing her unborn child – the heir to the estate. There are, of course, some striking similarities between Bennett's fictional heroine and her daughter, beyond their chiming names (Ellen/Esten): like Harriet Esten, the Countess of Castle Howel is 'bought' by a nobleman (and bears his child), while several pages of the novel are devoted to her gift of mimicry ('you should have been an actress' (II, p.72)). In 'the airy Regions of Fancy', the author does not spare her imaginary earl. The slapstick scene in which he discovers Ellen and her newly born son depicts him as a comic buffoon in nightshirt and nightcap, the victim of a savage attack launched on him by Winifred Griffiths. The author may reassure her sceptical readers that the reconciliation between husband and wife is a tender one – but within weeks Castle Howel is casually disposed of in a hunting accident.

It is not only Ellen's husband who suffers at the author's hand. Despite the thematic importance of Code Gwyn, she inflicts wilful damage on her portraits of Sir Arthur and Lady Meredith, making them morally responsible for bringing about the most bizarre event in the novel, the 'sale' of their granddaughter to Castle Howel. Initially, Bennett depicts Sir Arthur as a stereotypical poverty-stricken but hospitable 'shentleman of Wales'; he is

> of so easy, hospitable and benevolent a disposition, that, while he saw the long-familiar faces of his train of domestics, while his old coach held

together, and the almost foundered coach horses could draw his Lady and family to church, while that family were tranquil and happy, he seldom burthened his thoughts with the state of his finances. (I, p.10)

Lady Meredith, whose heart is said to be the seat of truth and her tongue the law of kindness, is one of that ubiquitous species in eighteenth-century society, 'the heiress of a noble Welch family' whose dignity 'far exceeded their wealth'; since Sir Arthur 'was of too thoughtless a turn' to repay the mortgage, her own estate had long passed into other hands. The Merediths are said to be devout: unlike Lord Claverton, who spends New Year's Day planning to keep Ellen for his hours of relaxation in a small box in the metropolis,

> the *simple* Knight, under whose hospitable roof he was entertained, not being able to go to church, read the lessons of the day to Mr. Griffiths, and while his as simple family were asking the blessing of the Being they served on the new year, a custom still adhered to in many parts of antient Britain. (I, pp.35–6)

Ellen herself has nothing but praise for her 'virtuous family', so that when she flees in disgrace to the north, she sheds no tears for past enjoyments but only for 'the recollection of the dear relatives of Code Gwyn':

> The years past under the protection of her virtuous family, were winged with happiness and peace, and she retraced their rapid progress with poignant regret; the few months that intervened were also winged; but one was the gentle motion of the summer breeze, the other the irresistible whirlwind; on the one, memory feasted with delight; from the other it shrunk with abhorrence: The remembrance of grandeur disgusted her, for had it not torn her from the innocent, cheerful and laudable avocations of her blameless life? (III, p.13)

Yet this same virtuous family, facing eviction from their ancestral estate, are partners in an essentially commercial transaction by which Ellen is handed over to Castle Howel in exchange for the repayment of the mortgage on Code Gwyn. Only in the fictional destinies of the Merediths is it possible to detect, perhaps, the author's barely suppressed anger against the buyers and sellers of the female body: Lady Meredith dies when she hears of Ellen's disgrace, Sir Arthur becomes senile.

Not even Winifred gets off scot-free. Although she plays an important role in defining the importance of Code Gwyn after Ellen herself leaves Wales, she is mocked for her coarse appearance, her uncouth Welsh speech, and her lower-class mimicry of her social superiors ('Ellen was the oracle of the parlour, Winifred gave her orations in the servant's-hall' (I, p.125)). Yet, despite the distorting and demeaning constraints of comic portraiture, she also performs a function similar to that of Mr Bently in *Anna* in giving voice to radical sentiments which are merely implicit in the author's jaundiced view of the upper classes. After making her usual complaint that 'I had rather be at Code Gwyn than any where' (that place where master and servant had danced together at the end of the day, 'without a frown on the brow of pride, or presumption in the bosom of poverty'), Winifred frightens the Castle Howel servants by criticizing the quality: 'I have peen, Cot help me, where lorts, and tukes, tukesses, and princes, and player people, and kings have peen, and lort knoes, they are no great things' (III, p.149). Like 'petlam' in her list of places that are outshone by Code Gwyn, the 'player people' are ostensibly inserted here for comic purposes – though Bennett herself, fresh from the Theatre Royal, Edinburgh, and her daughter's ducal ménage, may well be making her own private comment on 'things as they are'. At the end of the novel, the author certainly addresses her readers in much the same radical spirit as that shown by her Welsh maidservant. She refers to 'the monsters we meet at the end of all LANE's collections, men without error! And women without faults!', admits that her own hero and heroine are subject to the common frailties of human nature, and then – in the bitter spirit that is so characteristic of *Ellen, Countess of Castle Howel* – suggests that it would be rude to pry into secrets 'concealed, as in the present instance, by the impenetrable veil of IMMENSE RICHES' (IV, p.234). The immense riches in question are inherited by Percival Evelyn from his father and grandfather, villains both – the cruel nabob, Lord Claverton, and the ruthless self-made man, John Morgan Esq. (Both are killed off during the course of the novel, Morgan's fate being particularly nasty and highly symbolic, as his arm has to be amputated when it becomes trapped in an iron chest which contains some of his ill-gotten gains.) In capital letters, those immense riches stand alone as the last words of the novel, a final blast of authorial rage and bitterness.

12

Removing silver buttons

ELISA POWELL BY EDWARD 'CELTIC' DAVIES

Although *Twm Shon Catti* (1828) by T. J. Ll. Prichard has usually been identified as the first Anglo-Welsh novel,[1] there is at least one earlier contender for the position in *Elisa Powell, or, Trials of Sensibility* (1795), published anonymously in two volumes by G. G. and J. Robinson, but known to be the work of Edward 'Celtic' Davies (1756–1831). The early memoir by W. J. Rees[2] and more recent research by Frank R. Lewis[3] make it possible to appreciate the circumstances that made Edward Davies's experience – particularly the loss of Welsh as his first language and his long exile in England – prefigure that of many later 'Anglo-Welsh' writers. In addition, it is possible to discover in Davies's novel traces of his grand obsession with the cultural 'Renaissance' of eighteenth-century Wales. These factors make *Elisa Powell* unique among other fictions of Wales written at the time. It may be a clumsy attempt at the novel of sensibility but, despite its shortcomings, it remains a work of considerable historical interest.

Edward Davies was born in 1756 at Hendre-Einon, a farmhouse in the parish of Llanfaredd, Radnorshire, three miles from Llanfair-ym-Muallt (Buallt or Builth Wells). He was educated by his mother and various clergymen in the locality, and at the College Grammar School in Brecon. During his childhood, an accident with a gun permanently injured his sight. He suffered a less tangible handicap in being deprived of fluency in his native language:

> Although born in Wales, yet it was in that part of the Principality where the English language was spoken as well as the Welsh, and the service of the church was altogether in English, except, occasionally, a lesson would be read out of the Welsh Bible. As a knowledge of the Welsh language was considered by his parents to be injurious to their children in preventing their acquiring English, they were forbidden to

learn it. However, notwithstanding the discouragement shown to his acquiring Welsh, he gained some knowledge of it by attending to the conversations of his parents and their acquaintance, and from reading the Welsh Bible, and other books which belonged to his father.[4]

As a boy, he wrote a number of hymns, including one in Welsh in 1773, 'which shews that even then he was not inattentive to the literature of his country, although he had been discouraged from learning its language'.[5] For a time he taught at Hay-on-Wye and he was ordained in 1779. In 1783 he obtained the living of Chipping Sodbury in Gloucestershire where he combined his clerical duties with those of master of the grammar school. By the time he wrote his novel, he had tried his hand at three plays, *Owen, or, The Fatal Clemency*, *The Gold Mine* and *The Guardian*, and published two volumes of verse, *Aphtharte, the Genius of Britain* (1784) and *Vacunalia* (1788). Taunted by neighbours who claimed 'that the Welsh was a barren jargon',[6] he began studying in earnest the language and literature of his country, producing numerous transcriptions and translations of poetry and eventually publishing two weighty studies, *Celtic Researches* (1804) and *The Mythology and Rites of the British Druids* (1809). Having obtained the curacies of Olveston and Elberton in Gloucestershire and various preferments in Wales, he moved to Gower in 1813. *The Claims of Ossian* was published in 1825. He died in Bishopston in 1831 and is buried there.

There is a certain poignancy in the fact that, although his attempts to write poetry, drama and fiction in English gave way to prodigious efforts to study the history of the Welsh language and to make a scholarly appraisal of ancient Welsh poetry, his toil seems to have had little permanent value. Rees claimed that Davies acquired a profound knowledge of Welsh, acknowledging only that 'in consequence of not having long resided where it was currently spoken, he was never able to converse in it with fluency'.[7] Nowadays he is judged with much greater severity: 'he had only an imperfect knowledge of Welsh and no qualifications for the task of interpreting the older poetry in which he delighted.'[8] His work on the Druids has also been given short shrift.[9] It was Davies's misfortune that the form of the novel had not yet developed to a point where he might have used fiction to explore the cultural conflict that could never be resolved in life; as a consequence, *Elisa Powell* only dimly reflects his predicament.

It is possible that the impulse to try his hand at a novel originated in his correspondence with the Revd Richard Graves whose living at

Claverton, near Bath, was only twelve miles away from his own parish at Chipping Sodbury. Graves had had some literary success, particularly with *The Spiritual Quixote*, and three letters preserved in the Tonn Collection demonstrate how, in the guise of a grand old man of letters, he encouraged Davies in his literary labours.[10] In February 1788 Graves was principally concerned with Davies's tragedy, *Owen*, dealing with British resistance to the Romans.[11] He failed to persuade the managers of the Bath Theatre to put on the play but recommended 'one Lane in the City who buys every thing tho' chiefly in y^e *novel* way; which good or bad, are as saleable as a Newspaper'.[12] Referring to the success of his own novel, *Eugenius*, published three years previously, he suggested that Davies too might consider writing fiction:

> You write elegant Prose I would advise you, if you want to get money rather than fame to turn your hand to Novels – as I told Miss Seward who has written a Novel in Verse – But who attends to rhyme when eager to go through an interesting Tale?[13]

Seven years passed before Davies at last produced a novel, 'And agreeably to Mr. Graves's opinion, he received for this performance twenty guineas, the only direct sum he ever received for any of his literary works. This work was written during one school vacation.'[14]

Elisa Powell purports to be a series of letters collected by a Welsh curate (who takes no part in the actual events of the novel). It is set mainly in a Welsh spa, clearly based on Builth, though referred to throughout only by its initial. It is significant that, in a novel which conveys an essentially ambivalent attitude to his native country, Davies's central character is a young Englishman, the Revd Henry Stanley, who is in the process of buying an estate in the district and facing some hostility from the locals:

> Five centuries ago, we Englishmen robbed the Welch of their national independence. In defence of it, they had valiantly fought, seven hundred campaigns; at last they were compelled to yield it up; but it was resigned with indignant, haughty submission. They have never forgiven us; and, at this present day, I sojourn among them – 'nothing but an Englishman.' (I, pp.21–2)

Stanley tells his correspondent that the Welsh gentry have largely forgotten their nationality, 'but the populace still retain sufficient greatness of mind to contemn a refinement, which they consider as the badge of slavery, and to glory in their descent from the ancient Britons': they are in fact no worse off than they were under their native princes, but they still resent the loss of Liberty, which 'must be something necessary in the composition of human happiness' (I, pp.22–3).

Although these sentiments are put in the mouth of 'nothing but an Englishman', they represent a hardening of attitude since Davies considered the same issues in *Aphtharte, The Genius of Britain*, published in 1784 but (according to the prefatory 'Advertisement') actually written ten years previously, when he was sixteen years old.[15] In this youthful poem, Britannia's guardian power, Aphtharte, and her offspring, Liberty and Concord, are celebrating an auspicious day, the ascension of 'the Third George and Charlotte' to 'Britannia's awful throne'. It is Liberty who sings the praises of 'Britain's old worthies, and her native King', beginning with 'gallant NENNIUS' and his fight against the Romans and proceeding through a list composed of Cassibe'lan, Caradog, Arviragus ('The conduct and intrepidity he shewed in defence of his country gained him the name of the British Hector'), Boadicea ('Thy name shall ever live with Britain's fair'), Vortimer and Arthur. Liberty exhorts her listeners to consider how generous Albion bore many more brave sons of freedom: 'With hardy limbs she built her martial race, / And hearts to tear the mountains off their base.' Unlike the 'indignant, haughty submission' with which Stanley's Welshmen accept the Edwardian conquest of the thirteenth century, the Cambrians of *Aphtharte* are called upon to extend the hand of friendship to their Saxon conquerors:

> In vain, my Cambrians! To repel the foe
> All have ye done, that Virtue's self could do.
> Give now the friendly hand, since Heav'n ordains
> Odin's brave sons to share your happy plains:
> From your join'd blood a hardy race will rise,
> And Kings, whose names shall shine above the skies.[16]

Helping to promote that Hanoverian political consensus expressed in the concept of 'Great Britain', invented in 1707 when the Act of Union linked Scotland to England and Wales,[17] Liberty goes on to list the kings and queens of the realm, beginning with Alfred and ending with the Georges ('O'er CALEDONIA's realm, confirm thy sway').

But by the time Davies wrote *Elisa Powell*, Britannia had fought and lost the war of 'civil discord' in America,[18] and democratic ideas of individual liberty for the common man were beginning to fuse with notions of national independence. Davies both distances and validates the resentment of the Welsh 'populace' towards their conquerors – a tribute to their 'greatness of mind' – by using the device of a sympathetic English observer.

While his estate is being surveyed and mapped, Stanley spends a holiday in Builth, which is viewed, therefore, through the eyes of an English tourist, not by one for whom this was 'home'. He strolls over the Irfon bridge to the Park Wells, situated in a romantic glen a mile and a half out of town, and then visits the pump room, describing a picturesque group of Welsh peasants – such descriptions were becoming commonplace in the genre paintings of the day and in the accounts of pedestrian tourists through Wales, but were still rare in contemporary fiction:

> Arriving at a small octagon pump-room, I found a group of women in grey linsey-woolsey gowns, blue cloaks, and deep beaver hats. The knitting needles were clattering in every hand; for Welsh-women deem it the most awkward thing in the world to be unemployed. These fair Cambrobritons were interspersed with some men in loose great coats, or close-bodied, light-blue jerkins, sashed round with belts of leather. They scarcely condescended to take notice of a straggling Englishman. My appearance never interrupted their gleeful and vociferous conversation in the dialect of their country. (I, p.26)

The 'straggling Englishman' finds lodgings in a country house on the Radnorshire bank of the Wye, offering superior accommodation to paying guests and a pleasant view of the river:

> This hall is a charming place. Standing with a full south aspect on the lowest declivity of a craggy hill, it commands a view of the river, the bridge, and the town, at the distance of a short mile, bending like a crescent on the margin of the water; beyond which the ground rises in variegated swells of woody banks and smooth-matted hills, interspersed with winding glens: the whole prospect is bounded by the grand undulating lines of the Eppynt mountains. (I, pp.34–5)

Here Davies assembles a group of visitors: Stanley himself; Mr Powell of Morley Castle, Pembrokeshire, accompanied by his daughter, Elisa, and his niece, Jane Wilkins; Mrs Jones, wife of a respectable freeholder on the other side of the county, and her daughter, Maria; Watkins, a Brecon attorney; and Dr Pemberton, a distinguished antiquarian. They go boating and fishing on the Wye, take tea, look at garden insects through a microscope and converse on liberty and agriculture. All this may be of some sociological interest for a historian of the Welsh spas. But given the author's passion for Welsh literature, the interest of *Elisa Powell* lies mainly in his handling of his native culture – rare if not unique as subject matter in the eighteenth-century novel.

For it is Davies's 'idolatrous fondness' for Welsh literature that informs his portraits of Dr Pemberton and the local bard, Dewi ap Morgan, in *Elisa Powell*. Davies was one of that band of eighteenth-century Welshmen described by Prys Morgan as 'passionately devoted to rescue, restore and revive what they could of the old'.[19] His personal obsession with copying, translating and commenting on Welsh poetry was part of a literary crusade that had gathered momentum during the century, resulting in the publication of a number of anthologies of prose and verse, most conspicuously *Some Specimens of Antient Welsh Poetry* (1764), edited by Evan Evans ('Ieuan Fardd' or 'Ieuan Brydidd Hir'), and its counterpart for Welsh readers, *Gorchestion Beirdd Cymru* (1773), edited by Rice Jones of Blaenau. *Barddoniaeth Dafydd ab Gwilym* (1789), edited by William Owen Pughe[20] under the auspices of the Gwyneddigion Society, included items contributed by Edward Williams ('Iolo Morganwg'), which were not revealed as forgeries until over a century later.[21] In 1791, using the bardic name Iorwerth ap Dewi, Edward Davies sent the Gwyneddigion Society his 'Specimens of an English Metrical Translation of the more ancient Welsh Bards, and of Dafydd ab Gwilym', with an introductory essay on Welsh literature.[22] In his essay he points out that while 'the literary remains of the ancient inhabitants' are cherished by the Welsh themselves ('Venerated, even to idolatrous fondness, by the Welsh antiquarians') and superciliously overlooked by learned Englishmen, both parties are allowing the 'remains' to fall to dust. He is a passionate advocate of the need to preserve and elucidate the literature of the past: 'The reason of *our* partiality is well understood. It is natural to claim some merit upon the score of what *we* know, exclusive of others. Our backwardness in explaining the books which we alone understand; our supine neglect of their preservation are less accountable and excusable.' Davies himself could scarcely be accused of 'supine neglect': in 1792 he introduced himself to William Owen Pughe, congratulating him on his 'elegant edition' of Dafydd ap Gwilym 'and the specimens of our more ancient poetry which you published in the *Gentleman's Magazine*'.[23] The same year, Davies made transcripts of manuscripts lent him by Pughe and the Revd John Walters, rector of Llandough,[24] producing a huge volume of 745 pages which later became an invaluable source for the *Myvyrian Archaiology* (1801–7).[25]

In *Elisa Powell*, Davies uses his own translation of Welsh poetry to embellish the novel. In the 'Specimens', he had dismissed ap Gwilym's work as trifling: 'I call them trifles, for we must not dignify this bard's lucubrations, with a title of importance; but the world cannot always be intent upon serious affairs; and Dafydd knows, when he thinks proper, how to trifle with a grace.' Blithely unaware that Iolo Morganwg also knew how to trifle with a grace, Davies had included among his English translations items from Iolo's forgeries. (The unkindest cut of all was that Iolo actually had the gall to praise Davies as a translator.[26]) Long before his versions of Dafydd ap Gwilym (and Iolo) were printed in the *Cambrian Register*,[27] Davies included one of them in *Elisa Powell*. Maria Jones sings 'Address to the Summer', said to be a translation from Dafydd ap Gwilym, for the entertainment of her fellow guests at the boarding house in Builth. The English text of what is in fact a poem by Iolo Morganwg is given in full in the novel (I, pp.161–4). In the 'Specimens', where the poem is called 'Hymn to the Summer', Davies had already apologized for replacing the eighth stanza on the grounds of 'indelicacy and deficiency': 'Gwilym seldom descends to vulgarity, if he has anything better at hand; but it may be taken for a general rule, that, whenever his Pegasus flags, he lets his rider down in the dirt.' In the novel, he patches up Iolo's poem with an innocuous stanza filched from a genuine item by Dafydd ap Gwilym, and allows Maria to sing it in public. The author's misgivings are palpable, however. Although the performance naturally delights the antiquarian, Dr Pemberton, Stanley feels that it would scarcely be safe for such a handsome girl to indulge the doctor with any more treats of this kind: 'I suspect that the waggish bard has couched in his composition some ideas, which Maria, with all her vivacity, has too much innocence to comprehend' (I, p.165).

In creating a portrait of the antiquary, Dr Isaac Pemberton, Davies was in a sense personifying the recovery of Welsh history in the eighteenth century. Prys Morgan refers to the seminal work of Edward Lhuyd, Theophilus Evans, Henry Rowlands, Thomas Pennant and Philip Yorke, together with a number of county historians:

During a century of considerable anglicisation of language and manners, and considerable erosion of the ancient, traditional life, a great deal had been done to record, classify, and publicise the remains of the old language, its literature and its history, though the recovery was always adapted to the needs of the day. The sense of history, or perhaps of antiquarianism, affected all the other skills and arts, because it was an age which had discovered the past, especially the distant past, and had not yet become obsessed with progress, advancement or the future.[28]

Davies certainly shared the contemporary rage for 'the remains' of the Welsh language, and the literature and history of an ancient way of life. Even so, there is a certain ambiguity in his portrait of the antiquary; if Dr Pemberton is to be viewed in any way as the author's alter ego, it seems to be an identification riven with self-doubt. Like his author, Dr Pemberton has a passion for Welsh history and literature. He explains to Stanley that his love of literature began at the age of seven when, instead of giving him a crimson suit with glittering buttons, his grandmother cut down an old suit of his grandfather's and trimmed it with silver buttons engraved with the family crest. Young Pemberton cut off the buttons in disgust, but the chastisement he subsequently received from his grandmother taught him to respect his ancestry for ever after. Forced to wear mohair buttons as a badge of his disgrace, he quickly learned to appreciate the old helmet, relic of an ancestor who had fought with 'Glendour', and from the family history of the Pembertons and Merediths he proceeded to the history of Wales itself. He read David Powel's *Historie of Cambria, Now Called Wales* (1584), Camden's *Britannia* (1586), Aylett Sammes's *Britannia Antiqua Illustrata* (1676) and an unnamed manuscript treatise on the conquest of the Marches. Faring better than his author seems to have done, young Pemberton was taught to read Welsh by his grandmother 'and added to my stock the Drych y Prif Oesoedd, then just published' (I, p.158). Since Dr Pemberton is presented as a man in late middle age – he explains that he has come back to Wales to see one or two friends of his youth 'and to cast one more lingering look on those peaceful scenes that afforded me delight fifty years ago' (I, p.41) – this is presumably a reference to the widely circulated second edition of *Drych y Prif Oesoedd* (1740) by Theophilus Evans, which 'presented for the first time in two hundred years a view of Wales as a country with a history distinct from that of England'.[29] It was a work that had personal significance for Davies himself: as a budding antiquarian he had already quoted it in *Aphtharte*,[30] while the historian's grandson, Theophilus Jones, had been a schoolfellow at Brecon and remained ever afterwards 'my incomparable friend'.[31]

Although Dr Pemberton shares the interests of the author, he is nevertheless presented as a figure of fun, as if Davies (who was slightly built and self-effacing[32]) uneasily personifies in the gigantic stature and flamboyant personality of the antiquarian the absurd and unwieldy nature of his own grand obsession. Hence Watkins's description of his first meeting with Dr Pemberton:

> I had just had time to observe an enormous pair of boots, a brown cloak that would have covered a haystack, and a huge umbrella upon a pole as long and as large as one of Cromwell's pikestaves. I even ventured to lift my eyes toward the head of the prodigy. It was covered with a broad-brimmed hat, curling up, on each side, with a parallel bend; behind which an antique periwig swelled out like a thunder pillar: and on the opposite quarter, a nose of unconscionable length, like the bowsprit of a man of war, stretched forward. I saw his eyes, large and piercing, beneath two shaggy brows, like clear springs in the shade of a forest. In short I saw – (I, p.38)

Watkins is allowed to go no further: 'To these wild hyperboles, it was impossible to listen any longer: our peals of laughter stemmed the torrent of extravagance.' It is under Pemberton's ægis that Stanley visits the local bard, Dewi Morgan, allowing the author to satirize in these two characters the 'bardic nationalism' that had become his own private obsession.

Davies was certainly capable of laughing at himself: the engaging streak of self-mockery in 'Owen', one of the poems clearly written while he was still a schoolboy at Brecon, is directed at his own role as a Welsh bard. Said to be written by 'MORGAN AP JORWERTH AP DEWI, A WELCH TELYNWYR [sic] OR MINSTREL', the poem is a mock-heroic account of a fives tournament between Owen son of Howell and Morgan son of David. The opening sequence, in which the poet peers 'With low-arch'd eye' over his Cambrian harp, demonstrates his precocious talent for versification and a satiric view of the bardic tradition:

> COME to my hand, my Cambrian harp, resound
> The fame of Owen. From the fives-court he

> Glorious returns, shrin'd in a dusty cloud.
> The hero brings, deep nodding o'er his brow,
> The garland – keen his eye – his foot outstrips
> Brisk Eurus, and the racket loves his hand.
> By his bold gait I know him, while I peep,
> With low-arch'd eye, over the Cambrian lyre
> On Honddus' [sic] bank, stooping, intent to trace
> The soul of music, that divinely flies
> From string to string. Around, his friends, as night,
> Move clam'rous, should'ring to his presence – prone,
> They gaze, admiring, and repeat the tale,
> Echoing, with twirling hat, the jovial shout,
> Whilst old Brechinia's walls return the sound.[33]

In a companion piece, 'The Jail', said to be written by the same Morgan ap Jorwerth ap Dewi, the young poet finds himself in prison for debt, and here 'The absent lyre, which my fingers seek / Deluded' is anything but figurative: his harp is in the pawnshop.

> But ah! No more, dear Jenkin's sacred gift,
> Shall I revisit! Now detain'd in pawn
> By ruthless landlord, for the length'ning score
> Of potent ale – O may no rustic hand
> Thrum the smooth strings or force the tuneful key!
> May none, Ah me! the lovely tone profane.
> O chearful harp! Still must I think of thee,
> Though here I dwell, sequester'd and forgot,
> From now, from toil I rest, my British songs
> Unfinish'd, float in many an idle sheet.
> Dunwal of other days, Owen, and he
> Who feasted long the loyal swains, in proud
> Brechinia's vale – are robb'd of all their fame.[34]

The name of the schoolboy *telynwr* is echoed not only in the penname Davies used to endorse his translation of his 'Specimens' and prefatory essay presented to the Gwyneddigion Society (Iorwerth ap Dewi) but also in the name of the local bard, Dewi Morgan, a figure which both embodies and caricatures his enthusiasm for Welsh poetry. Stanley and the doctor ride 'among naked crags, gloomy woods, and solitary glens, on the south bank of the Irvon' (I, p.181) and eventually reach the bard's neat white cottage, set picturesquely between two broken points of rock, with a forest behind and a stream in front; but they are informed by 'A decent woman of fifty, in a blue woollen gown and high beaver, the malvina of this Cambrian Ossian'[35] (I, p.181) that he has gone to a farmer's wedding. They soon reach the spot:

> The first object that caught our attention was a large booth of fresh branches, erected on a narrow plain, as level as a bowling green; within which we descried the remains of a true old British figure, seated on a bank of turf and tuning an enormous treble harp. As we approached the place, he turned upon us a penetrating eye, shaded by a rough dusky brow, while, from a kind of garland that surrounded his head, a slip of green silk was suspended, to conceal the empty socket of the other. His nose was bold and aquiline; his forehead ample, square, and seamed with scars; and on each side of his head the thick curling locks, tinged with the first blossom of age, extended their volume to the breeze. His countenance altogether indicated a composition of manly intrepidity, honest frankness, and arch drollery. His whole dress, including the left stocking, was of one colour, the sky-blue of the ancient bards; but his right leg, being formed of true heart of oak, disdained a covering. (I, pp.182–3)

Stanley explains to his correspondent that Dewi Morgan was an illegitimate child, taught to play the harp by the sexton. Mutilated in the American wars, he returned to Wales and became so indispensable at country celebrations that on one occasion he was released from Brecon gaol by public subscription. The portrait is clearly based on the disabled ex-soldier, described among Davies's 'comrades dear' in 'The Jail', with grey hair 'thin waving, in the whistling blast', a forehead 'ridgy' with scars, a missing foot and only one eye, 'The single remnant of the grinding blade':

> Nor must be forgot, where, high, supreme,
> The old, grey officer sits, cow'ring huge,
> With locks, thin waving, in the whistling blast,
> Zealous for Britain's glory: much his grief,
> Should mortal wight affirm the dubious fate
> Of Jersey, Boston or old Gibralter.
> He thinks of former days; and shews his scars,
> Frowning tremendous, ridgy o'er his brow.

> He glories in his shorten'd nose, his hand
> Reft of a thumb, and foot that stumps the ground,
> Unequal: oft with deep, sonorous voice,
> Repeats his martial fame; how fierce he press'd,
> Mounted the breach, and burst through storms of fire,
> And urg'd the foe, confounded, to forsake
> Their silent thunders and proud banners vain;
> Trophies for Britons bold – His mighty soul
> Rekindles: round he throws his threatning eye,
> The single remnant of the grinding blade,
> And pants for arms, and rears the knotty hand,
> And seems, in spite of Albion's milder laws,
> Dealing revenge and ruin on the foe.
> Thus he supports the lofty soul, the breast
> Of conscious virtue, and the steady brow.[36]

There is no suggestion in 'The Jail' that the old soldier is also a bard – it is the poet himself who has lost his harp. But in *Elisa Powell* Davies reworks the description of 'The old, grey officer', refashioning in the process the prevailing image of the Welsh bard as purveyed by Thomas Gray and his imitators. Gray's figure of the ancient bard, sole survivor of the Edwardian massacre, was certainly acceptable to Iolo Morganwg and his circle – among Davies's manuscripts there still exists a printed sheet announcing the competition set for the Gorsedd sessions of 1798, a translation of Gray's poem into Welsh.[37] But Edward Davies chooses to clothe Dewi Morgan in the sky-blue robes of Iolo's new bardic dispensation: since his release from Brecon gaol, the old soldier has discarded military garb 'and vested [himself] with the unicoloured emblem of harmony and peace' (I, pp.188–9). He is delighted to see Dr Pemberton, promising him a choice collection of primeval bardism, transcribed in his own hand. This is a present that would have delighted the author himself, yet Dewi's own performance is treated with scant respect. The visitors are invited to stay to the wedding feast and the whole hillside brightens 'with a promiscuous cavalcade of both sexes and all ages, in their best attire' (I, p.192). The bridegroom leads the bride to the bard 'who received her with a voluntary on the Welsh harp, and an *original* epithalamium' (I, p.192). Davies provides the full English text, but not only does it read (perhaps inadvertently) as doggerel, it also causes some mirth among the wedding guests, 'amid the antic gigs and vociferation of part of his audience, and the peals of laughter of such as could not employ themselves otherwise' (I, p.194). About forty guests sit down in the barn to a plain but plentiful repast, with nappy Welsh ale to drink. At four o'clock, the younger guests assemble to dance on the green while the visitors jog back to Builth, wearing their bridal favours.

By the time Stanley goes on a longer tour with Dr Pemberton, he has fallen in love with Elisa Powell and has become immersed in her tragic history. The 'editor' admits to suppressing three letters on the manners and superstitions of the Welsh, the doctor's reflections on the grave of Llywelyn the Last[38] and other singular discoveries. The doctor then leaves for Dublin, hot on the trail of 'a complete copy of Aneurin's [sic] Gododin, the most ancient British poem now extant' (II, p.152). Prys Morgan describes the discovery of the Gododdin in 1758 as 'one of the great moments of the literary revival'.[39] As Lewis Morris told his brother, 'this discovery is to him [Evan Evans] and me as great as that of America by Columbus. We have found an epic Poem in the British called Gododin, equal at least to the Iliad, Aeneid, or Paradise Lost.'[40] Yet, at this point in *Elisa Powell*, Dr Pemberton is in effect laughed off the stage of the novel so that the author, himself a passionate devotee of Welsh poetry, can focus exclusively on what he perceives to be his proper business as a novelist, the morbid history of Elisa.

Janet Todd has described the fashion in mid-eighteenth-century novels for 'a sensibility that has wonderful powers and allure, with none of the strains of moral seriousness',[41] purveying a common fantasy 'of passive femininity sometimes made powerful through death but more usually through the extreme reverential attitude of others towards it'.[42] The heroes of such novels are exaggeratedly feminized, their creators insisting that tender sensibility is compatible with manliness.[43] It was to this unlikely territory, occupied mainly by female writers, that Davies turned his attention in the second volume of *Elisa Powell*, providing a history for the heroine which ultimately kills her and leaves Stanley (who might have accompanied Dr Pemberton to Dublin) longing for death himself. Having suffered attempted rape by her childhood sweetheart (while her parents favour the suit of a rival) and mourned both her brother's death in prison while awaiting trial for murdering the childhood sweetheart and the subsequent death of her mother, Elisa has suffered a 'settled melancholy gloom' and has been brought to Builth to recuperate. When her father dies of gout in the stomach, Elisa becomes consumptive; fortunately Stanley prefers a suffering Elisa and is more than willing to suffer himself:

> Elisa, cheerful, forgetful of the past, and alive to all the enjoyments of life, after what she has suffered, could never be my Elisa. She is more lovely in her grief. Her delicate sensibility folds itself about my heart, and suffers not a desire to escape. Oh that she would grant me one indulgence, which is in her power – to mix my tears with hers – to languish under the same sorrows – to sink into the same grave! (II, p.108)

Elisa does indeed sink into the grave. Whether Stanley sinks into the same one is left unresolved, but in either case it is a denouement designed, in W. J. Rees's view, 'to caution young persons against forming attachments, without the knowledge of their parents, and a reasonable hope of union, by marriage, which would produce happiness'.[44] One wonders.

It is only too evident that quite apart from his failure to write convincingly about 'sensibility', Davies also failed to produce an adequate fiction written at the interface of two cultures. His representation of his native country hints at that obsession with the language, history and literature of Wales which brought him into contact with many of the prominent figures involved in the eighteenth-century Welsh 'Renaissance'. But the literary conventions of the day were against him. Davies was uniquely placed to understand the quintessential Anglo-Welsh experience, yet in his novel he makes little use of his intimate knowledge of everyday life in Wales and nothing of the *hiraeth* he suffered at the loss of Welsh as his first language. He contented himself with an outsider's view of his place of birth, transformed his experience of exile into the persona of an English narrator and personified his own fascination with Welsh history and literature in the comic characters of the antiquarian, Dr Pemberton, and the bard, Dewi Morgan. Whether or not *Elisa Powell* can be described as 'the first Anglo-Welsh novel', it has to be acknowledged that in his solitary incursion into fiction, Edward 'Celtic' Davies came perilously close to ridiculing what he truly loved and esteemed.

13

Perdita, Wales and the monster

MARY ROBINSON'S WELSH NOVELS

In the museum devoted to the life and work of Howel Harris at Coleg Trefeca hangs a portrait of Mary Robinson, an exotic presence among the early Methodists. Acclaimed as one of the most beautiful women of her time, her brief career on the London stage culminated in her celebrated role as Perdita in *The Winter's Tale* and the notorious affair with the young Prince of Wales. In 1780 an illustrated sheet of verses beginning 'Polly is a sad slut' shows Perdita wearing what has been politely described as 'an elaboration of Welsh national costume'[1] – doubtless her dress was intended as an ironic compliment to her royal lover, though part of the joke may have been the fact that both she and her husband (who appears in the picture wearing stag's horns) were of Welsh descent. Indeed, she was one of the few writers of eighteenth-century 'Welsh' fiction to claim any connection with or personal knowledge of the country, offering in *Angelina* (1796), *Walsingham* (1797) and *The Natural Daughter* (1799) scenes set in the Breconshire countryside, and in *Memoirs of the Late Mrs. Robinson, Written by Herself* (1801) a lively account of her visits to Tregunter and Trefeca as a young married woman. *Walsingham* is of particular interest in its depiction of Brecknock man in the throes of early Romantic angst, and presents some remarkable parallels with *Fleetwood* (1805) by her distinguished mentor, William Godwin – with the distinct possibility that the literary 'influence' was not necessarily operating in the expected direction.

Mary Robinson was born in Bristol. In her *Memoirs* she gives her date of birth as 27 November 1758, though the baptismal register of St Augustine-the-Less shows that she was born two years earlier than she was willing to admit: '1758 July 19 Polle Daugh^t of Nicholas and Hester Darby Born Nov. 27th 1756'.[2] Her father, a Merchant Adventurer, was an American by birth. She claimed her Welsh descent through her mother, naming her great-grandmother as Catherine, daughter of Richard Seys of Boverton Castle in the Vale of Glamorgan. Like other writers of scandalous memoirs in the eighteenth century, Robinson was bent on making 'a mythology of her victimization' and sketching 'a drama of self-defense';[3] the exemplary character of Catherine Seys ('a woman of great piety, and virtue')[4] is clearly intended as a pointer to the author's own essential virtue ('subjugated by circumstances more than by inclination') in the face of a hostile world.[5] It has to be said, however, that while it is possible to find an Ann, an Elizabeth and a Margaret among the daughters of Richard Seys (d. 1714), there seems to be no record of a Catherine.[6]

Robinson claims that her Welsh grandmother, Catherine's daughter, was orphaned at an early age and brought up at Boverton Castle, and that she too was 'a woman of amiable and simple manners, unaffected piety, and exemplary virtue':

> My grand-mother Elizabeth, whom I may, without the vanity of consanguinity, term a truly good woman, in the early part of her life devoted much of her time to botanic study. She frequently passed many successive months with Lady Tynt of Haswell in Somersetshire, who was her god-mother, and who was the Lady Bountiful of the surrounding villages. Animated by so distinguished an example, the young Elizabeth, who was remarkably handsome, took particular delight in visiting the old, the indigent, and the infirm, resident within many miles of Haswell, and in preparing such medicines as were useful to the maladies of the peasantry. She was the village doctress; and, with her worthy god-mother, seldom passed a day without exemplifying the benevolence of her nature. (p.4)

There is no reason to doubt the substance of this, especially as Lady Tynte, wife of the second baronet, was the daughter of Sir Charles Kemys of Cefn Mably, a neighbour of the Seys of Boverton.[7] (There is, however, no record in the *Memoirs* of an unexpected and rather more colourful Welsh connection: as a poor relation of the Seys family, Iolo Morganwg's mother, Ann Matthew, may also have spent part of her girlhood at Boverton Castle.[8]) The *Memoirs* record that Elizabeth was 'wedded unhappily' and that her daughter was born in Bridgwater, Somerset. The parish register of St Mary, Bridgwater, duly records the baptism of Hester, daughter of Elizabeth and Jonathan Vinicot, on 22 May 1724.[9]

Mary Robinson, *c.*1782: drawing by Sir Joshua Reynolds

Mary, daughter of Hester, granddaughter of Elizabeth and possibly great-granddaughter of Catherine Seys of Boverton, was brought up in Bristol and educated at a school kept by Hannah More's sisters. Later, she moved to London with her mother and finished her education there. On 12 April 1774 she married Thomas Robinson, illegitimate son of Thomas Harris of Trefeca and Tregunter in the county of Brecknock.[10] Her father-in-law, born in 1715, was an older brother of Howel Harris, the great Methodist, and a younger brother of Joseph. As a tailor working in London, Thomas Harris had made a fortune out of army contracts; he acquired his Breconshire estate in 1768 and became sheriff of the county. He had certainly been married,[11] but he had also fathered three illegitimate children, William, Thomas and Elizabeth Robinson. Howel Harris had died the year before Mary's marriage, but the religious community he had set up in 1752, a 'Family' of up to two hundred people engaged in sixty or more trades, still flourished at Trefeca.[12] At nearby Tregunter, Thomas Harris and his family were living in what Mary described as a 'pretty little decorated cottage' while his new mansion was being built. It was to this cottage that Mary and her new husband came on their bridal visit (probably in August 1774), which began with a stormy crossing of the Old Passage to Chepstow and a journey by post-chaise to Tregunter.

Here, as elsewhere in the *Memoirs*, Robinson represents herself as a sensitive and melancholy young woman, fully alive (twenty-five years after the event) to the Romantic possibilities of the Welsh landscape:

> We passed through a thick wood, the mountains at every brake meeting our eyes covered with thin clouds, and rising in sublime altitude above the valley. A more romantic space of scenery never met the human eye! – I felt my mind inspired with a pensive melancholy, and was awakened from my reverie by the post-boy stopping at the mansion of Tregunter. (pp.46–7)

Moments later she is recalling how she was dressed for the occasion, making an unkind comparison between her own elegant person and the odd figure of her new sister-in-law, Elizabeth, and at the same time putting down a marker: she means to demonstrate that Thomas Harris and his family were vulgar and unpleasant, fitting relatives for her worthless husband whose dissolute behaviour would eventually precipitate her into the affair with the Prince of Wales. Even the 'excessive cordiality' of Harris's greeting is nicely gauged – before the visit was over he was confiding to his daughter-in-law that he wished he could have married her himself:

> Mr Harris came out to receive me. I wore a dark claret-coloured riding-habit, with a white beaver hat and feathers. He embraced me with excessive cordiality, while Miss Robinson, my husband's sister, with cold formality led me into the house. I shall never forget her looks or her manner. Had her brother presented the most abject being to her, she could not have taken my hand with a more frigid demeanour. Miss Robinson, though not more than twenty years of age, was Gothic in her appearance and stiff in her deportment; she was of low stature, and clumsy, with a countenance peculiarly formed for the expression of sarcastic vulgarity – a short snub nose, turned up at the point, a head thrown back with an air of *hauteur*; a gaudy-coloured chintz gown, a thrice-bordered cap, with a profusion of ribbons, and a countenance somewhat more ruddy than was consistent with even pure health, presented the personage whom I was to know as my future companion and kinswoman! (p.47)

Her father-in-law, looking like 'a venerable HAWTHORN', generally wore a brown fustian coat, a scarlet waistcoat edged with narrow gold, a pair of woollen spatterdashes and a gold laced hat. Every day he rode out on a small Welsh pony and was scarcely at home except at mealtimes. He was a regular churchgoer and justice of the peace and frequently fined the rustics for swearing, 'though every third sentence he uttered was attended by an oath that made his hearers shudder' (p.48). (The Breconshire squire in *Angelina* behaves in much the same way.[13]) The household was completed by the housekeeper, Mary Edwards, 'and a more overbearing, vindictive spirit never inhabited the heart of mortal than that which pervaded the soul of the ill-natured Mrs Molly' (p.48).

Mary spent her time in 'this uninteresting circle' by drinking ale with the squire, visiting Lady Huntingdon's 'methodistical seminary' or riding out with Elizabeth, who was resplendent 'in a camlet safeguard, with a high-crowned bonnet' (which sounds remarkably like a Welsh hat), while she herself wore a fashionable habit 'and looked like something human'. The seminary, founded in 1768 for the preparation of young men for the mission field, occupied a farmhouse, Trefeca Isaf, which can still be seen on the road between Trefeca and

Talgarth.[14] A year after Mary's visit, Sir Thomas Gery Cullum described the seven young students as

> dressed chiefly in black, very grave and attentive to their Business... I could not help pitying the Situation of these young Men, who from a settled Gloom on their Countenances seemed rather under the Influence of a religious Melancholy than actuated by the Design of spreading false Doctrines in the World.[15]

Mary gives no indication of her effect on the class of 1774.

The three-week visit was a success: Thomas Harris assured Mary that he would leave his estate to Tom. However, by the time the young couple made their second visit to Wales later that year, things did not look so promising. Tom was hiding from his creditors and Mary was near her confinement. One of the reasons for fudging the dates in the *Memoirs* was almost certainly to disguise the fact that Mary was already pregnant when she was married: her 'drama of self-defense' required a state of perfect chastity until she began her affair with the Prince of Wales. Since Tregunter House was barely finished, she was sent to Trefeca House, 'a spacious mansion at the foot of a stupendous mountain' (p.75). She admits that part of the building had been 'converted into a flannel manufactory' and that 'the inhabitants were of the Huntingdonian school', then continues in Romantic mode:

> Here I enjoyed the sweet repose of solitude: here I wandered about woods entangled by the wild luxuriance of nature, or roved upon the mountain's side, while the blue vapours floated round its summit. O, God of Nature! Sovereign of the universe of wonders! In those interesting moments how fervently did I adore thee! (pp.75–6)

The baby was born and her baptism recorded in the parish register: 'Maria Elizabeth, daughter of Thomas Robinson and Mary his wife, baptized Oct. 25, 1774, by Rev. John Jones, Talgarth'.[16] (Maria Elizabeth Robinson was to become one of the few eighteenth-century novelists known to have been born in Wales.[17]) At two days old, 'my little darling, enveloped in the manufacture of her own romantic birth-place, made her first visit to her kind but unsophisticated countrywomen' (p.78). Shortly afterwards, still fleeing their creditors, Mary and her family decamped to Monmouth where they stayed with her grandmother, descendant of the Seys. Elizabeth Vinicot received them with affection and hospitality: 'How different were these moments from those I had passed with the low-minded inhabitants of Tregunter' (p.82). Mary accompanied her 'amiable and venerable relative to church' and indulged her Romantic tastes by wandering by the River Wye and exploring the antique remains of the castle. On the day she left Monmouth, 'an execution arrived for a considerable sum'. In London, Tom was arrested for debt and the family spent the next fifteen months in the King's Bench.

While her husband was in prison, Mary Robinson published her first volume of poems. On 10 December 1776, she made her debut on the London stage, with the encouragement of Garrick himself. She paid her last recorded visit to Tregunter 'on the second year after my appearance at Drury-lane theatre' (p.112) and received a warmer welcome than before. However, when Thomas Harris died in 1782, his extensive property was left to Anna Maria and Samuel Hughes (Joseph Harris's daughter and son-in-law), while Tom Robinson received an annuity of one hundred pounds.[18] The only benefit which accrued to Mary was the lasting effect that her visits to Trefeca and Tregunter had upon her writing.

By 1787 Mary Robinson's stage career was over, her affair with the Prince of Wales was a thing of the past and she was permanently crippled by '*a violent rheumatism*', said to have been contracted after a miscarriage during her sixteen-year relationship with Colonel Banastre Tarleton.[19] From this date until her death, she wrote prolifically. Described by Coleridge as 'a woman of undoubted Genius',[20] she produced several volumes of verse (including a handful of poems on Welsh subjects),[21] as well as two plays and an essay on women's rights. She wrote for the periodicals of the day, contributing verses to the *Morning Post* under the pen-name of Smollett's comic Welsh spinster, Tabitha Bramble, of Brambleton Hall, near Crickhowell (only a few miles from Tregunter). She also published seven novels, three of which include scenes set in Tabby's home territory.

In *Angelina* (1796),[22] a rambling epistolary novel, the young heroine, Sophia Clarendon, falls in love with Charles Belmont but has to escape the clutches of the debauched Lord Acreland – who, many years before, married then abandoned the unfortunate Angelina. There are a number of Welsh characters in the novel, including Sir Philip and Lady Watkins of Kidwelly, the Revd Mr Evan Jones (revealed as Angelina's father) and Old Morgan and his wife. Only Belmont, however, is given specifically 'national' traits when he stands up to Sophia's father, the boorish Sir Edward Clarendon, who 'has more than once given offence to this Cambrian hero, whose high mind, and irritable temper, soon reduced the Knight to terms of accommodation' (I, p.162). The Welsh scenes occur early in the novel when Sir George Fairford discovers Angelina's retreat in Breconshire, in countryside 'that would have done honour to the fancy of a Claude de Lorraine, and would scarcely have received additional splendour from the pencil of a Salvator Rosa!' (I, p.214). The vividness – one might say the virulence – of the brightly lit landscape suggests both the powerfully focused beam of memory and the transformation of the remembered scene through the filter of Italian art:

> The valley presented a long track of verdant meadow land, which was bounded on each side by stupendous mountains, their summits hidden with clouds, through which the rays of the declining sun penetrated, in columns of brilliant light, which, as they descended towards the base of the mountains, gave the green turf the brightness of the emerald. The slope, which was skirted by a winding narrow wood, was sprinkled over with sheep and goats, and here and there a shepherd boy sat on the declivity, singing or whistling, as his fancy or occupation permitted. (I, p.50)

As befits a woman who has been abandoned by her husband after a clandestine marriage, Angelina has hidden herself away in a lonely cottage built into the ruins of a castle, deep in a wood between two stupendous mountains, with a foaming cataract rushing beside it – a retreat which is both civilized and romantically wild, a tribute to the chatelaine's impeccable taste as well as a pointer to the vulnerability that requires castle walls to protect her from discovery and attack. A much grimmer metamorphosis of the author's brief incarceration in Trefeca House appears in *The Natural Daughter* when Mrs Sedgley takes refuge in a solitary habitation, situated (like Maria Elizabeth Robinson's birthplace) 'at the foot of a bleak and barren mountain near Crickhowel' (I, p.228). Her plight is even more pitiable than Angelina's since she has been forcibly wed in revolutionary France (to Marat's *valet-de-chambre*, no less) and is now pregnant. She is still not safe, even in her retreat: 'My real name and situation was whispered about with malevolent avidity: I was shunned, abhorred, and driven from the sanctuary of compunction to seek a new asylum – among strangers' (I, p.228). When she returns to the cottage, she finds it burnt to ashes. Both Angelina and Mrs Sedgley hide away until the world is convinced that they are women of unblemished character – thus pre-empting the 'plot' of the *Memoirs* in which Robinson deals with her own 'fallen' state by attempting as best she can (she fudges dates, she prevaricates) to establish not only the legitimacy of her daughter but also her conception within the bonds of marriage (with Tom Robinson cast as a villain somewhere between Lord Acreland and Marat's *valet-de-chambre*). In this sense, it is possible to read Robinson's autobiography as both a recapitulation and a transformation of the novels; like other female writers of scandalous memoirs in the eighteenth century, she attempts, in Felicity Nussbaum's terms, to 'radically redefine the fall, away from the notion of an irrecoverable act that condemns women to solitude and retreat [exemplified in Angelina's ruined castle and Mrs Sedgley's cottage], and toward an argument for contesting cultural universalization of the female'.[23]

In the same year that *Angelina* came out, Mary Robinson was introduced to William Godwin by Robert Merry, Hester Lynch Piozzi's 'Della Crusca'.[24] It seems likely that she became acquainted with Mary Wollstonecraft at about the same time.[25] By 1798, Robinson was identified by *The Anti-Jacobin Magazine* as a literary disciple of Godwin and his wife. Lashing out against 'the voluptuous dogmas of Mary Godwin and her more profligate imitators', the journal dismissed Mary Robinson's 'trash' along with the work of Mary Hays, Charlotte Smith and Elizabeth Inchbald: these writers were the 'unprincipled disciples of Godwin and his wife' – 'the spawn of the monster'.[26] In May 1799 'The Unsexed Females' by the Revd Richard Polwhele bade the reader 'See Wollstonecraft, whom no decorum checks', asserting her sovereignty over humbled man with the help of Anna Laetitia Barbauld, Mary Robinson, Charlotte Smith, Helen Maria Williams, Anna Yearsley and Mary Hays, though at the end of the poem these erring women abandon their leader at the entreaty of a supernatural voice: Hannah More is calling them to order.[27] Robinson pays tribute to Wollstonecraft in her essay, *A Letter to the Women of England, on the Injustice of Mental Insubordination* (1799), where she argues that it will require '*a legion of Wollstonecrafts*' to undermine the poison and malevolence that affect the lives of women.[28] In *Angelina* Miss Juliana Pengwynn is a Welsh bluestocking who upholds a woman's right to education and independence and is impeccably radical in her thinking. It has been suggested that on occasion

Robinson herself was prepared to defend the slave trade,[29] but the fictional Miss Pengwynn deplores the fact that her brother-in-law's estate has been acquired by means of 'the barbarous traffic of your fellow creatures', while her niece reflects on the human degradation that underpins her comfortable existence: 'I pity the sable sons of slavery . . . And while I take my morning beverage, I often think with horror, that it was cultivated under all the agonies of torture and oppression' (II, p.29).

This is not to suggest that Mary Robinson was directly 'influenced' by either of the Godwins, though few critics allow her either intellectual or political autonomy. While acknowledging that she had expressed advanced political views in her poetry and fiction before the appearance of Godwin's *Enquiry Concerning Political Justice* (1793), M. Ray Adams nevertheless refers to her 'discipleship', suggesting that *Walsingham* 'reflects the association with Godwin and his circle begun the year before' and noting that 'Mrs. Robinson had not read Godwin on inequality for nothing'.[30] Similarly, while Gary Kelly recognizes that novelists like Mary Robinson and Mary Hays might themselves have exerted 'influence' in the opposite direction, he is scathing about their effect on Godwin's work: 'The extravagance of their language and the emotional intensity of their thinly disguised autobiographies were, unfortunately, all too easy to imitate, and it was their example which Godwin seems to have followed, rather than the philosophical restraint and chaste language of other novels he read at this time – *Clarissa*, or the novels of Fanny Burney.'[31] Yet, in identifying numerous literary sources for *Fleetwood*, Kelly makes no reference to *Walsingham*. Peter Garside implies a reciprocal influence, suggesting that the distorting effects of tyranny on the hero's mind in *Walsingham* may recall the analysis of 'order and insubordination' in *Caleb Williams*, while anticipating later psychological studies by Godwin, notably in *Fleetwood*, though the comparison is not developed.[32] Godwin had certainly read some of Mary Robinson's fiction;[33] whether he absorbed ideas from a writer more usually considered a mere acolyte must remain a matter for speculation, though by comparing *Walsingham* and *Fleetwood*, both set in Wales and both concerned with ideas about man and nature that relate to and offer a critique of early Romanticism, it is possible to demonstrate a number of suggestive parallels between the two works.

Walsingham, or, The Pupil of Nature (1797)[34] came out a year after *Angelina*. *Fleetwood, or, The New Man of Feeling* was published eight years later.³⁵ Both Walsingham and Fleetwood are brought up as solitary children in wild Wales, with occupations, as Walsingham puts it, 'romantic, almost to incredibility'. Both are allowed to run wild in the Welsh mountains – much like the stripling in *The Minstrel*, written by the Scottish poet referred to in *Walsingham* as 'the inspired Beattie':

> LO! where the stripling, wrapt in wonder, roves
> Beneath the precipice o'erhung with pine;
> And sees, on high, amidst th'encircling groves,
> From cliff to cliff the foaming torrents shine:
> While waters, woods and winds in concert join,
> And Echo swells the chorus to the skies.
> Would Edwin this majestic scene resign
> For aught the huntsman's puny craft supplies?
> Ah! no: he better knows great Nature's charms to prize.³⁶

As 'a wild inhabitant of the Welsh mountains', Walsingham belongs to the primitive tribes of the earth: he is addressed contemptuously as 'my man of copper', his tawny physiognomy suggesting that he had 'first seen the light of day in the wilds of Otaheite'; Fleetwood is likewise referred to as 'a solitary savage'. Both novels examine the psychological effects of such an upbringing – and both appear to question the role of 'nature' in the education of the developing child.

Robinson's hero, Walsingham Ainsworth, 'born in a small village on the borders of South Wales' (I, p.21), is brought up by his aunt and uncle on an estate which clearly recalls the situation of Tregunter: 'An opening which led towards Abergavenny broke the towering amphitheatre of nature which nearly encircled Glenowen' (IV, p.322). After Sir Edward's death, Lady Aubrey gives birth to a posthumous child, 'Sir Sidney', and moves to Nice. Her nephew remains behind at Glenowen and, left to the tender mercies of the steward and housekeeper, wanders about on his own 'like a wild inhabitant of the mountains'. The effect of an unhappy childhood is made quite explicit:

> The solitude in which I was condemned to waste my infant hours, implanted the first roots of that melancholy which has never ceased to be the prominent characteristic of my nature. For nothing can be more certain, than that the general tenor of the mind through life fashions its bent from the impressions of that period, when reason begins to dawn, and memory takes root in the young and opening fancy. (I, p.70)

But, although melancholy blights Walsingham's life, as it would later blight Fleetwood's, he develops a love of his fellow creatures even in these unpromising circumstances. In one of the poems written into the novel, he wanders 'upon the brow of mountain steep', and like Beattie's Minstrel ('Even sad vicissitude amused his soul') occasionally allows a tear of pity to roll down his cheek:

> With ebon locks unkempt and mean attire,
>   A mountain weather-beaten wight was I;
> And passing meek, save when resentful ire
>   Bade from my glance the living light'nings fly,
>   To think that vice should virtue's place supply.
> For though no classic knowledge grac'd my mind,
>   From legends old, or feats of chivalry,
> Still round my heart the wond'rous instinct twin'd,
> Which throbb'd through ev'ry vein, the love of human kind.[37] (I, p.74)

As Walsingham has nothing human on which to bestow his affections, they have imperceptibly attached themselves to inanimate objects. From the bleak and barren summit of the mountain where he had once wandered with his uncle, he contemplates the tranquil scene below, 'and I fancied that the objects of my attention, as though grateful for my pains, looked more fresh and lovely by every sigh that escaped from my bosom' (I, pp.77–8).

Like Walsingham, Godwin's hero, Fleetwood, is also brought up among 'the sublime and romantic features of nature'. Just as Walsingham is described as the descendant of Sir Sidney Waller, 'a gallant general, who lost his life on the same day, and in the same cause as the immortal Hampden' (I, pp.21–2), Fleetwood is named for one of Cromwell's generals and is brought up in a Cromwellian house at the foot of Cader Idris,[38] suggesting that both are likely to hold radical political views. Fleetwood's father has retreated into Merionethshire as a desolate widower; although he is fond of his son, the child is emotionally neglected and very lonely. Constant familiarity with mountains and precipices, the roaring of the ocean and the dashing of waterfalls gives a 'wildness' to his ideas and 'an uncommon seriousness' to his temper. Unlike Walsingham's cautious simile ('as though grateful') that establishes a tentative emotional link between himself and the landscape, Fleetwood's mind is fully in accord with the mysterious power that operates in nature. Like the animal and vegetable kingdoms,

'Even the clouds, the winds and the streams present us with the image of life, and talk to us of that venerable power, which is operating every where, and never sleeps' (I, p.5). Like Walsingham, Fleetwood experiences 'the love of human kind', though he is honest enough to admit that while his sympathy flows 'from a celestial source', his charity is nourished by self-complacency – he enjoys exhibiting an 'honourable character'. But, despite the fact that both Walsingham and Fleetwood grow up in the Welsh mountains, 'nature' scarcely seems to prepare them adequately for adult life: indeed, both characters are shown to be capable of dissolute, even brutal, behaviour, in ways that seem deliberately shocking in a 'pupil of nature' or a 'new man of feeling'. In effect, while both writers appear to accept the Romantic doctrine of the primacy, even the divinity, of nature, neither assumes that its influence is likely to have a lasting, benign influence on a man's life. Indeed, it is possible that both subtitles are bitterly ironical.

In a plot conspicuous for its bizarre twists and turns, Walsingham eventually acquires a tutor, the Revd Mr Hanbury, and falls in love with Isabella, Hanbury's sister; Isabella meanwhile becomes inseparable from 'Sir Sidney'. Plunging into a series of picaresque adventures in Bath and London, Walsingham seduces his landlady's daughter, Amelia, believing her to be Isabella; when Amelia later agrees to marry Walsingham's uncle, Colonel Aubrey, she catches a glimpse of her seducer at the wedding and promptly collapses and dies. Walsingham also has to deal with conflicting feelings for 'Sir Sidney'. It is clear that he is attracted to the young cousin he has been taught to hate – so much so that, on a first reading of the novel, one may even suspect that it is in fact a thinly disguised apologia for homosexuality. But at the end of the novel Lady Aubrey reveals the true gender of her child ('The ill-fated Sidney is my daughter!'). The estate is handed over to its rightful (male) owner – and Sidney marries Walsingham.

As Adams points out, 'the Pupil of Nature, plumped down amid the sophistries and inanities of high life, has little opportunity to develop the virtues which were implanted in him earlier'.[39] Walsingham himself reflects on the mental chaos that afflicts the growing boy:

> Alas! from the period that reason begins to shoot, the mind of man is a chaos of perpetual warfare; the affections of our early days combat with the propensities of nature, and struggle in the fetters of contradiction. The passions succeed; the stormy passions! Pride, ambition, *love!* (I, p.123)

The ambiguities of the terms used here, 'reason', 'affections' and (notoriously) 'the propensities of nature', point up the inconsistencies of Walsingham himself as a coherently realized fictional character, and one would broadly agree with the verdict of *The Analytical Review* in regretting the loss of a potentially philosophical novel through the author's inability to conceive the work as a whole. Nevertheless, when the same reviewer remarks that 'the reader, wholly losing sight of "the pupil of nature", perceives only the author',[40] one would now prefer to regard this apparent failure of technique as a bold experiment in narrative perspective. In the text of *Walsingham*, the 'author' is subsumed in the 'I' of the young male narrator: just as the plot requires 'Sir Sidney' to stride through the action in male dress in the way in which Mary Robinson herself strode through her breeches parts on the stage at Drury Lane,[41] so Walsingham is required by his female author to live as a young man, ultimately to carry out the quintessentially male crime of what would now be called date rape. The female author 'is' the drunken young man who abuses Amelia, but s/he conspicuously fails to explain or justify the disjunction between the sensitive 'pupil of nature' and the grown man ('I was a villain'). This can certainly be read as the bungling of an inefficient writer – or, alternatively, as a bitterly feminist demonstration of, indeed identification with, 'Things as they are'.

Before the rape takes place, Amelia's likeness to Isabella – and indeed to Mary Robinson herself – is established at a masked ball, held in London. Amelia is dressed in 'Cambrian habit', which is much like the peasant costume observed by Sir George Fairford in *Angelina* when he takes shelter at a Breconshire turnpike during a shower of rain:

> The village was crowded with lads and lasses, who were all thronging to a small farm, where it was their weekly custom to regale themselves with cakes and cyder. – The girls wore petticoats of fine stuff, striped with a variety of colours; short blue jackets, and large round beaver hats, the simple bands of which were decorated with field flowers. They all appeared to be cheerful and healthy. I contemplated these happy mountaineers near half an hour, and then set out on my evening's walk towards the ruin. (I, pp.211–12)

Amelia wears a similar costume but it is in fact 'a species of disguise', only 'half concealing her bosom'; there is a certain raffishness in her appearance, not unlike that of the 'sad slut' herself in the cartoon of 1780:

> my heart throbbed with agony when Amelia presented herself in the simple habit of a Welsh peasant girl – a species of disguise in which I had often seen Isabella, when she entered into the spirit of the village *fêtes* near Glenowen, and which always rendered her more beautiful than the most studied adornments of fashion could have done. As she came into the room I started as though I had seen a spectre. – The short jacket, half concealing her bosom, and the large black hat, adorned with a wild bouquet of flowers, which shaded her countenance, throwing her features into shadow, concealed every dissimilarity, and she was the exact counterpart of Isabella. (III, p.29)

The fatal encounter takes place after a second masked ball: Amelia, a tall and beautiful figure (like her author), has now exchanged her Welsh costume for 'a black gauze robe spangled with silver'. Although the male 'I' claims that Amelia is a willing victim, he admits full responsibility for the rape: 'all the claims of unprotected innocence, all the laws of honour were violated – and – I was a villain!' (III, pp. 92–3). It is as if, in a daring masochistic act of the imagination, the author brings about the downfall of the 'sad slut' herself by adopting the persona of her abuser. But the author fails, even so, to wreak fictional vengeance on the rapist. To roar and holler with him in Werther-like anguish suffices. It is, after all, Amelia who dies.

It would seem at least a possibility that in *Fleetwood* Godwin has seized on the tormented figure of Walsingham and attempted to make a more coherent psychological study of a child whose upbringing in wild Wales fails to give him the moral strength required in adult life, though even here it is difficult to recognize the sensitive boy in the misogynous man whose jealousy nearly destroys his wife. Just as the subtitle of *Walsingham* seems misplaced or ironical (to be replaced, perhaps, by Walsingham's own description of himself as 'the very fool of nature'), so does Godwin's subtitle call into question the moral calibre of Fleetwood as a successor to Harley in Mackenzie's *The Man of Feeling*. It is as if Harley's tearful hypersensitivity to the sufferings of others has been metamorphosed into the nervous irritability of a man who (like his father before him) is so self-centred that he is unable to bear the proximity of other people. In this respect, B. S. Tysdahl's description of Fleetwood as a man with 'a tendency to moral solipsism'[42] seems more convincing than Kelly's notion that in *Fleetwood* Godwin fixed his own variety of Romanticism after exploring 'the possibilities for wholeness and progress in human life'.[43]

Godwin, as the narrator of Fleetwood's story, seems only too aware of the difficulties he faces in making the deterioration of his hero's character psychologically convincing. He admits that nothing could be more opposite than 'the Fleetwood of Merionethshire and the Fleetwood of the university', pointing out rather lamely that 'It is the first step only that costs a struggle' (I, p.49) before lamenting his fall as a pupil of nature who has forgotten his lessons: 'Oh, Cader Idris! oh, genius of the mountains! oh, divinity, that presidest over the constellations, the meteors, and the ocean! how was your pupil fallen!' (I, p.54). Neither of his mentors, Ruffigny in Switzerland or Macneil in the Lake District, significantly helps him revert to 'the simplicity and guilelessness' of his Merionethshire character. As an adult he can find no consolation in the Welsh landscape, lamenting the loss of the visionary years of childhood in a passage which might almost stand as a synopsis of the great elegiac opening of 'The Immortality Ode' (which first appeared in print in 1807, two years after *Fleetwood* was published):[44]

> The landscape was as if it had lost the prismatic illusion, which clothes it to the sense of sight in such beautiful colours. The fields were no longer green, nor the skies were blue; or at least they afforded no more pleasure to my eyes, than they would have done if the grass had been withered, and the heavens shrouded in pestilence and death. The beautiful and the bold forms of valley and mountain, which had frequently delighted me, seemed to my eye loathsome and tame and monotonous. (II, p.114)

Macneil diagnoses Fleetwood's problem as being too much alone: he needs to become 'one of the great congregation of man'. Although he has been personally acquainted with Rousseau, Macneil calls into question the most sacred tenet of early Romantic doctrine when he suggests that solitary communing with nature can be overdone. Like Christ returning from the wilderness, a man who has been alone with the grand exhibitions of nature needs 'the interchange of sentiments and language'. When Fleetwood takes his young wife to live in Merionethshire, she re-enacts his own boyhood experiences, recognizing that the beauties of nature, from the tremendous precipice to the frailest herb, 'are all alike the productions of that mysterious power, which is every where at work' (III, pp.28–9). But, as a daughter of Macneil, she is also dependent on 'the interchange of sentiments and language' (by going to a dance in Barmouth, for instance) and is literally driven mad by her husband's misogyny. When the marriage fails, Fleetwood's repudiation of nature is, by implication, as misguided as his jealous reference to Mary's supposed infidelity: 'Nature herself is the great parent-hypocrite, deluding us onward from the cradle to the grave. Her daughters do but inherit the same treacherous smiles, and tempt us to damnation!' (III, pp.159–60). He appears to have learned nothing.

In *Walsingham* and *Fleetwood*, both Robinson and Godwin appear to question the moral basis on which their fictions seem initially to be predicated. The pupil of nature is capable of brutality; the new man of feeling is a sensualist, incapable of forming loving relationships. Yet both are rewarded with a happy ending. Walsingham's remorse for Amelia's death is enacted on a stormy night 'among the stupendous rocks' of the Avon Gorge: 'I had outraged the very laws of Nature, and her dreadful artillery was pointed at the devoted wretch who had been her pupil, and was destined to become her victim' (IV, p.192). This Romantic act of contrition appears to deal adequately with Walsingham's guilt: he marries Sidney without any obvious qualms of conscience. When Fleetwood suspects Mary of infidelity, he too has a Werther-like episode 'on one of the heaths of Hampshire', flourishing a brace of pistols and wallowing and roaring aloud as he measures his length on the earth. But, unlike *Walsingham*, Godwin's novel culminates in an act of forgiveness which (despite the author's avowed atheism) ultimately eschews Romantic in favour of Christian symbolism. Like the Blessed Virgin herself, Mary freely forgives Fleetwood as an act of grace. If the portrayal of Fleetwood to this point in the novel suggests what Tysdahl refers to as Godwin's 'sombre view of man's possibilities',[45] his 'true remorse' seems to imply at least the desire for spiritual renewal under the ægis of Mary, represented here and elsewhere as a divine being: 'She threw back her veil, and I saw the godlike irradiations of innocence' (III, p.340).

There is almost certainly another Mary – though scarcely one who emitted 'godlike irradiations of innocence' – inscribed in Godwin's text. It has been claimed that in the character of Mrs Kenrick, Fleetwood's disreputable kinswoman, Godwin left a pen-portrait of Mary Robinson herself:[46]

> She was of exquisite beauty, tall, graceful and captivating. Her tastes were expensive, and her manners gay. Her demeanour was spirited and

impressive, her passions volatile, and her temper violent. With all this, she was by no means destitute of capacity. She was eloquent, witty and sarcastic; exhibiting, when she pleased, the highest breeding, and delivering her remarks with inexpressible vivacity and grace. Thus endowed, she was surrounded, wherever she appeared, with a little army of suitors. Every youth of fashion, who had the courage to look up to her, became her professed admirer; and, among these admirers, it was pretty universally believed, that all had not offered up their incense in vain. (III, p.97)

Appropriately, Mrs Kenrick is given Welsh connections: she has been divorced by her first husband, a Welsh squire, and is widowed when her second husband, an apothecary in a small market town in Montgomeryshire, dies of a broken heart. She resolves 'to make that figure by dissoluteness and effrontery, which, if she had set out right in life, she might have made by elegance, accomplishments and virtue'. Eventually she sinks into obscurity, 'by all neglected and by all despised' (III, p.105).

That this may well be a chilling epitaph for Mary Robinson is suggested by the circumstances of the last months of her life, spent at her daughter's cottage at Englefield Green, near Windsor. She wrote a number of letters to Godwin at this time,[47] assuring him that 'it is unimportant to me where I pass my days, if I possess the esteem and friendship of its best ornaments, among which I consider *you*'.[48] On 28 August 1800, she wrote that she was now greatly debilitated: youth and beauty had fled and she felt 'abused, neglected, – unhonoured, – unrewarded'.[49] Godwin and his friend Marshal visited her at Windsor at the beginning of September.[50] A month later, she wrote that she was 'still so feeble, and depressed in Spirit'.[51] She died on 26 December 1800 and it would seem that few mourned her passing. Her daughter recorded that 'The funeral was attended only by two literary friends, greatly valued by the deceased, whose friendship and benevolence had cheered her while living and followed her to the grave.'[52] One of the mourners was probably Dr John Walcot.[53] The other was William Godwin. His Journal for 31 December recorded, as laconically as ever, 'Funeral at Old Windsor'.[54]

Notes

Notes to Preface

1. Jane Austen's letter to her sister Cassandra (18 December 1798), quoted in Margaret Anne Doody and Douglas Murray (eds), *Catharine and Other Writings* (Oxford: Oxford University Press, 1993), p.xiv.
2. Ibid., p.xv.
3. Ibid.
4. Ibid., p.76.
5. Ibid., p.77.
6. Ibid., pp.79–80.
7. Ibid., p.170. *Tour through Wales* consists of one letter from Elizabeth Johnson to Clara in which the writer's mother gallops through Wales while her daughters run alongside, managing to take 'a great many Drawings of the Country', but wearing out their shoes ('we were obliged to have them both capped and heelpeiced at Carmarthen'); as a last resort the girls borrow a pair of blue satin slippers 'of which we each took one and hopped home from Hereford delightfully'.
8. Ibid., pp.171–2. In *A Tale*, Wilhelminus's 'retreat' in Pembrokeshire consists of a neat cottage on the borders of an extensive forest and about three miles from the sea, which he reaches after travelling for three days and six nights without stopping and 'following a track which led by it's side down a steep Hill over which ten Rivulets meandered'. The cottage consists of two 'destitute' rooms and a closet but once they are furnished, Wilhelminus puts up a large party of vistors in 'two noble Tents' ('A couple of old blankets, each supported by four sticks') in an open spot in the forest adjacent to the house.
9. Jane Austen, *Northanger Abbey* (1818), ed. R. Brimley Johnson (London: Collins, 1953), p.153.
10. Katie Trumpener, *Bardic Nationalism: The Romantic Novel and the British Empire* (Princeton: Princeton University Press, 1997), pp.18–19.
11. Jane Austen, *Tour through Wales*, in Doody and Murray, *Catharine*, p.170.
12. W. J. Hughes, *Wales and the Welsh in English From Shakespeare to Scott* (Wrexham: Hughes, 1924), pp.206–7.
13. Dorothy Blakey, *The Minerva Press 1790–1820* (London: Oxford University Press, 1935).

14. James Henderson, 'The Gothic Novel in Wales (1790–1820)', *National Library of Wales Journal*, XI (1959–60), 244–54, and Emerson Robert Loomis, 'The Problem of the Gothic Novel in Wales', ibid., XIII (1963–4), 67–9.
15. See Appendix to the present study for a cumulative list of eighteenth-century fictions of Wales.
16. Gwyn Jones, *The First Forty Years: Some Notes on Anglo-Welsh Literature* (Cardiff: University of Wales Press, 1957), p.9.
17. Ibid., p.7, quoting Dr Johnson.
18. The term is borrowed from Tony Curtis (ed.), *Wales: The Imagined Nation: Studies in Cultural and National Identity* (Bridgend: Poetry Wales Press, 1986).
19. Trumpener, *Bardic Nationalism,* p.xi.
20. Ibid., p.xii.
21. Ibid., p.113.
22. Prys Morgan, 'Keeping the Legends Alive', in Curtis, *Imagined Nation*, p.30.

Notes to Chapter 1

1. Roger Thompson (ed.), *Samuel Pepys' Penny Merriments* (London: Constable, 1976), p.11.
2. For an account of the chapmen and their wares, see Margaret Spufford, *The Great Reclothing of Rural England: Petty Chapmen and their Wares in the Seventeenth Century* (London: Hambledon Press, 1984).
3. Spufford, *The Great Reclothing*, pp.18, 62, refers to two Welsh chapmen, one who operated at Llanblethian in the Vale of Glamorgan until his death in 1667, and another, John Lloyd, who worked with horse and pack from Norton, Radnorshire.
4. John Ashton, *Chap-Books of the Eighteenth Century* (London: Chatto & Windus, 1882), pp.ix–x. Quotations are from the facsimile published by the Seven Dials Press (1969).
5. Margaret Spufford, *Small Books and Pleasant Histories: Popular Fiction and its Readership in Seventeenth-Century England* (Cambridge: Cambridge University Press, 1981), points out that as well as the three volumes of *Penny Merriments*, the Pepys Collection at Magdalene College, Cambridge, comprises four volumes of *Vulgaria* and one volume of *Penny Godlinesses*, that is, 215 items in all. The Pepys Collection is noted in Garfield H. Hughes, 'Llyfrau Samuel Pepys', *Journal of the Welsh Bibliographical Society*, vol.ix, no.3 (December 1963), 135.
6. Thompson, *Penny Merriments*, p.19. Extracts from *The Merry Tales of the Mad-Men of Gotam*, by A.B. Doctor of Physick [thought to be Andrew Boorde], printed for J. Clark, W. Thackeray and T. Passinger, are included in Ashton, *Chap-Books*, pp.275–87 and Thompson, *Penny Merriments*, pp.243–6. Ashton identifies Gotham as a village about six miles from Nottingham. Spufford, *Small Books and Pleasant Histories*, 51, notes that it is a chapbook which mocks 'the clodhopping countryman come to town'.

7   A small number of woodcuts, showing a Welshman walking along the road to London, were used time and time again to illustrate the chapbooks and other popular publications of the day. See the illustration in Peter Lord, *Words with Pictures: Welsh Images and Images of Wales in the Popular Press, 1640–1860* (Aberystwyth: Planet, 1995), p.44, a version used to illustrate a single sheet of verses, *The Welsh Fortune-Teller, Or, Sheffery Morgan's Observation of the Stars, as he sat upon a Mountain in Wales* (1689). The hero wears a leek in his hat, carries a pike over his shoulder, and advances with a piece of cheese on the point of his dagger; mountains and goats adorn the background.

8   E. Vincent Evans, 'Andrew Boorde and the Welsh People', *Y Cymmrodor*, XXIX (1919), 44–55, includes an extract from *The Fyrst Boke of the Introduction of Knowledge*, taken from the reprint edited for the Early Text Society by F. J. Furnivall (London: Trubner, 1870).

9   W. J. Hughes, *Wales and the Welsh in English Literature* (Wrexham: Hughes, 1924), pp.30–1, refers to *A Hundred Mery Talys* (1525), *The Merie Tales of Skelton* (1567) and *Tales and Quick Answers* (1567).

10 Hughes, *Wales and the Welsh*, pp.32–5, refers to two lost plays, *The Welshman's Prize* and *The Prince's Masque*, Peele's *Edward I* (1593), Chettle's *Patient Grissel* (1603), R.A.'s *Valiant Welshman* (1615) and Ben Jonson's antimasque *For the Honour of Wales* (1619).

11 Hughes, *Wales and the Welsh*, p.41, refers to the *Catalogue of Civil War Tracts* (Aberystwyth, 1911).

12 Gwyn A. Williams, *When Was Wales? A History of the Welsh* (Harmondsworth: Penguin Books, 1985), p.131.

13 Peter Gaunt, *A Nation Under Siege: The Civil War in Wales 1642–48* (London: HMSO, 1991), p.25.

14 Ibid., p.29.

15 Ibid.

16 Ibid.

17 *The Welsh-Mans Postures, Or, The true manner how her doe exercise her company of Souldiers in her own Countrey in a warlike manners with some other new-found experiments, and pretty extravagants fitting for all Christian podies to caknow. Printed in the yeare. When her did her enemy jeere* (1642).

18 *The Welch-Mans Warning-Piece. As it was delivered in a Sermon in Shropshire at the Assembly when the Resolution was agreed upon. And Now published for the cood of all her Country-men in these parts. By Shon ap Morgan. In the Anti-Prelation Yeer. 1642. Wherein her gives Kot thanks, that her was no Beshit.* (London: printed for Robert Wood and Henry Marsh, 1642).

19 *The Welsh Doctor: Or The Welch-man turned Physitian, being a New Way to Cure all Diseases in these times . . . By Shinkin ap Morgan, Professor of her Medicall Arts and Sciences. Printed for the good of her Country-men, this present yeare* (1643).

20 Based on the account given in Gaunt, *A Nation Under Siege*, p.30.

21 *The Welsh-mans publique and hearty Sorrow and Recantation, That ever her tooke up Armes against her cood Parliament, declaring to all the world how her hath been abused by faire urds and flatterings, telling what booties and honours her should get if her*

Notes 193

would but helpe to conduct her King to her crete Councell the Parliament. Also her new Oath and Protestation never to beare Armes against her cood Parliament any more. By Shon ap Morgan Shentileman. Printed and published for the use and benefit of all her loving Countrymen in her Kingdome and Principallity of Wales (1647). The copy in the British Library has the date emended by hand to 1646.

22 See Lord, *Words with Pictures*, pp.37–45, for further references to the Welsh in the popular press during the Civil War.

23 Quoted by Lord, *Words with Pictures*, p.47, from the 1738 edition, *The Briton Described, or a Journey thro' Wales*, printed by J. Torbuck.

24 Spufford, *Small Books and Pleasant Histories*, p.182.

25 Ibid., p.183.

26 Ibid. Spufford cites K. W. G. Goodman, 'Hammerman's Hill: The Land, People, and Industry of the Titterstone Clee Hill Area of Shropshire, from the Sixteenth to the Eighteenth Centuries' (University of Keele: Ph.D. thesis, 1978) and T. C. Mendelhall, *The Shrewsbury Drapers and the Welsh Wool Trade in XVI and XVII Centuries* (Oxford, 1953).

27 Spufford, *Small Books and Pleasant Histories*, p.183.

28 Lord, *Words with Pictures*, p.37, reproduces *The Welsh Man's Inventory*, published by W[illiam] O[ly].

29 *The Pleasant History of Taffy's Progress to London; with the Welshman's Catechism*, printed for F. Thorn, near Fleet-Street, is dated [1709?] in the British Library Catalogue. Ashton, *Chap-Books*, pp.475–7, gives an extract from this edition.

30 Compare *The Honour of Welshmen Or The Valiant Acts of St. Taffy of Wales*, printed by P. Lillicrap in Clarkenwell Close (1667), a single sheet of verses [British Library, C.40.m.11 (81), not listed in the General Catalogue], which satirizes the Welsh and their patron saint who was capable of killing ten thousand pagans ere he went to dinner.

31 In *The Welch Wedding Betwixt Ap-Shinkin and Shinny*, for example, a single sheet of verses to be sung to the tune 'The Devonshire Frolick' or 'The Country Farmer', printed in London by J. Deacon at the Angel in Gultispur-street and dated [1691?] in the British Library Catalogue, Shinny asks Shinkin to invite her cousins, Welch Mary and Sary, Welch Robin and William with Tom besides; Shinkin agrees to invite them all and more besides – Cozen Taffie, Hukin and Sukin 'and old *Shon-ap-Morgan*, with hur own Son'. The celebrations end in drunken squabbles.

32 The satirical association between the Welsh and mouse-traps (the mice also have a predilection for cheese) reaches its apotheosis in *Muscipula, sive, Cambro-muo-machia* (1709), a poem in Latin by E. Holdsworth, which went through several editions. English translations included *Taffy's Triumph* (1709), written in Miltonic verse, and involving the council of Cambria's chiefest pride in the construction of a mouse-trap, *Taffi's Master Piece* (1709), *The Mouse-Trap, or, The Welsh Engagement with the Mice* (1709), *The Mouse-Trap, or, the Welshmen's Scuffle with the Mice* (1709). There were several further editions, including Richard Graves's version in *The Reveries of Solitude* (Bath, 1793). The *Muscipula* provoked a reply, *Choirochorigraphia, sive, Hoglandiae*

Descriptio (1709), a satire on Hampshire by William Richards, written at the request of Edward Lhuyd. See Hughes, *Wales and the Welsh*, pp.53–4, 202.

33 See illustration on p.6 of this volume.

34 Pepys's collection of *Penny Merriments* includes an edition of *The Distressed Welch-Man*, by Hugh Crumpton, printed by W. T[hackeray] and sold by J. Conyers (listed in Thompson, *Penny Merriments*, p.298). Quotations in the present essay are from the edition printed by T. Norris at the Looking Glass on London-bridge, dated [1700?] in the British Library Catalogue.

35 Pepys's collection of *Penny Merriments* includes an edition of *The Welch Traveller*, with publication details missing. Thompson, *Penny Merriments*, pp.204–8, prints an extract. The British Library Catalogue lists an edition of [1671?] with a mutilated title-page, an edition printed by William Whitwood (London, 1671), an edition printed and sold in Aldermary Church-yard (London, [1780?]) and a limited edition printed by J. O. Halliwell (London, 1860). Ashton, *Chap-Books*, pp.344–8, includes an extract from the Aldermary edition and an illustration from a Newcastle edition [n.d.] which gives the author as Humphrey Cornish. Quotations in the present essay are from the Aldermary edition.

36 The *DNB* identifies Humphrey [*sic*] Crouch or Crowch (*fl.* 1635–1671) as the publisher of *A Whip for the Back of a Backsliding Brownist* (c.1641) and other broadsides of the same date. Nine works, including *The Welch Traveller* ('an amusing attack on the Welsh'), bear his name as author. *The Distressed Welch-Man* is one of a number of works initialled H.C. and attributed to Crouch.

37 *The Unfortunate Welch-Man; Or The Untimely Death of Scotch Jockey*, printed for J. Deacon at the Angel in Gultispur-street, is dated [1690?] in the British Library Catalogue.

38 Lord, *Words with Pictures*, pp.43–5, refers to *Crete Wonders foretold by Her Crete Prophet of Wales* (1647), mocking the Welshman's facility for predicting the future. In *The Welsh Fortune-Teller*, a single sheet of verses printed by T. Conyers of Ludgate-hill, to be sung to 'Touch of the Times', Sheffery Morgan observes the stars as he sits on a mountain in Wales and celebrates the accession of William of Orange (in 1689).

39 Lord, *Words with Pictures*, p.47.

40 Ibid., pp.49 and 80–1.

41 Pepys's *Penny Merriments* includes the edition of *The Life and Death of Sheffery Morgan* printed by J. Deacon (1683). Thompson, *Penny Merriments*, pp.200–3 includes extracts from this edition. The Bodleian Library Catalogue lists an edition of [1695]. The British Library Catalogue lists editions printed in Newcastle in [1780?] and [1785?] and an Edinburgh edition of [1820?]. Ashton, *Chap-Books*, pp.341–3, includes an extract from a Newcastle edition [n.d.]. Quotations in this essay are from the Newcastle [1780?] edition.

42 Pepys's *Penny Merriments* includes an edition of *The Wonderful Adventures, and Happy Successes of Shon ap Morgan* printed by J. Deacon (listed by Thompson, *Penny Merriments*, p.300). The British Library Catalogue lists *Shon ap Morgan, Shentleman of Wales, Journey to London*, printed in Stone-cutter-Street

[London, 1770?]. Quotations in this chapter are from the edition in the Salisbury Library (Drogheda, 1808).

Notes to Chapter 2

1 Unless otherwise stated, biographical information about Aubin is taken from William H. McBurney, 'Mrs. Penelope Aubin and the Early Eighteenth-Century Novel', *Huntington Library Quarterly*, XX (1957), 245–67.
2 *The Stuarts: A Pindarique Ode* (1707), *The Welcome: A Poem to His Grace the Duke of Marlborough* (1708) and *The Extasy. A Pindarick Ode to the Queen* (1708).
3 Antoine-François Prévost, *Le Pour et Contre*, IV, lviii (1734), 294–8. References are to the facsimile edition (Genève: Slatkine Reprints, 1967), I.350–1.
4 *A Dictionary of British and American Women Writers 1660–1800*, ed. Janet Todd (London: Methuen, 1984), p.34.
5 Preface to *The Life of Charlotta du Pont* (1722), quoted by George Frisbie Whicher in *The Life and Romances of Mrs Eliza Haywood* (New York: Columbia University Press, 1915), p.174. Whicher comments that Aubin was perhaps the only *romancière* not dependent in some measure on the sale of her work.
6 The novels were *The Strange Adventures of the Count de Vinevil* (1721), *The Life of Madam de Beaumount* (1721), *The Life of Charlotta du Pont* (1722), *The Noble Slaves* (1722), *The Life and Amorous Adventures of Lucinda* (1722), *The Life and Amorous Adventures of Lady Lucy* (1726) and *The Life and Adventures of the Young Count Albertus* (1728). Aubin translated several French romances: *The Adventures of Prince Clermont and Madam de Ravezan* by Louise Gomez de Beaucours (1722), *The Illustrious French Lover* by Robert Challes (1727) and *The Life of the Countess of Gondez* by Marguerite de Lussan (1729). She also edited a translation by her friend J. Mornington Gibbs of *The Doctrine of Morality* by Le Roy, Sieur de Gomberville (1721), reprinted as *Moral Virtue Delineated* (1726).
7 Philip H. Highfill, Kalman A. Burnim and Edward A. Langhans, *A Biographical Dictionary of Actors, Actresses, Musicians, Dancers, Managers & Other Stage Personnel in London, 1600–1800* (Carbondale and Edwardsville: Southern Illinois University Press, 1978), I. p.175, records a benefit for Mrs Aubin at Lincoln's Inn Fields on 2 January 1724 at a performance of *The Spanish Friar*.
8 Ibid.
9 According to *Boswell's Life of Johnson*, ed. George Birkbeck Hill, rev. L. F. Powell (Oxford: Clarendon Press, 1934), I. p.463, Johnson pronounced on female Quaker preachers on 31 July 1763: 'Sir, a woman's preaching is like a dog's walking on his hinder legs. It is not done well; but you are surprized to find it done at all.'

10 For an account of the Revd John Henley (1692–1756), see Graham Midgley, *The Life of Orator Henley* (Oxford: Clarendon Press, 1973).
11 Highfill et al., *Biographical Dictionary*.
12 Ibid.
13 See *The Dunciad Variorum* (1729), Book III, ll.195–202, for Alexander Pope's satirical portrait of Henley.
14 McBurney, 'Mrs. Penelope Aubin', 245n., citing 'Henry Stonecastle', *The Universal Spectator* (16 August 1729).
15 Prévost cites 'Bavius' in *The Grub Street Journal*, no.111, but McBurney, 'Mrs. Penelope Aubin', 246, finds no mention of Aubin in that issue (17 February 1731) or elsewhere in the periodical.
16 Arthur H. Scouten (ed.), *The London Stage 1660–1800 Part 3: 1729–1747* (Carbondale: Southern Illinois University Press, 1961), p.101.
17 Virginia Blain, Patricia Clements and Isobel Grundy (eds), *The Feminist Companion to Literature in English* (London: B. T. Batsford, 1990), p.39.
18 See John Richetti's chapter on 'The Novel as Pious Polemic' in *Popular Fiction Before Richardson: Narrative Patterns 1700–1739* (Oxford: Clarendon Press, 1969). Janet Todd, *The Sign of Angellica: Women, Writing and Fiction, 1660–1800* (London: Virago, 1989), p.87, refers to Aubin's novels as examples of 'the moral mode' that dominated fiction during the 1720s and 1730s. Jane Spencer, *The Rise of the Woman Novelist: From Aphra Behn to Jane Austen* (Oxford: Blackwell, 1986, reprinted 1993), p.88, comments that 'Aubin's work is intended to demonstrate that the passions can be controlled by virtue'.
19 Aubin's Preface to *The Strange Adventures of the Count de Vinevil* (1721), quoted from the second edition of 1728.
20 McBurney, 'Mrs. Penelope Aubin', 265, is sceptical about Henri Roddier's thesis in 'Robert Challes, inspirateur de Richardson et de l'abbé Prévost', *Revue de Littérature Comparée*, XXI (1947), 5–38, that Aubin's translation of Challes's *Les Illustres Françaises* provided Richardson with inspiration for both *Pamela* and *Clarissa* ('Any direct or considerable effect of Mrs. Aubin on Richardson seems unlikely'). However, Wolfgang Zach, 'Mrs. Aubin and Richardson's Earliest Literary Manifesto', *English Studies*, LXII (1981), 271–85, has since argued that in the Preface to the collected edition of Aubin's novels (1939) Richardson offered (anonymously) a theory of the rules for writing fiction only a year before the publication of *Pamela*.
21 Donald A. Stauffer, *The Art of Biography in Eighteenth Century England* (New York: Russell & Russell, 1970, first published in 1941), p.76.
22 Mary Anne Schofield, *Masking and Unmasking the Female Mind: Disguising Romances in Feminine Fiction, 1713–1799* (London and Toronto: Associated University Presses, 1990), p.35. Catherine Craft-Fairchild, *Masquerade and Gender: Disguise and Female Identity in Eighteenth-Century Fictions by Women* (Pennsylvania: Pennsylvania State University Press, 1993), p.5, comments that while Mary-Anne Schofield's study of masquerade usefully resurrects many neglected works, she ignores ways in which writing by women upheld or promoted ideologies of inferiority and subservience, assuming 'that each

woman writer wished to be as feminist as she possibly could, self-censoring her radical views only to allow her works to gain public acceptance'.

23 Jerry C. Beasley, 'Politics and Moral Idealism: The Achievement of Some Early Women Novelists', in *Fetter'd or Free? British Women Novelists 1670–1785*, ed. Mary Anne Schofield and Cecilia Macheski (Athens: Ohio University Press, 1986), p.231.

24 Linda Colley, *Britons: Forging the Nation 1707–1837* (London: Pimlico, 1994), p.66, cites Julian Hoppit, 'The Use and Abuse of Credit in Eighteenth-century England', in N. McKendrick and R. B. Outhwaite (eds), *Business Life and Public Policy* (1986). Because of the Mint's incapacity to produce enough silver and copper coin, credit played a more vital part in Britain's economy than in that of almost any of its competitors.

25 Gwyn A. Williams, *When Was Wales? A History of the Welsh* (Harmondsworth: Penguin Books, 1985), p.139.

26 Aubin refers to Defoe's work in the Preface to her first novel, *The Strange Adventures of the Count de Vinevil* (1721), published the same year as *The Life of Madam de Beaumount*: 'As for the Truth of what this Narrative contains, since Robinson Crusoe, has been so well receiv'd, which is more improbable, I know no reason why this should be thought a Fiction.' McBurney traces a number of borrowings from Defoe in Aubin's work, suggesting that Madam de Beaumount's cave, the rocky refuge of Domingo and Isabinda, several hermitages and the hut on the Summer Islands 'all owe something to the ingenuity of Defoe' ('Mrs. Penelope Aubin', 258).

27 In *The Strange Adventures of the Count de Vinevil*, there are several domestic spaces which invite comparison with Crusoe's hut and Madam de Beaumount's cave – the priest's cottage deep in the woods near Constantinople where Ardelisa and Nanette take refuge from a Mohammedan after the murder of Ardelisa's father, the cave (furnished with jewelled crucifix and church-plate) where Don Fernando lives a penitent's life of tears, fasting and prayer, and the large tent ('their Tarpaulin Palace') erected on the uninhabited island of Delos after a shipwreck.

28 Introduction to Ann Radcliffe, *A Sicilian Romance*, ed. Alison Milbank (Oxford: Oxford University Press, 1993), p.xxiii. Milbank's discussion focuses on Julia's stay with her incarcerated mother in the vault under the castle and their rescue by her brother Hippolytus.

29 I have taken the definition of 'space' from Michael Rosenblum, 'Smollett's *Humphry Clinker*', in John Richetti (ed.), *The Cambridge Companion to the Eighteenth-Century Novel* (Cambridge: University Press, 1996), pp.177, 179: 'Narrative is now figured as a kind of representational "space" whose boundaries are authorized by the culture within which acts of representation take place. With the right kind of tinkering, what is "inside" the narrative field can be shown to refer to what is "outside" the field, to what lies beyond in "space" of history. Because the borders of fictional works are no longer considered inviolable (they are in Bakhtin's figure, "permeable" rather than absolute), events inside can be taken to refer to events outside, and events from history can provide the clues for what is really happening inside the

novel.' He refers to Edward Said's contention that 'History is something concealed in the margins, peripheries, or palimpsestic depths of the text; or to switch from spatial to temporal modalities, it is something to be briefly glimpsed in the text before it gets covered over.'

30 'The Court being removed to the other Side of the Water and beyond Sea, to take the Pleasures this Town and our dull Island cannot afford; the greater part of our Nobility and Members of Parliament retired to Hanover or their Country-Seats, where they may supine sit, and with Pleasure reflect on the great Things they have done for the publick Good.' Quoted by McBurney, 'Mrs. Penelope Aubin', 247.

31 Ibid.

32 R. B. Dooley, 'Penelope Aubin: Forgotten Catholic Novelist', *Renascence*, XI (1959).

33 Zach, 'Mrs Aubin and Richardson's Earliest Literary Manifesto', 273, suggests that the attempted seduction of Pamela in a summer-house derives from Aubin's scene in *The Life of Madam de Beaumount.*

34 Colley, *Britons*, p.72.

35 In *The Life and Adventures of Lady Lucy,* Henrietta is captured by robbers and taken to a cottage where she is looked after by two poor Irishwomen who speak nothing but their native tongue 'which tho' we are all born in the same Kingdom . . . yet we are not able perfectly to understand'. The thieves are all gentlemen 'ruin'd either by their own Imprudence and Vices, or by the change of Affairs in this Kingdom'.

36 John Davies, *A History of Wales* (Harmondsworth: Penguin Books, 1994), p.286ff.

37 Ibid., p.297. For an account of *Gweledigaethau Y Bardd Cwsc*, see Gwyn Thomas, *Ellis Wynne* (Cardiff: University of Wales Press, 1984).

38 Davies, *History of Wales.*

39 *The Extasy: A Pindarick Ode To Her Majesty The Queen*, printed for the author (1708), p.16.

40 Williams, *When Was Wales?*, p.139.

41 *The Stuarts, A Pindarique Ode. Humbly Dedicated to Her Majesty of Great Britain,* printed for John Morphew (1707), p.11.

42 Davies, *History of Wales*, p.294, points out that although the Nonconformists of Wales could feel relatively secure during the reign of William III, Anne had no sympathy for them. The Toleration Act found no favour among diehard Tories: their success in 1711 in outlawing occasional conformity and their enthusiasm for the Schism Bill were expressions of their opposition to the principle of toleration.

43 Tsar Peter of Russia declared war in 1700 on Charles XII, King of Sweden (reigned 1697–1718). Aubin presumably refers to the defeat of the Swedes at the Battle of Poltava in 1709.

44 The phrase is taken from J. Paul Hunter, *Before Novels: The Cultural Contexts of Eighteenth Century English Fiction* (New York: W. W. Norton & Co., 1990), pp.353–4, who discusses the relationship between the early novel and travel

literature which increasingly 'chronicles the developing awareness of cultural coloration and the deterioration of belief in universal truths'.

Notes to Chapter 3

1. John Eagles, 'The Beggar's Legacy', *Essays Contributed to Blackwood's Magazine* (Edinburgh: William Blackwood and Sons, 1857), p.495.
2. Barrett J. Mandel, 'Full of Life Now', in James Olney (ed.), *Autobiography: Essays Theoretical and Critical* (Princeton: Princeton University Press, 1980), p.53.
3. John Richetti, *Popular Fiction Before Richardson 1700–1739* (Oxford: The Clarendon Press, 1969), p.60.
4. *The Voyages, Travels and Adventures, of William Owen Gwin Vaughan, Esq.*, was printed for J. Watts and sold by J. Osborn (London, 1736). A second edition was printed for T. Lownds (London, 1760). The author's name appears on the title-page of the edition 'Printed, and Sold by the Editor' (Dublin, 1754). Quotations in this essay are from the Dublin edition.
5. *A Genuine Account of the Life and Transactions of Howell ap David Price, Gentleman of Wales*, printed for T. Osborne, 1752.
6. *The Admirable Travels of Messieurs Thomas Jenkins and David Lowellin* (London, 1783). The British Library catalogue lists further editions of 1785 and 1792. The Bodleian Library has *The Life, Voyages, and Travels,* of *Thos. Jenkins, & David Lowellin*, printed by A. Swindells and sold by J. Sadler and T. Thomas (Manchester, [1800]). Quotations in this essay are from the 1783 edition.
7. Donald F. Stauffer, *The Art of Biography in Eighteenth Century England* (New York: Russell & Russell, 1941, 1970), pp.209–10.
8. [William] Williams, *The Journal of Llewellin Penrose, A Seaman*, ed. John Eagles (London: John Murray and William Blackwood, 1815), 4 vols. An abridged edition, printed for Taylor and Hessey (London, 1825), appeared without the author's name, 'for the perusal of Young Persons'. William Williams, *Mr. Penrose. The Journal of Penrose, Seaman*, ed. David Howard Dickason (Bloomington: Indiana University Press, 1969), based on the original manuscript, is unexpurgated and unabridged. Quotations in this essay are from Dickason's edition.
9. Dickason, *Mr. Penrose*, p.13.
10. Jeremy Gavron, 'Late rescue for history's castaway', *Guardian* (30 January 1999), reports that while researching burial customs in Madagascar, Pearson 'found a world that matched Drury's descriptions in detail after detail, from the names and locations of mountains and rivers to customs of bee-keeping and the use of spears to dig up wild yams'.
11. Richetti, *Popular Fiction*, p.104.
12. William Rufus Chetwood (d. 1766), bookseller and author, was prompter at Drury Lane in 1722–3 and probably remained so until he moved to the Smock Alley Theatre, Dublin in 1741–2. He was imprisoned for debt on more than one occasion and died in poverty. His works include *The Voyages,*

Dangerous Adventures and Imminent Escapes of Captain Richard Falconer (1720) and *The Voyages and Adventures of Captain Robert Boyle* (1726). (*DNB*)
13. Richetti, *Popular Fiction*, p.111.
14. Martin C. Battestin with Ruthe R. Battestin, *Henry Fielding: A Life* (London: Routledge, 1989), pp.133–4.
15. Ibid., p.133.
16. Scott's letter to Daniel Terry (10 November 1814), thanking him for sending *The Voyages and Adventures of Captain Robert Boyle* and *The Travels of William Bingfield Esq.* (1753), is quoted in J. G. Lockhart, *Memoirs of Sir Walter Scott* (London: Macmillan, 1900), II, p.305.
17. Richetti, *Popular Fiction*, p.61.
18. Ibid.
19. Mandel, 'Full of Life Now', p.53.
20. Stauffer, *Art of Biography*, p.208.
21. Ibid.
22. Ibid., p.209. Stauffer refers to the Count de Benyowski's *Memoirs and Travels* (1790).
23. Ibid.
24. Ibid., 210. Gavron, 'Late rescue', points out that although Drury's *Pleasant and Surprising Adventures* was accepted as fact by his contemporaries, Defoe was first proposed as the author by Victorian critics, a claim substantiated by Defoe's biographer, John R. Moore in 1945. Drury acknowledged the help of an editor 'and though Parker Pearson has his doubts, it may be that Daniel Defoe had a hand in the journal after all'.
25. Benjamin West (1738–1820), born in America, spent a period in Italy before arriving in England in 1763 where he became historical painter to King George III and President of the Royal Academy from 1792 to 1805.
26. John Eagles (1783–1855) was born in Bristol and educated at Winchester and Oxford. He hoped to become a landscape painter but he entered the church, serving in parishes in Bristol, Devon and Herefordshire. From 1831 he contributed to *Blackwood's Magazine*, writing chiefly on art. He produced three volumes of poetry, two of them published posthumously. He died in Clifton and is buried there, though there is also a tablet in Bristol Cathedral commemorating him as 'SCHOLAR, PAINTER, POET'.
27. Eagles, 'The Beggar's Legacy', p.497.
28. In addition to his edition of *Mr. Penrose*, see also D. H. Dickason, *William Williams: Novelist and Painter of Colonial America 1727–1792* (Bloomington, Indiana: Indiana University Press, 1970).
29. In his letter to Thomas Eagles (10 October 1810), West records that 'He [Williams] . . . informed me that he was a Welshman by birth . . . but brought up at a Grammar School in Bristol', quoted by Dickason, *William Williams*, p.13. Dickason, however, modifies West's statement, claiming only that Williams's family 'was of immediate Welsh extraction'. West's original letter is in private ownership but a copy made by Thomas Eagles, now deposited in the Lilly Library, Indiana University, is printed in full in D. H. Dickason,

'Benjamin West on William Williams: A Previously Unpublished Letter', *Winterthur Portfolio*, VI (1970), 128–33.

30   Dickason, *William Williams*, p.10, refers to the baptism recorded in the parish register of St Augustine-the-Less, Bristol, of William, son of William and Elizabeth Williams, on 14 June 1727.

31   Ibid., pp.16, 26–7. Dickason refers to West's letter to Thomas Eagles in which he describes how he was invited to dinner by Colonel (formerly Captain) Hunter after he moved to London around 1762. When Hunter discovered from West that he had learned painting from William Williams, he exclaimed on the 'singular event' that he too remembered Williams as a young seaman with a penchant for drawing. He absconded from the ship before Hunter could offer him a job on his estate in Norfolk, Virginia. Some years later, after Hunter had settled in Norfolk as a wealthy merchant and banker, Williams visited him, confessed that he had been bound to him as a boy, and hoped to recompense him for leaving his service. Hunter claimed that he frequently visited Williams and his family in Philadelphia.

32   Accounts of Benjamin West's meeting with William Williams vary. Helmut von Erffa and Allen Staley, *The Paintings of Benjamin West* (New Haven and London: Yale University Press, 1986), pp.449, 523, refer to John Galt's account (1816), in which a relative, Mr Pennington, presented the eight-year-old West with his first paint and canvases and took him to stay in Philadelphia for a few days where he was already working on a landscape when he first met Williams; William Carey (1820) claimed that West was residing with his brother-in-law in Philadelphia when he accidentally saw and copied one of Williams's landscapes. The *DNB* entry for West has the most colourful account of all, claiming that he was first given instruction on art by a Cherokee, given his first colours by Pennington, and at nine years old burst into tears when he saw a landscape by Williams and declared his intention of becoming a painter.

33   Von Erffa and Staley, *Paintings of Benjamin West*, p.209, date 'The Battle of La Hogue' *c*.1775–80 (reproduced as nos.90 and 91). West told Thomas Eagles in 1810 that he had included a likeness of Williams 'in one of the Boats, next in the rear of Sir George Rook'. Von Erffa and Staley identify Williams as the prominent figure with his hand on a cannon and wearing a feathered hat on the extreme left of the composition. They acknowledge, however, that Flexner (1952), p.41, makes a different identification. The original hangs in the National Gallery of Art, Washington D.C. and a copy, probably by John Trumbull, in the Metropolitan Museum, New York.

34   Thomas Eagles (1746–1812) was a Bristol merchant, fellow of the Society of Antiquaries, a lover of the classics, art and music and a man of active benevolence. (*DNB*)

35   St Peter's Hospital was a workhouse (*An Account of the Hospitals, Alms-Houses, and Public Schools, in Bristol,* printed for H. Farley for T. Mills, Bristol, 1775).

36   The Merchants' Hospital in King Street, Bristol, provided thirty-one apartments for seamen and seamen's widows, under the direction of the Society of

Merchant Adventurers (ibid.). It still stands today, inscribed with twelve lines of verse beginning 'Freed from all storms the tempest and the rage / Of billows, here we spend our age . . .' Dickason, *William Williams*, p.10, records that William Williams's name first appears in the paybook for the almshouse on 26 May 1786.

37 Eagles, 'The Beggar's Legacy', pp.492–3, gives a detailed description of the portrait 'as it is now before me.' It now hangs in the Francis DuPont Winterthur Museum, Indiana.

38 Dickason, *William Williams*, pp.10–11, refers to the almshouse paybook which records Williams's death on 27 April 1791 and the parish register for St Augustine-the-Less which records his burial on the same day. He records the mutilated inscription on what is likely to be William Williams's tombstone in the burial ground of St Augustine-the-Less on College Green.

39 Ibid., pp.185–7. Dickason reprints the two wills (in the possession of Major Graham-Clark of Abergavenny, a descendant of John Eagles).

40 Nicholas Pocock (1741–1821) went to sea and kept detailed logbooks illustrated with wash drawings. He exhibited at the Royal Academy from 1782–1812 and is well-known for his watercolours of Bristol and Iceland and his illustrations for the 1804 and 1811 editions of William Falconer's *The Shipwreck*. (Penrose claims in the *Journal* to have known Falconer.) Edward Bird (1772–1819) was apprenticed to a firm producing japanned wares in Wolverhampton before setting up as a drawing master in Bristol. His pictures of domestic life have been much admired though he became historical painter to Princess Charlotte in 1812. He died a bankrupt. A memorial to Bird is placed directly below that of John Eagles in Bristol Cathedral. Dickason attributes two of the illustrations in the 1825 edition of the *Journal* to Bird.

41 Percy G. Adams, *Travel Literature and the Evolution of the Novel* (Lexington: University of Kentucky, 1983), p.133, states unequivocally that 'whatever suggestions William Williams took from his life as a sailor before settling in Philadelphia at the age of twenty . . . his account of Penrose is another attractive fiction that employs techniques necessary for inventing a Crusoe or a Quarll; that is, he had a library of travel books and a lively tradition to work with. All the best local color, in fact, comes, or could have come, from that library.'

42 Dickason, *William Williams*, p.9, notes that 'There was a farm family named Pen-Rhos in the area (distinguished in local tradition by their interest in the arts), but no Llewellin or Owen – his fictional father's given name'. Dickason found no record in the 'faded vellum parish registers in a mountaintop fourteenth-century church in South Wales' of a William Williams between 1700 and 1730. He also refers to an unsuccessful search of the registers of Eglwysilan and Bedwas, carried out many years earlier by one Evan Evans (letter to Zoe King written in 1857, deposited in the Lilly Library). In fact, the name William Williams occurs four times among the baptisms registered in Eglwysilan between 1700 and 1730 – in 1708, 1711, 1714 and (a year after Penrose), William Williams, son of David Williams, baptized on the 9th December 1726 (Glamorgan Record Office).

43 J. W. Damon Powell, *Bristol Privateers and Ships of War* (Bristol: J. W. Arrowsmith Ltd., 1930), p.157.
44 Dickason, *Mr. Penrose*, p.33, cites *The Eclectic Review*, new ser.V (April 1816), 395–8.
45 Ibid., p.22.
46 Dickason, *William Williams*, p.78.
47 Ibid., p.137.
48 Ibid.
49 Eagles, 'The Beggar's Legacy', p.495.
50 Dickason, *Mr. Penrose*, p.25–6.
51 Gwyn A. Williams, *When Was Wales? A History of the Welsh* (Harmondsworth: Penguin Books, 1985), pp.124–5.
52 John Davies, *A History of Wales* (Harmondsworth: Penguin Books, 1994), p.255.
53 Ibid., p.288.
54 Williams, *When Was Wales?*, p.156.

Notes to Chapter 4

1 Other editions of *The True Anti-Pamela* appeared in 1742, 1770 and in Dublin [1770?]. Quotations in this chapter are from the facsimile of the 1741 edition reproduced from the copy in the Beinecke Library, Yale (New York: Garland Publishing, 1974). In the printed text, most names are incomplete; in the Beinecke Library copy, many of the blanks have been filled in, apparently by a contemporary reader.
2 Authorship attributed to Haywood in Margaret Anne Doody, *A Natural Passion: A Study of the Novels of Samuel Richardson* (Oxford: The Clarendon Press, 1974), p.72.
3 James Olney, 'Autobiography and the Cultural Moment: A Thematic, Historical and Bibliographical Introduction', in *Autobiography: Essays Theoretical and Critical* (Princeton: Princeton University Press, 1980), p.21.
4 Georges Gusdorf, 'Conditions and Limits of Autobiography', in Olney, *Autobiography*, p.43.
5 Ibid., p.44.
6 Leigh Gilmore, 'Policing Truth: Confusion, Gender, and Autobiographical Authority', in Kathleen Ashley, Leigh Gilmore and Gerald Peters (eds), *Autobiography & Postmodernism* (Amherst: University of Massachusetts Press, 1994), p.73.
7 Mary Powell was the daughter of William Powell (d. 1723) of the Great House, Llantilio Crossenny, and his second wife, Elizabeth née Smith. Her half-brother, Mathew Powell, son of William Powell and his first wife, Penelope née Evans, inherited the Great House on his father's death. Parry refers to the funeral of Mathew's wife, Abigail née Hill, on 14 April 1732. Mary inherited her half-brother's estate on his death in 1738. She married

John Lewis of Llwyn Fortun in Carmarthenshire, who had acted as her lawyer in a suit against Parry, and bore two sons and two daughters between 1743 and 1751. See J. A. Bradney, *A History of Monmouthshire* (London: Mitchell Hughes and Clarke, 1907), I, pp.94–8. According to her memorial in the parish church, Mary Powell died in 1760, aged forty-five. By this reckoning, she was three years younger than Parry though in *The True Anti-Pamela* he gives her date of birth as 10 October 1711, a few months before his own.

8 Olney, *Autobiography*, p.22.
9 Barrett J. Mandel, 'Full of Life Now', in Olney, *Autobiography*, p.53.
10 Roy Pascal, *Design and Truth in Autobiography* (London: Routledge & Kegan Paul, 1960), p.19.
11 Olney, *Autobiography*, pp.10–11.
12 W. J. T. Collins, 'A Scandal of Old Monmouthshire', *Monmouthshire Review*, I, 1 (January 1933), 22.
13 The lines from Swift's *Libel on Dr. Delany* are quoted in *Boswell's Life of Johnson*, ed. George Birkbeck Hill, rev. L. F. Powell (Oxford: Clarendon Press, 1934), I, p.127n. Money troubles forced Sir Richard Steele (1672–1729) to leave London in 1724. He died in Carmarthen.
14 Richard Smallbroke, DD (1672–1749) was consecrated to the see of St David's in 1724; an active prelate, he enforced the reading of the Athanasian creed and is said to have mastered the Welsh language sufficiently to officiate in it. He was translated to Coventry and Lichfield in 1731. (*DNB*)
15 J. G. Hooper, 'A Survey of Music in Bristol with Special Reference to the Eighteenth Century' (University of Bristol, MA thesis, 1963), pp.25–7, identifies Nathaniel Priest with the organist of the same name who was appointed to Bangor Cathedral from 1705–8 and was the composer of a Service in F. Priest is first referred to as organist at Bristol Cathedral in 1724, with simultaneous appointments at Christ Church and All Saints, Bristol. That he was a competent all-round musician is indicated by his benefit concert at St Augustine's Back Theatre, Bristol, in 1728. In 1734 he was succeeded as Cathedral organist by James Morley.
16 According to Parry, Miss D–g's father was the owner of P–t–n and P–t–n Passage in Gloucestershire and also rented an estate known as The Ponds or Weston-hall in Dorchester, thirty miles from Charles-town in South Carolina. Apart from Miss D–g herself, other members of the family mentioned in the text are Mrs D–g (daughter of a Lombard Street goldsmith), her son Tommy, a cornet in the Duke of Argyll's regiment, and two younger boys still at school in Uxbridge. *Gloucestershire Notes and Queries*, II (1884), 500, refers to the Doning (or Dunning) family of Purton, their house on the cliffs between Purton Ferry and Severn Bridge, and the flatstones in the chancel of St Peter's, Lydney, which record the deaths of numerous members of the family between 1637 and 1742.
17 Hooper, 'A Survey of Music', p.26, quotes from the newspaper article in question without realizing that the absconding choirboy was later to enjoy notoriety of a different kind.

[18] *The Beggar's Opera*, first produced in Lincoln's Inn Fields in January 1728, was transferred to Bath and Bristol after the London run of sixty-three nights. The first Bristol performance by the Bath Company of Comedians took place in May 1728, probably in the Long Room at the Hot Well. So great was its popularity that, in spite of Puritan protests, it was transferred to the Comedians' Great Booth in Bridewell Lane near St James's Church. See Hooper, 'A Survey of Music', pp.75, 88–9, quoting *Felix Farley's Bristol Journal* (18 May 1728) and the *Gloucester Journal* (28 June 1728).

[19] Mandel, 'Full of Life', pp.52–3, counters 'the notion held by most critics who have struggled with the problem . . . that autobiographies are inspired by an impulse undifferentiated by the impulse that produces fiction' and states unequivocally that 'At every moment of any true autobiography (I do not speak here of autobiographical novels) the author's intention is to convey the sense that "this happened to me," and it is this intention that is always carried through in a way which, I believe, makes the result different from fiction.'

[20] Bradney, *History of Monmouthshire*, I, p.98, records that Elizabeth Powell (half-sister to Mary's father) married Thomas Jeffries [Jeffereys in the marginal notes on the Beinecke copy of *The True Anti-Pamela*] of Penrhos [Penrose in Parry's text] at Llanvapley on 9 May 1713. Parry later refers to Thomas and his son Dicky in his account of storming the parlour at the Great House.

[21] Monmouth Record Office, Cwmbran, Q/P.B.1, PART I.

[22] By his own account, Parry was indicted at Newport Quarter Sessions on 5 May 1736 for stealing gold coins from Matthew Powell and for assaults on Mary Haines, Powell's housekeeper, and Jane Greyswood, Powell's tenant. None of these cases came to trial at the Chepstow Quarter Sessions on 6 July 1736 but he was indicted again for the assault on Jane Greyswood. He was tried at the Caerleon Quarter Sessions on 6 October 1736, found guilty of assault but not of forcible entry, and fined one shilling. In the summer of 1737 he was tried at Monmouth Assizes for forcible entry and the assault on Mary Haines and found guilty on both counts. In October 1737 he waited for several days for sentencing at Westminster Hall and again in the Hilary Term, 'but my Name was never mention'd' (p.306).

[23] At the Newport Quarter Sessions, Parry told the Clerk that he thought he might have had another indictment against him 'for a forcible Entry into the Body of *Parthenissa*. If you had any such Thing, I would have pleaded guilty to that, instead of traversing, and I don't question but that I shall convince eighteen out of twenty thro' the whole County of what I assert. "There is no body here that says any thing of that, (replied P[hillip] M[organ][the Powells'attorney]) we have nothing to do with it"' (p.258).

[24] See the account of 'Perry, Mr [fl. 1740–1741], actor, singer' in Philip H. Highfill, Kalman A. Burnim and Edward A Langhans (eds), *A Biographical Dictionary of Actors, Actresses, Musicians, Dancers, Managers & Other Stage Personnel in London, 1600–1800* (Carbondale: Southern Illinois University Press, 1978), II, p.268.

[25] Ibid.

26 Olney, *Autobiography*, p.25.
27 *The Life and Surprizing Adventures of James Wyatt . . . Written by Himself* (London, 1748), printed and sold by E. Duncomb in Butcherhall-Lane, T. Taylor at the Meuse Back-Gate and E. Cook at the Royal-Exchange.

Notes to Chapter 5

1 Basil Willey, *The Eighteenth Century Background: Studies on the Idea of Nature in the Thought of the Period* (London: Chatto & Windus, 1961), p.2, quoting Leslie Stephen.
2 Ibid., p.240.
3 Quotations in this essay are taken from *The History of Ophelia* printed in *The Novelist's Magazine*, XIX, for Harrison and Co., Paternoster-Row, London, 1785.
4 Deborah Downs Miers, 'Springing the Trap: Subtexts and Subversions', in Mary Anne Schofield and Cecilia Macheski (eds), *Fetter'd or Free? British Women Novelists 1670–1785* (Athens: Ohio University Press, 1986), p.309.
5 Sarah Fielding, *The Adventures of David Simple*, ed. Malcolm Kelsall (Oxford: Oxford University Press, 1994), p.5.
6 Letter to the Revd Leonard Chappelow (15 March 1795), quoted in Martin C. Battestin with Ruthe C. Battestin, *Henry Fielding: A Life* (London: Routledge, 1993), p.381. Mrs Piozzi's source was Dr Arthur Collier (1707–77) who had tutored her in the classics when she was a girl. He had also helped Sarah Fielding with her Greek and Latin in the 1740s. See the Introduction to *The Correspondence of Henry and Sarah Fielding*, ed. Martin C. Battestin and Clive T. Probyn (Oxford: Clarendon Press, 1993), pp.xxxii, xxxix, and *Thraliana: The Diary of Mrs. Hester Lynch Thrale (Later Mrs. Piozzi) 1776–1809*, ed. Katharine C. Balderston (Oxford: Clarendon Press, 1942), I, pp.78–9, where Mrs Thrale records that Dr Collier had taught Sally Fielding with 'prodigious Assiduity', and goes on to quote Dr Johnson: 'He used to mention Harry Fielding's behaviour to her as a melancholy instance of narrowness; while She read only English Books, and made English Verses, it seems, he fondled her Fancy, & encourag'd her Genius, but as soon [as] he perceived She once read Virgil, Farewell to Fondness, the Author's Jealousy was become stronger than the Brother's Affection, and he saw her future progress in literature not without pleasure only – but with Pain.'
7 *Xenophon's Memoirs of Socrates* (1762), translated by S.F., included notes by James Harris (1709–80), a nephew of the 3rd Earl of Shaftesbury.
8 Until her death in 1755, Jane Collier (sister of Dr Arthur Collier) was Sarah Fielding's closest companion. In 1751 they lived together at Beauford Buildings, Westminster. See Battestin and Probert, *Correspondence of Henry and Sarah Fielding*, pp.xxii, xxvii. For an account of the collaboration between Fielding and Collier, see Carolyn Woodward, 'Who wrote *The Cry*? A Fable for our Times', *Eighteenth-Century Fiction*, IX, 1 (October 1996), 91–7.

9   Battestin and Probert, *Correspondence of Henry and Sarah Fielding*, pp.xxxvi–xxxvii. Mrs Montagu's scheme for a female community included her sister, Sarah Scott, as well as Mrs E. Cutts, Mrs Freind and Sarah Fielding.
10 Ibid., p.157n.
11 *The Adventures of David Simple*, p.xii.
12 Ibid., p.7.
13 Willey, *Eighteenth Century Background*, pp.57–75, discusses the 'natural morality' of Anthony Ashley Cooper, 3rd Earl of Shaftesbury. He includes an extract from the dialogue between Theocles and Philocles from *The Moralist: A Philosophical Rhapsody* (1709), later reprinted in the *Characteristicks*, to illustrate 'how the philosophical passion for the best-of-possible-worlds could already, in the opening eighteenth century, pass into fondness for "the country" and for what is "natural", in contrast to town life and the "artificial"'.
14 Jane Spencer, *The Rise of the Woman Novelist: From Aphra Behn to Jane Austen* (Oxford: Blackwell, 1993), p.121, discusses Fielding's *The Countess of Dellwyn* (1759) as a 'cool, detached, ironical narrative' in which the author's moral scheme is evident at all times, 'perhaps excessively so'.
15 Patricia Meyer Spacks, *Imagining a Self: Autobiography and Novel in Eighteenth-Century England* (Cambridge, Mass.: Harvard University Press, 1976), p.71.
16 Quoted by Willey, *Eighteenth Century Background*, p.57.
17 *The Adventures of David Simple*, p.xiii.
18 Leslie Stephen, *History of English Thought in the Eighteenth Century* (London: Harbinger Books, 1962) (first published 1876), II, pp.62–3.
19 Terry Eagleton, *The Rape of Clarissa: Writing, Sexuality and Class Struggle in Samuel Richardson* (Oxford: Basil Blackwell, 1982), p.71.
20 Quotations are from *The Cry; A New Dramatic Fable*, printed in three volumes for R. and J. Dodsley, Pall-mall, London, 1754.
21 Spencer, *Rise of the Woman Novelist*, p.208.
22 The discussion of the *Characteristicks* in *The Cry* (II, pp.276–309) deals with 'that freedom of thought and enquiry, which he [Shaftesbury] asserts to be the distinguishing prerogative of the human mind' (II, p.276), with his contention that ridicule is the test of truth, 'that all belief in revelation or tradition had in it something very ridiculous, and therefore could not suit with the dignity of human wisdom' (II, p.277), and with Cylinda's 'exaltation of my own understanding, in being thus made sole judge to myself of right and wrong' (II, p.279), unfettered by the paltry fear of punishment or the selfish hope of reward.
23 Woodward, 'Who wrote *The Cry*?', 93, referring to Mrs Piozzi's claim that the critique of Shaftesbury's philosophy in *The Cry* was written by Arthur Collier, is too well disposed to the idea of collaborative writing to query Collier's role: 'Certainly, one or another of the people in the Fielding–Collier circle might have enjoyed writing such a critique, especially as Arthur Collier, senior, was known as a philosopher, and Anthony Ashley Cooper . . . was the uncle of James Harris, close friend to both Sarah Fielding and Jane Collier.'

²⁴ *Remarks on Clarissa* (1749), printed for J. Robinson, p.49. The essay was published anonymously but is generally attributed to Sarah Fielding.

Notes to Chapter 6

¹ See *Johnson's Juvenal: London and The Vanity of Human Wishes*, ed. Niall Rudd (Bristol: Bristol Classical Press, 1981, 1988), p.27, for a discussion of the identity of Johnson's 'Thales' (usually understood as Thales of Miletus, a pioneer of Greek natural philosophy), the replacement for Juvenal's Umbritius. Richard Holmes, *Dr Johnson and Mr Savage* (London: Hodder and Stoughton, 1993) discusses the vexed question of whether Thales represents Richard Savage, but concludes that the rescue operation, masterminded by Pope, to send the hapless poet away from London to mend his fortunes in Bristol, almost certainly took place after the publication of *London*. Savage moved on to south Wales, probably early in 1740. Certainly, Johnson's account of his departure from London in his *Life* (1744) was rather more acerbic than his sorrowful farewell to Thales in *London*:

> As he was ready to entertain himself with future Pleasures, he had planned out a Scheme of Life for the Country, of which he had no Knowledge but from Pastorals and Songs. He imagined that he should be transported to Scenes of flow'ry Felicity, like those which one Poet has reflected to another, and had projected a perpetual Round of innocent Pleasures, of which he suspected no Interruption from Pride, or Ignorance, or Brutality . . . he could not bear to debar himself from the Happiness which was to be found in the Calm of a Cottage, or lose the Opportunity of listening without Intermission, to the Melody of the Nightingale, which he believ'd was to be heard from every Bramble, and which he did not fail to mention as a very important Part of the Happiness of a Country Life. (*Life of Savage*, ed. Clarence Tracy (Oxford: The Clarendon Press, 1971), p.111.)

² Quotations from *London* are from Rudd's edition which includes both Juvenal's Latin text and Johnson's version. E. L. Bloom and L. D. Bloom, 'Johnson's *London* and its Juvenilian Texts' and 'Johnson's *London* and the Tools of Scholarship', *Huntington Library Quarterly*, XXXIV (1970–1), 1–23 and 115–39, provide a scholarly comparison between Johnson's poem about 'London and the English [*sic*] countryside' and the Latin original.

³ *Boswell's Life of Johnson*, ed. George Birkbeck Hill, rev. L. F. Powell (Oxford: Clarendon Press, 1934), I, p.118.

⁴ It is not usual to suspect Johnson of a sense of humour. Bloom and Bloom, 'Johnson's *London* and its Juvenilian Texts', 22, point out that the variant 'Me quoque ad Eleusinam Cererem, vestramque Dianam' in the version of Juvenal published with *London* in 1738, alluding to Ceres and her sanctuary at Eleusis, permitted Johnson 'to speak of the "wilds of Kent" and its silently drawn image of Canterbury as the spiritual source of the satirist's strength'. Rudd,

Johnson's Juvenal, p.38, will have none of this; he also rejects an allusion to the family home of Johnson's friend, Elizabeth Carter, and the fact that Kent was 'deconverted' by the Danes and thus became the bastion of paganism. Noting John Oldham's reference to his native Kent in his version of the Third Satire, Rudd suggests a more superficial explanation of Johnson's 'wilds of Kent' 'based on rhyme and on the hint from Oldham'.

5   According to Rudd, *Johnson's Juvenal*, p.8, 'Cambria's solitary shore' was Johnson's rendering of Juvenal's 'empty Cumae'. It was 'the gateway to Baiae . . . and a delightful stretch of coast offering beauty and seclusion'. Cumae was an old Greek colony on the coast near Naples and Baiae, a fashionable resort.

6   References in this essay are to *The Parasite* (Dublin, 1765), printed for P. Wilson, J. Exshaw, S. Cotter, H. Saunders, E. Watts, J. Potts and J. Williams, 2 vols.

7   *Letters from Altamont in the Capital, to his Friends in the Country*, printed for T. Becket and P. A. De Hondt (London, 1767).

8   *The Contemplative Man, or, The History of Christopher Crab, Esq. of North Wales* printed for J. Whiston (London, 1771), 2 vols.

9   References in this essay are to *The Expedition of Humphry Clinker*, ed. Lewis M. Knapp, rev. Paul-Gabriel Bouce, for The World's Classics (Oxford: Oxford University Press, 1984).

10 Philip Jenkins, *The Making of a Ruling Class: The Glamorgan Gentry 1640–1790* (Cambridge: Cambridge University Press, 1983), pp.242–4.

11 Geraint H. Jenkins, *The Foundations of Modern Wales 1642–1780* (Oxford: The Clarendon Press/Cardiff: University of Wales Press, 1987), p.389, quoting Hugh Owen, *The Life and Works of Lewis Morris*, p.262.

12 Although the humour of *The Parasite* is more cynical than the relatively good-natured comedy of *The Contemplative Man*, some similarities of style and content suggest at least the possibility that they came from the same pen. Dick Swallow is born and bred in Wrexham while Christopher Crab lives within 'twelve Welch miles' of the same town; Dick is apprenticed to an apothecary, while Trundle, an apothecary, is a frequent visitor to the Crab household; Dick obtains spurious medical qualifications from Scotland, while Christopher studies medicine at Oxford; the author of *The Parasite* leaves blank pages in imitation of *Tristram Shandy* while the author of *The Contemplative Man* refers to Sterne in a whole chapter devoted to digression and quotations. The parallels are merely suggestive but receive some further support from the fact that like the fictitious Dick Swallow and Christopher Crab, Herbert Lawrence – thought to be the author of *The Contemplative Man* – was himself a medical man from a Denbighshire family.

13 Entry in the *OED* under 'picaresque'.

14 The Revd Charles Jenner (1736–74) was the son of Dr Charles Jenner, chaplain to King George II, prebendary of Lincoln and archdeacon of Bedford and Huntingdon. At Cambridge, the younger Charles won the Seatonian Prize for Poetry on two occasions, following in the footsteps of Christopher Smart, who won it five times. He married Rebecca Thomson in 1764 and

obtained the livings of Claybrooke in Leicestershire and Craneford in Northamptonshire. He died of a cold caught at Vauxhall Gardens. In addition to *Letters from Altamont*, he published several volumes of verse, two plays, *Letters from Lothario to Penelope* (1771) and a novel, *The Placid Man, or Memoirs of Sir Charles Beville* (1770).

15 Entry on Charles Jenner in the *DNB*.

16 In *Thraliana: The Diary of Mrs. Hester Lynch Thrale (Later Mrs. Piozzi) 1776–1809*, ed. Katharine C. Balderston (Oxford: Clarendon Press, 1942), I, p.131, Hester Thrale refers to Herbert Lawrence as 'my Relation, very distant indeed, but he *is* related to the Cottons, and his family have been called Cousins by us – not only at Election times but at all Times'. (The principal seat of the Cottons, her mother's family, was Llewenni Hall near Denbigh.) She recalled that 'We were once good Friends, and he loved my Father much, and made verses in my Praise when I was but 12 or 13 Years old, & tutour'd me, & thought me more obliged to mind what he said, than I thought myself'. (II, p.710)

17 Mary Hyde, *The Thrales of Streatham Park* (Cambridge, Mass.: Harvard University Press, 1977), p.11, refers to Hester Thrale's description of her father's death in 1762 when Lawrence 'our medical Friend' was summoned to dinner because '*All of us* were *Ill*'. She quotes extensively from Mrs Thrale's 'Family Book' which refers to Lawrence's treatment of the children's ailments and gives a harrowing account of the death of Harry in 1776 after Lawrence failed to respond to an urgent call for help. *Thraliana*, I, p.130, records that she shut her heart against him in that fatal year, but later there was a rapprochement: 'when a Man of 75 Years old begs Pardon, & writes Epigrams, – 'tis surely Time to make up' (II, p.711). James L. Clifford, *Hester Lynch Piozzi (Mrs Thrale)* (Oxford: Clarendon Press, 1941), lists thirteen letters she received from Lawrence between 1758 and 1788, nine of them deposited in the John Rylands Library, Manchester.

18 In *Thraliana* there are a number of references to Lawrence's verses and witticisms. Clifford, *Hester Lynch Piozzi*, p.73, records that Herbert supported Wilkes in the 1768 election and during the following summer sent Mrs Thrale newspaper cuttings of the poems and articles which he had written to further the popular cause.

19 Although Lawrence had expected something better from the author of *Roderick Random*, he confesses that Matthew Bramble has some originality about him as 'the principal Conduit-Pipe thro' which our Author conveys his own real Sentiments of Men and Things' (II, p.112). He recognizes that 'This most unfaithful Portrait of poor Old *England* does mend upon us when Mr. *Bramble* quits *London*' (II, p.115) and that he was at a loss to guess the author's design until 'Mr. *Bramble* had crossed the Tweed; and then I found that *England* was sacrificed, and, as it were, thrown into Shadow, in order to bring the *Mother* Country forwards, and shew her in a more brilliant Light' (II, p.115–16). Although the book abounds in masterly strokes, Lawrence hates that Hottentot, Captain Lismahago, 'and the ridiculous Letters of Mrs. *Tabitha*

Bramble, and her Maid *Jenkins*, are too childish to amuse the meanest Capacity' (II, p.117).

20 Ann Jessie Van Sant, *Eighteenth Century Sensibility and the Novel: The Senses in Social Context* (Cambridge: Cambridge University Press, 1993), p.104.

21 John Sekora, *Luxury: The Concept in Western Thought, Eden to Smollett* (Baltimore: John Hopkins University Press, 1977), p.281.

22 The information that Bramble 'had the honour to sit in the last parliament but one of the late king, as representative for the borough of Dymkymraig' [literally, 'No Welsh'] (p.98) occurs in a conversation with the old duke of N[ewcastle]. In his letter to Sir Watkin Phillips of Jesus College, Oxford, written from Argyllshire on 3 September, Bramble's nephew Jery comments on the great affinity between 'Gaelick' and 'Welch': 'I was not a little surprised, when asking a Highlander one day, if he knew where we should find any game? he replied, *'hu niel Sassenagh,'* which signifies *no English*: the very same answer I should have received from a Welchman, and almost in the same words' (p.240).

23 In the same letter to Sir Watkin, Jery explains that their landlord's name is plain Dougal Campbell, 'but as there is a great number of the same appellation, they are distinguished (like the Welch) by patronimics; and as I have known an antient Briton called Madoc-ap-Morgan, ap-Jenkin, ap-Jones, our Highland chief designs himself Dou'l Mac-amish mac-'oul ich-ian, signifying Dougal, the son of James, the son of Dougal, the son of John' (pp.240–1).

24 Weary of Tabby's 'intolerable scolding', Matthew Bramble closes his letter of 19 May by asking Dr Lewis, 'Can't you find some poor gentleman of Wales, to take this precious commodity off the hands of / yours, / M. BRAMBLE' (p.78).

25 In his letter of 18 July, Jery tells Phillips that 'If I had never been in Wales, I should have been more struck with the manifest difference in appearance betwixt the peasants and commonality on different sides of the Tweed.' The boors of Northumberland are lusty fellows while Scottish labourers are beggarly, their cattle as meagre and stunted as themselves. Jery goes on to quote his uncle: 'Though all the Scottish hinds would not bear to be compared with those of the rich counties of South Britain, they would stand very well in competition with the peasants of France, Italy, and Savoy – not to mention the mountaineers of Wales, and the red-shanks of Ireland' (p.214).

26 Sekora, *Luxury*, p.243.

27 Ibid., p.286.

28 *Humphry Clinker*, p.xiv.

29 Jean B. Kern, 'The Old Maid, or "to grow old, and be poor, and laughed at"', in Mary Anne Schofield and Cecilia Macheski (eds), *Fetter'd or Free? British Women Novelists 1670–1785* (Athens: Ohio University Press), p.201, notes the representation of 'old maids' in eighteenth-century novels by male authors as sex-starved, frustrated and disagreeable stereotypes: 'The model is familiar in Bridget Allworthy and Tabitha Bramble who harass their bachelor brothers in *Tom Jones* and *Humphry Clinker*.'

30 *Humphry Clinker*, p.358, translates as 'O my countryside, when shall I see you!', citing Horace, *Satires*, II.vi.60.
31 *Humphry Clinker*, p.362, translates Horace, *Satires*, II.vi.62 as 'The happy forgetfulness of life's cares'.

Notes to Chapter 7

1 Quoted from *The Reveries of Solitude* (Bath and London, 1793), in Clarence Tracy, *A Portrait of Richard Graves* (Toronto: University of Toronto Press, 1987), p.8.
2 In a letter to his friend, Thomas Hearne, Richard Graves (senior) wrote: 'it hath pleased God to visit me with one of the Greatest Afflictions that could have befallen me in this world, the Loss of the nearest and dearest Relation, who has left me the Father of 6 poor motherless Children'. See *Remarks and Collections of Thomas Hearne*, ed. C. E. Doble, D. W. Rannie et al. (Oxford: Oxford Historical Society, 1884–1918), VIII, p.46. Quoted by Tracy, *Richard Graves*, p.8.
3 In his essay 'On Health' in *The Invalid: with the Obvious Means of Enjoying Health and Long Life* (1804), pp.22–3, Graves implies that his mother had cared for him tenderly and that after her death his health had declined in the hands of servants. Cited by Tracy, *Richard Graves*, p.9.
4 Graves refers in *Recollection of Some Particulars in the Life of the late William Shenstone, Esq.* (1788), p.49, 'to a distant relation, a Mr M–rg–n, of W–rl–s, in Essex' with a footnote explaining that W–rl–s was near Waltham Abbey. Quoted by Tracy, *Richard Graves*, p.8, who has traced a typescript history of Warlies in the Essex Record Office at Chelmsford, in which Richard Morgan Esq. of London (d. 1740) is recorded as admitted tenant in 1720 of the copyhold estate of Warlies; a document in the Harrowby MSS Trust indicates that Morgan Graves inherited properties in Middlesex bequeathed to him by Richard Morgan of Warlies, Essex.
5 Tracy, *Richard Graves*, p.9.
6 Tracy claims that there are Welsh scenes in all four of Graves's novels (ibid., p.8). In *Columella, or The Distressed Anchoret* (1779), however, the only reference appears to be the brief appearance of a Welsh captain who annoys Columella during his residence in Bath by urinating against the wall of his house (II, pp.200–2).
7 For Holdsworth's *Muscipula* (1709), see Ch. 1, n.32.
8 George Whitefield (1714–70) was born at the Bell Inn, Gloucester – which features in *Tom Jones* and again in *The Spiritual Quixote* where it is said to be under the management of Whitefield's sister. Unlike Graves, who went up to Pembroke College funded by an Abingdon scholarship, Whitefield was a servitor at the same college, waiting on other undergraduates and receiving his education as payment. Both matriculated on 7 November 1732 and graduated in July 1736. See entries for Graves and Whitefield in the *DNB*.

9   Tracy, *Richard Graves*, pp.41, 45–6, citing *The Journal of the Rev. Charles Wesley*, ed. Thomas Jackson (1849), refers to the long conversation between Charles Wesley and Richard Graves on 10 October 1737 when the latter admitted that formerly religion had been his chief pleasure in life. Wesley hoped that he would be one of those whose life fools count madness, 'no other than what you once laboured after, till the gentleman swallowed up the Christian'.
10 *The Journal of the Rev. John Wesley, A.M.*, ed. Nehemiah Curnock (London: Charles H. Kelly, n.d.), II, p.151n. Prior to being 'carried away by his friends' in July 1737, Charles Caspar Graves had breakfasted at Oxford with Charles Wesley on 2 May 'and owned with tears he had never felt any true joy but in religion'. On 4 July, Wesley encouraged Graves, who was 'in an excellent temper', 'to go on in the narrow way' and strongly recommended stated hours of retirement. On 11 July, shortly before being removed by his friends as 'stark mad', Graves took Wesley to see the quarries at Bath where the latter 'narrowly missed being dashed to pieces'.
11 Tracy, *Richard Graves*, pp.43–4, claims that in the summer of 1737 Charles Wesley spent a month at Mickleton as the guest of Morgan Graves. There was still trouble to come, however. Curnock, *Journal of John Wesley*, III, p.40n, referring to Charles Wesley's *Journal* for 25 July and 10 October 1737, records that on 2 October, after expostulating with his relatives, Wesley took Charles Caspar Graves to Stanton Harcourt, where he remained some time. Tracy, *Richard Graves*, pp.41, 45–6, using the same source, reports the conversation between Charles Wesley and Richard Graves on 10 October which seems to have begun with some acrimony but ended amicably enough: 'Being determined not to leave England till I had come to a full explanation with Dicky Graves, this morning I went to his rooms; talked the whole matter over, and were both entirely satisfied.'
12 In his *Journal* for 16 August 1742, John Wesley includes the full text of the letter written by Charles Caspar Graves to the Fellows of St Mary Magdalen College in December 1740 (Curnock, *Journal of John Wesley*, III, pp.40–1).
13 Ibid., III, pp.40–2.
14 Tracy, *Richard Graves*, p.45.
15 Ibid., p.81, quoting *Public Characters of 1799–1800* (printed by Richard Phillips, St Paul's Churchyard), p.386.
16 The Religious Societies, consisting of small groups of godly people, had flourished within the Church of England since the 1670s. In the early days of Methodism, both Whitefield and the Wesleys were gladly received by the societies which already existed at Bristol and elsewhere. There were at least five of them in Bristol, known by the name of the street in which they met (Nicholas Street, Baldwin Street, Gloucester Lane, Back Lane and Castle Street). The Bristol Societies flourished under the influence of Whitefield (the early months of 1739 saw the beginning of his 'field preaching' to the Kingswood miners) and John Wesley, who took over Whitefield's work in Bristol later in 1739 and opened the 'Society room' in Horsefair in 1741. See

John Wesley in Wales 1739–1790: Entries from his Journal and Diary relating to Wales, ed. A. H. Williams (Cardiff: University of Wales Press, 1971), pp.xvi–xvii; Rupert E. Davies, *Methodism* (Harmondsworth: Penguin Books, 1963), pp.71–3; the entry for George Whitefield in the *DNB*.

17 References in this essay are to *The Spiritual Quixote*, ed. Clarence Tracy (London: Oxford University Press, 1967), which contains indispensable notes on Graves's use of Whitefield's and Wesley's journals.

18 Whitefield's entry in his *Journal* for 7 February 1739, when he was setting out from London to Windsor ('Lord, send thy angel before me to prepare my way'), was probably coupled in Graves's mind with the entry for 7 March 1739 when Whitefield was about to visit Wales: 'Our business being in haste, God having, of his good providence, sent one to guide us, we rode all night' (*Spiritual Quixote*, p.486).

19 In addition to the references to Whitefield's *Journal* of 7 February and 7 March 1739, Graves also echoes the entry for 18 May 1739: 'As the walls of Jericho once fell down at the sound of a few ram horns; so I hope even this foolishness of preaching, under God, will be a means of pulling down the Devil's strong holds, which are in and about the city of London' (*Spiritual Quixote*, p.488).

20 Williams, *John Wesley in Wales*, pp.xviii–xx, claims that there were already a number of Religious Societies in Wales in 1738–9. He notes that, in time, members were obliged to make their choice, between the Calvinism of Whitefield and the Arminianism of the Wesleys:

> The Cardiff society, for example, threw in its lot with John Wesley, and in this way an open Religious Society of Anglicans and Dissenters became the first Arminian or Wesleyan Methodist society in Wales. In November 1746 some of its members talked of breaking away from Wesley and sought Howell Harris's advice. Harris refused, and the refusal does him credit; 'as they had chosen Bro. Wesley', he wrote, 'I would advise them to go to him & be advis'd by him.'

Williams records Wesley's numerous visits to Cardiff between 1739 and 1790.

21 Whitefield observed in his *Journal* for 9 March 1739, 'I think Wales is excellently well prepared for the gospel of Christ . . . People make nothing of coming twenty miles to hear a sermon' (*Spiritual Quixote*, pp.488–9).

22 Albert M. Lyles, *Methodism Mocked: The Satiric Reaction to Methodism in the Eighteenth Century* (London: The Epworth Press, 1960), p.148.

23 Geoffrey F. Nuttall, *Howel Harris 1714–1773: The Last Enthusiast* (Cardiff: University of Wales Press, 1965), p.3, quoting Dr R. T. Jenkins.

24 Ibid.

25 Howel Harris, born at Talgarth in 1714, experienced a religious conversion at Llangasty Tal-y-Llyn Church on 18 June 1735. He was never ordained but saw his calling as an 'exhorter'; it was a source of pride that he was 'sent out' as a field preacher before Whitefield, Wesley or Daniel Rowland. In 1742 an Association of Welsh Societies was set up and a year later an alliance was formed with the corresponding Methodist movement in England. In the

Calvinist controversy which soon erupted, the Welsh reformers sided with Whitefield though Harris himself resolutely supported the Wesleys in their bid to unify the movement. Similarly, he was steadfastly opposed to secession from the Church of England. Appointed as Whitefield's deputy during his visits to America, he officiated at the Moorfields tabernacle for a period, but after the rift with Daniel Rowland in 1750, he withdrew to Trefeca where he set up the 'Family' [Mary Robinson would meet some surviving members of the commune on the birth of her daughter at Trefeca in 1774]. When a French invasion was threatened, he became captain of a militia unit, resigning his commission in 1762. In 1768, the Countess of Huntingdon built a seminary at Trefeca Isaf for the training of evangelical preachers. Harris died in 1773 and was buried in Talgarth church. An estimated 20,000 people attended his funeral (*Dictionary of Welsh Biography*; Nuttall, *Howel Harris*; Eifion Evans, *Howel Harris, Evangelist 1714–1773* (Cardiff, University of Wales Press, 1974)).

26 Meeting in a shady spot at noonday, the travellers talk about pre-existence, predestination, election and reprobation. When the stranger declares that he would sooner renounce his Bible than believe Whitefield's Calvinistic doctrines, Wildgoose concludes that he must be a follower of John Wesley. 'No,' replies the stranger; 'I am John Wesley himself.' Graves bases his anecdote on Wesley's account in his *Journal* for 20 May 1742 of a conversation he had with a stranger on the road to Northampton (*Spiritual Quixote*, pp.326, 491).

27 Whitefield had first met Harris in March 1739, on the day of his arrival in Wales, when Harris was twenty-five and Whitefield twenty-four. Six weeks earlier Whitefield had written: 'Mr. Howel Harris, and I, are correspondents, blessed be God! May I follow him, as he does Jesus Christ! How he outstrips me! Fye upon me, fye upon me.' Whitefield now wrote in his journal: 'my heart was knit closely to him. I wanted to catch some of his fire . . . A divine and strong sympathy seemed to be between us . . . Blessed be God, there seems to be a noble spirit gone out in Wales' (Nuttall, *Howel Harris*, pp.21–2). In November 1741, Whitefield married Elizabeth James of Abergavenny (Harris had also been interested in the lady). On 5 January 1743, Whitefield and Harris were present at the first joint conference of the Welsh and English Calvinistic Methodist Associations, held at Watford, near Caerffili. Afterwards, 'Harris could write with conviction, "I see God sent you to Wales"' (Evans, *Howel Harris*, p.47). At the second joint conference at Carmarthen in April 1743, Harris was chosen as Whitefield's deputy during his absences abroad.

> The ups and downs of his relations with Whitefield . . . include such expressions as 'longing for Mr. Whitefield as the dove for her mate'; 'parting with dear Mr. Whitefield, blessing the hour I ever saw him, weeping on his neck, and he embracing me too'; 'weeping for love to Brother Whitefield'; and 'we kissed and parted, and immediately I was filled with joy'. (Nuttall, *Howel Harris*, p.50)

28 Whitefield notes in his *Journal* for 8 March 1739: 'I did not observe any scoffers within; but without, some were pleased to honour me so far, as to trail a dead fox, and hunt it about the hall. – But, blessed be God, my voice prevailed' (*Spiritual Quixote*, p.488).

29 Williams, *John Wesley in Wales*, p.36, in John Wesley's entry for 6 May 1748, recording a visit to Llangefni.

30 On 3 and 4 May 1748, at Rhyd-sbardun, and Bodlew in the parish of Llanddaniel-fab, William Williams, Pantycelyn, preached in Welsh and John Wesley in English. On the afternoon and evening of 6 May, Wesley preached at Llanfihangel, six miles from Llangefni, and at Glan-y-gors, probably a farm a mile from Nantannog. On both occasions, William Jones of Trefollwyn Blas repeated in Welsh the substance of what Wesley had said (ibid., pp.35–7).

31 Reproduced in Peter Lord, *Words with Pictures: Welsh Images and Images of Wales* (Aberystwyth: Planet, 1995), p.17 (detail) and in colour between pp.80 and 81.

32 For example, in William Webster's *A Casuistical Essay on Anger and Forgiveness . . . In Three Dialogues between a Gentleman and a Clergyman* (1750), pp.94–5, Generosus, the country squire, describes a visit to the poverty-stricken clergyman, Clericus:

> Through the defects of the Timbers, the Rain had made many Gutters down the dirty Walls; the Furnuture was, a Couple of old Maps, the *Bottom* of an old *Windsor* Chair, and a *Rush* one, *quite whole*, a large brown Table, a great *Bin* for *Corn*, with a rusty Lock to it, but quite empty, and a monstrous Chimney without a Grate.

In his poem 'To the Reverend and Learned Dr. Webster', Christopher Smart similarly focused on the penury of the inferior clergy:

> Behold where poor unmansion'd Merit stands,
> All cold, and crampt with penury and pain;
> Speechless thro'want, she rears th'imploring hands,
> And begs a little bread, but begs in vain.

33 Geraint H. Jenkins, *Literature, Religion and Society in Wales, 1660–1730* (Cardiff: University of Wales Press, 1978), p.4, quoting Erasmus Saunders, *View of the State of Religion in the Diocese of St. David's* (1721).

34 Jenkins, *Literature, Religion and Society*, p.3, quoting Norman Sykes, *Church and State in England in the Eighteenth Century* (1934), p.364.

35 Prys Morgan, *A New History of Wales: The Eighteenth Century Renaissance* (Llandybïe: Christopher Davies, 1981), pp.13–39, devotes a chapter to 'Merrie Wales and its Passing', with a note on the Methodists' view of the Welsh as a heedless, reckless, feckless people and their claim to have totally transformed Welsh life.

36 John Wesley recorded a similar event on 5 May 1747 when after the collapse of the wall his congregation 'appeared sitting at the bottom, just as they sat at the top' (*Spiritual Quixote*, p.489).

37   Wesley recorded on 4 December 1742 that J– B– of Tanfield-Leigh 'came riding thro' the town, hollowing and shouting and driving all the people before him, telling them, "God had told him, he should be a king, and should tread all his enemies under his feet" ' (ibid.).
38   Graves conflates John Wesley's *Journal* for 11 August 1740 and George Whitefield's *Journal* for 20 March 1739 (*Spiritual Quixote*, pp.489–90).

Notes to Chapter 8

1   Quotations from *Eugenius, or, Anecdotes of the Golden Vale* are taken from the second edition, printed for J. Dodsley (London, 1786) in two volumes.
2   *The Metamorphoses of Ovid*, trans. Mary M. Innes (Harmondsworth: Penguin Books, 1955, 1961), p.34.
3   Quoted in Basil Willey, *The Eighteenth Century Backgound* (London: Chatto & Windus, 1940, 1961), p.202.
4   Ibid., p.203.
5   Thomas Pennant, *A Tour in Wales* (1784), printed for Benjamin White at Horace's Head in Fleet Street, 2 vols. References are to the facsimile (Wrexham: Bridge Books, 1991), with an introduction by R. Paul Evans.
6   Pennant states that since about five hundred persons are employed at the Parys Mountain, it is estimated that together with their families, nearly eight thousand people get their bread from these mines.
7   A. L. Owen, *The Famous Druids* (Oxford: Clarendon Press, 1962), p.76, quotes Henry Rowlands's antiquarian study of Anglesey, *Mona Antiqua Restaurata* (1723), in which he refers to the original inhabitants of the island, 'so near in descent, to the Fountains of true Religion and Worship, as to have one of *Noah's Sons* for Grandsire or Great-grandsire'.
8   Gwyn A. Williams, *The Welsh in their History* (London: Croom Helm, 1982), p.34.
9   Thomas Pennant, *The History of the Parishes of Whiteford and Holywell* (London, 1796), p.215.
10   From John Jones's 'Holyhead', quoted in Dewi Roberts, *The Old Villages of Denbighshire and Flintshire* (Llanrwst: Gwasg Carreg Gwalch, 1999), p.92.
11   An account of the industrial schools in M. G. Jones, *The Charity School Movement: A Study of Eighteenth Century Puritanism in Action* (Cambridge: University Press, 1938), pp.154–62, shows that their development was closely related to the Sunday school movement inaugurated by Robert Raikes in Gloucester in 1782 (only twenty miles or so from Claverton). Graves's reference to the school in *Eugenius* predates by two years the schools described in *The Œconomy of Charity* (1787) by Sarah Trimmer, whose 'belief in the moral value of industrial schools ran parallel to her passionate conviction that the religious well-being of the country was bound up with the Sunday school'. She describes a school for girls in Brentford where spinning, learnt on a wheel given by a benevolent lady, knitting and plain needlework were taught, while

a school for boys gave twenty children instruction in carding and spinning coarse wool. Twice a week, for two hours in the evenings, a master attended to teach them to read and write. Neither school lasted more than two years. Sir Thomas Eden, *The State of the Poor* (1797) concluded that 'The experience of eight years has proved that although schools of industry may flourish for a while under the active zeal of the first promoters, yet, when after a few years' trial they are left to the superintendance of less interested administrators, they dwindle into the ordinary state of the parish poor house.'

12 Ann Bermingham, *Landscape and Ideology: The English Rustic Tradition 1740–1860* (London: Thames & Hudson, 1987), pp.79–80, quotes *The Annals of Agriculture*, vol.14, pp.166–7, in her discussion of aesthetic responses to the industrial landscape at the end of the eighteenth century. She equates Young's description of Coalbrookdale with *Joseph Arkwright's Mill, View of Cromford, near Matlock*, painted in 1783 by Joseph Wright of Derby, and contrasts both with Uvedale Price's description of cotton mills in Derbyshire as ugly, unwanted intrusions into picturesque nature (*An Essay on the Picturesque* (1842), p.152) and John Sell Cotman's depiction in *Bedlam Furnace, near Madeley* (1802) of the smoky furnaces befouling and deadening natural vegetation: 'In Wright as for Young nature sustains its integrity in the presence of industry; for Cotman as for Price, industry overpowers nature.'

13 Bermingham, *Landscape and Ideology*, p.80.

14 Nicolaes Berchem (1620–83).

Notes to Chapter 9

1 'Autobiography 1756–72', transcribed from a manuscript in the Abinger Collection in the Bodleian Library, Oxford, in *Collected Novels and Memoirs of William Godwin*, ed. Mark Philp (London: William Pickering, 1992), I, pp.18, 22. All the details of Godwin's family in this paragraph are taken from the same source.

2 Ibid., I, p.8.

3 Godwin refers to Robert Sandeman (1718–71) as

> a celebrated North-country apostle, who after Calvin had damned ninety-nine in a hundred of mankind, has contrived a scheme for damning ninety-nine in a hundred of the followers of Calvin. Calvin had sufficiently guarded against the merit of good-works; but Sandeman undertakes to show a flaw in the passport for the elect, and demonstrates that, after we have dispossessed the devil of the battery of good-works, he gains possession of the citadel by imposing on us the merit of faith. In a word, he incontestably shows that many reputed orthodox divines have represented faith as an act of the will or a disposition of the heart, whereas God scorns to save or damn a man but according to the right or wrong judgment of . . . his understanding. (Ibid., I, p.30)

4   'Autobiographical Fragments', in Philp, *Collected Novels and Memoirs*, I, p.42.
5   Ibid., I, p.43. Godwin refers to Samuel Clarke, *A Discourse Concerning the Being and Attributes of God* (1716), first published as *A Demonstration of the Being and Attributes of God* (1705).
6   'The Principal Revolutions of Opinion', in Philp, *Collected Novels and Memoirs*, I, p.53. Godwin's manuscript is dated 10 March 1800.
7   Ibid. Basil Willey, *The Eighteenth Century Background* (London: Chatto & Windus, 1961 edn), pp.7, 155–6, defines deism or natural religion as reaching God 'not only through the starry heavens above, but also through the moral law within: through Reason as well as Nature'. In Holbach's *Système de la Nature* (1770) and the work of the other Encyclopedistes, the Nature philosophy of the century worked itself out to its ultimate conclusions and touched on revolutionary issues: ' "Nature" is seen no longer as a christianized demi-urge, working obediently under heavenly auspices, but as a defiant Titaness who would dethrone the established gods and overturn all earthly altars and thrones, the symbols of priestcraft and tyranny.'
8   Some notions of Godwin's Socinianism (or Unitarianism) can be gleaned from the works of Joseph Priestley (1733–1804) whose early life closely paralleled Godwin's own: he too had a Calvinistic upbringing, attended a dissenting academy and became a Presbyterian minister. After reading Lardner's *Letter on the Logos*, Priestley became a Socinian, 'one who holds that God is the only proper object of worship, and who rejects the Trinitarian doctrine of Christ's divinity, and the Arian doctrine of his pre-existence'. Priestley nevertheless demonstrated in his *History of the Corruptions of Christianity* (1782), published two years before *Imogen*, that he believed in the final resurrection and also retained from traditional doctrine the belief in the miracles and the resurrection of Christ.' See Willey, 'Joseph Priestley and the Socinian Moonlight', *Eighteenth Century Background*, pp.168–204.
9   Philp, *Collected Novels and Memoirs*, I, p.53.
10 William Godwin, *Imogen: A Pastoral Romance From the Ancient British* (New York: The New York Public Library, 1963), reprinted from *The Bulletin of the New York Public Library* (January–June, 1963). Quotations in the present essay are taken from this edition. For a more recent edition by Patricia Clemit, see Philp, *Collected Novels and Memoirs*, II, pp.163–267.
11 Marken's references (*Imogen*, pp.13–14) are to John Toland, *A Critical History of the Celtic Religion and Learning: Containing an Account of the Druids* (1720), William Cooke, *An Enquiry into the Patriarchal and Druidical Religion, Temples* (1754), John Smith, *Gaelic Antiquities: Consisting of a History of the Druids* (1780) and Hugh Blair, *Dissertation on the Poems of Ossian, the Son of Fingal* (1783).
12 *Imogen*, p.14.
13 Ibid., p.109.
14 Ibid., p.115.
15 Ibid., p.120.
16 A. L. Owen, *The Famous Druids: A Survey of Three Centuries of English*

Literature on the Druids (Oxford: Clarendon Press, 1962), p.100. My debt to this comprehensive and entertaining study will become only too apparent in the course of this essay.

17 Ibid., pp.1–2.
18 Ibid., p.27.
19 Ibid., p.238, quoting *Archaeologia*, VII (1784), 304.
20 John Aubrey's *Proposals for Printing Monumenta Britannica* (1693) failed to interest a sufficient number of subscribers, though his theories found their way into print through his influence on other scholars. See the account in Owen, *Famous Druids*, pp.102–9.
21 Ibid., p.109.
22 See Chapter 12 for Iolo Morganwg's forgeries and his contributions to the *Myvyrian Archaiology of Wales*.
23 Owen, *Famous Druids*, p.195.
24 In *Mona Antiqua Restaurata* (1723), the Revd Henry Rowlands, Vicar of Llanidan in Anglesey, presumed that the original inhabitants of the island

> so near in descent, to the Fountains of true Religion and Worship, as to have one of *Noah*'s Sons for Grandsire or Greatgrandsire, may well be imagin'd, to have carried and convey'd here some of the Rites and Usages of that true Religion, pure and untainted, in the first propagating them; tho' I must confess they soon after became . . . abominably corrupted.

With the development of language, laws and religion, Druidism came into being and in the course of time, the 'infatuated Monkish *Druids*' lapsed into idolatry. See the account of Rowlands in Owen, *Famous Druids*, pp.73–82.
25 Patricia Clemit, *The Godwinian Novel: The Rational Fictions of Godwin, Brockden Brown, Mary Shelley* (Oxford: Clarendon Press, 1993), p.17.
26 Ibid., p.29. Owen, *Famous Druids*, p.149, offers a number of examples of this association of ideas, not least William Mason's heroic verse drama, *Caractacus* (1759), which documents the struggles of the great British chief against the might of Rome in the first century, the Druids providing the play with its philosophical background: 'in their firmness Caractacus's resolution is deeply rooted'.
27 Owen, *Famous Druids*, p.65.
28 Ibid., p.117.
29 Ibid., pp.122–3.
30 Ibid., p.121.
31 Ibid., pp.62–5.
32 *Imogen*, p.114.
33 In *Imogen*, the reference to Mona occurs just before the sacrifice of Arthur: 'In this hour of calamity the Druids came forth from their secret cells, and assembled upon the heights of Mona' (p.33). In the *Annals*, Tacitus describes the massacre of the Druids by Suetonius Paulinus on Mona in AD 60 when the Roman soldiers were confronted by armed warriors, women wearing brands

and Druids 'lifting up their hands to heaven and pouring forth dreadful imprecations' (Owen, *Famous Druids*, p.23).

34 Don Locke, *A Fantasy of Reason: The Life and Thought of William Godwin* (London: Routledge & Kegan Paul, 1980), p.344.

35 Ibid.

36 At the end of *Fleetwood* (1805), for instance, written nearly twenty years after his final rejection of Christianity, the hero is reconciled to his wife in the language of Christian discourse (*forgiven, remorse, angelic, pardon, the pains of hell*): 'It is from the hour in which we are forgiven, that the true remorse commences. That I could have ever acted thus toward the angelic creature who condescends to pardon me for what I acted, – this is the sensation that is sharper than all the pains of hell!'

37 B. J. Tysdahl, *William Godwin as Novelist* (London: The Athlone Press, 1981), p.25. He suggests that Godwin lacks the tact which Milton or Johnson in *Rasselas* could command:

> Young people must be taken out of the world, so to speak, to undergo the difficulties which will steel them so that they can be happy and good ever after. Had he read *Imogen*, Johnson would certainly have been sarcastic about their reward: they go back to the world of men in which there is really no choice, no challenge, and no tension.

38 Ibid., p.23.

39 *Imogen*, p.110.

40 Owen, *Famous Druids*, p.20.

41 Ibid., p.155.

42 Ibid., p.12.

43 Willey, *Eighteenth Century Background*, p.160, quoting Holbach's *La Système de la Nature*.

44 Ibid.

45 As John Ray had written in the Preface to *The Wisdom of God Manifested in the Works of Creation* (1691), the works of creation '*serve to Stir up and Increase in us the Affections and Habits of Admiration, Humility and Gratitude*'. It was a view ultimately derived from the Psalms of David and Ray goes on to quote from Psalm 8 and to comment: '*The holy Psalmist is very frequent in the Enumeration and Consideration of these Works, which may warrant me doing the like, and justifie the denominating such a Discourse as this, rather Theological than Philosophical.*' Examples of eighteenth-century poets who wrote in this vein include Addison, Pope, Thomson, Boyse and Smart. Godwin was 'brought up' on the hymns of Isaac Watts and presumably knew 'The Universal Hallelujah', a paraphrase of Psalm 48 in which it is the duty of the creatures to praise the Creator. Watts writes,

> Let the shrill birds his honour raise,
> And climb the morning-sky:
> While grovelling beasts attempt his praise
> In hoarser harmony.
> (Chalmers's *English Poets* (1810), XIII, p.27)

In *Imogen,* Godwin writes: 'Praise him, ye beasts, in different strains! And let the birds, that soar on lofty wings, and scale the path of heaven, bear, in their various melody, the notes of adoration to the skies!' (p.36)

46 *Imogen,* p.110.
47 Philp, *Collected Novels and Memoirs,* I, p.53.
48 Locke, *Fantasy of Reason,* pp.13–14.
49 *Imogen,* p.110.
50 There are no druids in 'Edwin and Angelina', but Owen, *Famous Druids,* p.178, quotes from *The Druid's Monument, A Tribute to the Memory of Dr. Oliver Goldsmith* (1774) in which a group of Druids often meet near the Isis to discuss Goldsmith's works. They are particularly fond of the story of Angelina and Edwin.
51 *Imogen,* p.111.
52 Ibid.
53 Locke, *Fantasy of Reason,* p.50, quoting Godwin, *Enquirer* (1797), p.27.
54 Ibid., p.52, quoting C. Kegan Paul, *William Godwin: His Friends and Contemporaries* (1876), I, p.79.
55 Ibid., pp.53–4.

Notes to Chapter 10

1 See Jane Aaron, 'Seduction and Betrayal: Wales in Women's Fiction, 1785–1810', *Women's Writing,* I, 1 (1994), 65–76, and *Pur Fel Y Dur* (Caerdydd: Gwasg Prifysgol Cymru, 1998), pp.80–5. See also Francesca Rhydderch, 'Dual Nationality, Divided Identity: Ambivalent Narratives of Britishness in the Welsh Novels of Anna Maria Bennett', *Welsh Writing in English: A Yearbook of Critical Essays,* III (1997), 1–17.
2 *Memoirs of Charles Lee Lewes* (London: Richard Phillips, 1805), IV, p.199.
3 W. Goldwin, *A Description of the Antient and Famous City of Bristol,* revised by I. Smart (London, 1751), p.33.
4 J. F. Fuller, 'A Curious Genealogical Medley', *Miscellanea Genealogica et Heraldica,* Fourth Series, V (1914), 244–7.
5 Anna Maria Bennett's father is named as John Evans in Thomas Pye's will (Public Record Office, PROB 11/1136). The marriage of Harriet Bennet and James Esten at Tooting Graveney on 24 February 1784 was witnessed by Anna Maria Bennet and John Evans (Greater London Record Office).
6 Sir Thomas Pye's will, drawn up in 1785, refers to Anna Maria's husband, Thomas Bennet, as a custom house officer. *The European Magazine* (1790) describes both her father and husband as custom house officers. See under 'Anna Maria Bennett' in Virginia Blain, Patricia Clements and Isobel Grundy (eds), *The Feminist Companion to Literature in English* (London: B. T. Batsford, 1990), p.82.
7 Sir Thomas Pye (1713?–85), known variously as 'Nosey' and 'Goose Pye', was knighted and promoted to the rank of admiral in 1773. He is said to have

been a man of limited ability who achieved high office through the interest of his uncle, the Earl of Bathurst. See under 'Sir Thomas Pye' in the *DNB* and a number of references in N. A. M. Rodger, *The Wooden World: An Anatomy of the Georgian Navy* (London: Collins, 1986).

8 Lewes, *Memoirs*, IV, p.203.

9 Ibid., IV, pp.202–3. Lewes claims that when mistaken reports of Pye's death appeared in the press, he wrote reassuring notes to Mrs Bennett at Tooting and to a current favourite, Miss Louisa Ellis, but placed the notes in the wrong envelopes. The enraged Mrs Bennett 'never after saw the Admiral'. *The Annual Register* (1784–5), p.253, gives the date of Pye's 'death' as 23 February 1785.

10 *Commissioned Sea Officers of the Royal Navy* (National Maritime Museum), I, p.61, records Thomas Pye Bennett's promotion to Lieutenant on 9 May 1781. Candidates had to be at least twenty years old to obtain promotion from midshipman.

11 When Harriet Esten died in Kensington on 29 April 1865, she was reputedly a hundred years old (*Gentleman's Magazine*, June 1865). For an account of her acting career see under 'Mrs James Esten' in Philip H. Highfill, Kalman A. Burnim and Edward A. Langhans (eds), *A Biographical Dictionary of Actors, Actresses, Musicians, Dancers, Managers & Other Stage Personnel in London, 1600–1800* (Carbondale: Southern Illinois University Press, 1978), V, pp.104–10. Her portrait is reproduced in Fuller, 'Genealogical Medley', facing p.244.

12 Although in his will Pye gives his name to five of Anna Maria Bennett's children, only Polly is directly referred to as his daughter.

13 *Anna, or, Memoirs of a Welch Heiress* (1785) was followed by *Juvenile Indiscretions* (1786), *Agnes de Courci* (1789), *Ellen, Countess of Castle Howel* (1794), *The Beggar Girl and her Benefactors* (1797) and *Vicissitudes Abroad, or, The Ghost of my Father* (1806). Mrs Bennett's obituary announced a sequel, *Vicissitudes at Home*, but it seems to have remained unpublished. *De Valcourt* (1800) is sometimes attributed to Anna Maria Bennett but it is neither listed on the title-pages of her novels nor referred to in her obituary; the style and content of the novel suggest that it is unlikely to be her work. *Faith and Fiction* (1816) and *Emily* (1819), sometimes attributed to Anna Maria Bennett, are the work of Elizabeth Bennett. *The Cambridge Bibliography of English Literature* also attributes *Henry Bennet and Julia Johnson* [1794?] to A. M. Bennett.

14 Lewes, *Memoirs*, IV, pp.203–4.

15 Highfill et al., *Biographical Dictionary*.

16 *Gentleman's Magazine*, LXXVIII, part 1 (1808), 180.

17 Rhydderch, 'Dual Nationality, Divided Identity', 1.

18 Ibid., 13.

19 Elizabeth Lewis (d. 1733), daughter of Thomas Lewis of Soberton, Hants. ('Lewis of the Van'), married in 1730 Other Windsor, 3rd Earl of Plymouth (1707–32).

20 Charlotte Herbert (d. 1733), daughter of Philip, 7th Earl of Pembroke,

married as her second husband in 1703 Thomas, 1st Viscount Windsor (d. 1738), son of the 1st Earl of Plymouth by his second wife. A plan of the Dowlais Iron Company's furnace (1763) at Merthyr Tydfil, reproduced in Donald Moore (ed.), *Wales in the Eighteenth Century* (Swansea: Christopher Davies, 1976), p.123, shows that Charlotte's daughter-in-law Alice owned part of the land on which the iron works was built. In *Anna*, Mrs Herbert of Llandore Castle owns the local iron works (inherited from her grandmother).

21   Philip Jenkins, *The Making of a Ruling Class: The Glamorgan Gentry 1640–1790* (Cambridge: Cambridge University Press, 1983), p.xxi, refers to the failure to produce male heirs as a 'violent caesura . . . a demographic catastrophe that thoroughly changed the character and composition of the Welsh gentry'. He describes the early eighteenth century as 'an age of heiresses': from roughly thirty great estates, there were eleven occasions between 1721 and 1750 when a squire died leaving his property to an heiress, and five more between 1751 and 1780 (ibid., p.40).

22   The list of gentry élite in Glamorgan 1670–90 includes Herbert of Friars, the Mansells of Briton Ferry and Margam, and the Turbervilles of Penlline and Sker (ibid., pp.25–6). Jenkins refers to Llanmihangel, belonging to the Edwin family, as 'another great estate' (ibid., p.40).

23   A description of Y Fan, built on a low hill less than a mile from Caerffili Castle, is included in *An Inventory of the Ancient Monuments in Glamorgan Volume IV: Domestic Architecture from the Reformation to the Industrial Revolution Part I; The Greater Houses* (Cardiff: HMSO, 1981), pp.191–203.

24   Rhydderch, 'Dual Nationality, Divided Identity', 4–6, comments on Anna's namelessness until she is finally discovered to be a Trevannion: 'The obsession with the social significance of naming evident in Bennett's Welsh novels becomes itself a textual marker of an anxiety focused on the relationship between changing inheritance patterns, that is, weakened kinship and emergent Britishness.'

25   Quotations from *Anna* in this essay are taken from the fourth edition (1796), printed for William Lane at the Minerva Press.

26   A perpetual fund of first-fruits and tenths, known as Queen Anne's Bounty, was granted by charter of Queen Anne and confirmed by statute in 1703 for the augmentation of the livings of the poorer Anglican clergy. In *Agnes de Courci* (1789), Julia Neville disguises herself as Betsy 'the orphan daughter of a poor clergyman, who was come up to London to be apprenticed by the fund, a charitable institution as she [Mrs Arnold] explained, for the benefit of the children of the inferior clergy' (III, p.8).

27   Kathryn R. King, 'Of Needles and Pens and Women's Work', *Tulsa Studies in Women's Literature*, XIV, 1 (Spring 1995), 77–93, discusses text/textile and pen/needle figures in women's writing, with particular reference to Jane Barker's *A Patch-Work Screen for Ladies* (1723) and Charlotte Smith's *Old Manor House* (1794). Her references to other studies of the significance of needlework in women's writing include Cecilia Macheski, 'Penelope's Daughters: Images of Needlework in Eighteenth-Century Literature', in

Mary Anne Schofield and Cecilia Macheski (eds), *Fetter'd or Free? British Women Novelists 1670–1785* (Athens: Ohio University Press, 1986), pp.85–100, and Josephine Donovon, 'Women and the Rise of the Novel: A Feminist-Marxist Theory', *Signs: Journal of Women in Culture and Society*, XVI, 3 (1991), 441–62. Interestingly in terms of Anna Maria Bennett's possible identification with her heroine, Donovon sees textile production as furnishing Barker with legitimizing models for her own art as a writer, though King questions the link between a 'use-value ethos' and an essentially ornamental screen produced by a gentlewoman in an aristocratic setting. It is not impossible that Bennett's anxieties, as expressed in the text of *Anna* and explored in the present essay, may reflect her own questioning of the use and value of a novel which rejects the mantua maker in favour of the Welsh heiress.

28 Isaac Wilkinson was associated with the Merthyr iron industry from 1757 to 1771. See W. H. Chaloner, 'Isaac Wilkinson, Potfounder', in L. S. Pressnel (ed.), *Studies in the Industrial Revolution* (London: University of London, The Athlone Press, 1960), pp.23–51. In *Anna*, Bennett's Wilkinson is given a potentially interesting history – after being brought up in a workhouse, he is apprenticed to a whitesmith and eventually becomes manager of the iron works at Llandore – but, in order to make him eligible to marry Patty Herbert, it is eventually revealed that he is a sprig of the nobility, the son of the villain Gorget.

29 Eric Pawson, *Transport and Economy: The Turnpike Roads of Eighteenth Century Britain* (London: Academic Press, 1977), pp.153, 283, notes that Brecon and Monmouth were connected by a weekly coach to London in 1763, that is, before the turnpiking of all the main roads in Breconshire in 1767. Anna's journey thus seems to belong to the period 1763–6.

30 *The European Magazine* (1790), cited in Blain et al., *Feminist Companion*, describes Bennett's brother as a reputable City attorney.

31 King, 'Of Needles and Pens', 84. Like Anna, Monimia is orphaned from birth and brought up by a series of surrogate mothers. However, she is allowed to do only the plainest of needlework; when later in the novel she becomes a seamstress to relieve her family's financial distress, she sews *secretly* to spare her husband's feelings.

Notes to Chapter 11

1 J. G. Lockart, *Memoirs of Sir Walter Scott* (London: Macmillan, 1900), I, p.259. In 1799, Scott sent a version of *The House of Aspen* to Monk Lewis; the play was read and much recommended by 'the celebrated actress, Mrs Esten' and taken up by J. P. Kemble. But, although rehearsed for the stage, it was later abandoned. According to Dorothy Blakey, *The Minerva Press 1790–1820* (London: Oxford University Press, 1935), p.54, three of Anna Maria Bennett's novels were in the library at Abbotsford.

2 See the entry under 'Esten, Mrs James' in Philip H. Highfill, Kaman A. Burnim and Edward A. Langhans (eds), *A Biographical Dictionary of Actors,*

Actresses, Musicians, Dancers, Managers & Other Stage Personnel in London, 1600–1800 (Carbondale and Edwardsville: Southern Illinois University Press, 1978), V, pp.104–10.

3   James Boaden, *Memoirs of the Life of John Philip Kemble, Esq.* (London: Longman, 1825), II, p.26.
4   Ibid., II, p.27.
5   Highfill et al., *Biographical Dictionary*.
6   In the letter to Colonel Hunter that prefaces *Agnes de Courci*, Anna Maria Bennett acknowledges the compliment he has paid to *Anna*, and proceeds to the subject 'dearer to my heart, than the vital stream which animates it':

> Where shall a mother, whose existence is in her children, who fancies she sees in them every perfection, whose anxious solicitude for their welfare is the business of her life? where shall she find a language? how put into words her thankful gratitude to the invaluable friend; whose open heart, and supporting hand, was extended to her beloved child! whose goodness and penetration, removed the veil, which humility had cast over a timid young female; who encouraged, and upheld her; who by a noble perseverance, and steady kindness, called forth those sparks of genius, which but for him, would have shrunk, like the delicate sensative, from the rude touch of envy, and oppression; and who, when emulative pride had rendered her more worthy, procured for her, the first of all protections; that of – women of *virtue*! and men of *honor*! . . . May the benevolent kindness you have so happily in your power, and still more happily in your will, to communicate to others; be a perpetual source of peace, and tranquility to yourself. And may every being for whom you are interested, flourish like, HARRIET ESTEN, under the genial warmth of your protecting friendship; and like her also; ever remember, to *whom* they are ultimately indebted, for the success, which the sanction, and good wishes of so worthy a man must ensure.

7   Harriet Hunter Wildman Esten married Thomas Darby Coventry of Henley-on-Thames at St George, Hanover Square, on 21 December 1809 (Highfill et al., *Biographical Dictionary*).
8   Ibid. J. F. Fuller, 'A Curious Genealogical Muddle', *Miscellanea Genealogica et Heraldica*, Fourth Series, V (1914), 244–7, gives an account of Harriet Esten's connection with Douglass, 8th Duke of Hamilton (1756–99).
9   Highfill et al., *Biographical Dictionary*. For accounts of the dispute about the lease of the Theatre Royal, Edinburgh, see *Memorial for Robert Playfair, writer in Edinburgh, Trustee for the Creditors of John Jackson, late Manager of the Theatre-Royal, Edinburgh, and for Mrs. Harriet Pye Esten, Lessee of the said Theatre-Royal* (1793), *Memoirs of Charles Lee Lewes* (London: Richard Phillips, 1805) and James C. Dibdin, *The Annals of the Edinburgh Stage* (1888), pp.206–22.
10 Elizabeth Whitlock (Stephen Kemble's sister) and her husband were engaged by Harriet Esten in 1793. See entry for 'Whitlock, Mrs Charles Edward' in Highfill et al., *Biographical Dictionary*, XVI, pp.45–51.

11 *Ellen, Countess of Castle Howel* was published by William Lane at the Minerva Press (London, 1794), 4 vols. Quotations in this chapter are taken from this edition.
12 Highfill et al., *Biographical Dictionary*, refers to Harriet Esten's daughter as Anne Douglas Hamilton (born July 1794, married 3rd Baron Rossmore 25 June 1820, died childless 20 August 1844). Her portrait is reproduced in Fuller, 'Genealogical Medley', facing p.244.
13 Francesca Rhydderch, 'Dual Nationality, Divided Identity: Ambivalent Narratives of Britishness in the Welsh Novels of Anna Maria Bennett', *Welsh Writing in English: A Yearbook of Critical Essays*, III (1997), 1–17.
14 Ibid., 6–7.
15 The term is Jane Aaron's ('that passionate libidinousness which was considered the hallmark of the wild Welsh hoyden') in a study of some later manifestations of the literary stereotype. See 'The Hoydens of Wild Wales: Representations of Welsh Women in Victorian and Edwardian Fiction', *Welsh Writing in English: A Yearbook of Critical Essays*, I (1995), 23–39.
16 Fanny Burney, *Evelina, or, The History of a Young Lady's Entrance into the World* (Oxford: Oxford University Press, 1991), [p.7].
17 Rhydderch, 'Dual Nationality, Divided Identity', 9–10.
18 Sophia Lee (1750–1824), with her sister Harriet, ran a school at Bath from the early 1780s to 1803. By the time *Ellen* appeared in 1794, she had published a comedy, *The Chapter of Accidents* (1780), an historical novel, *The Recess* (1783–5), which went through five editions by 1804, and a ballad, *A Hermit's Tale* (1787). See entry for Sophia Lee in Virginia Blain, Patricia Clements and Isobel Grundy (eds), *The Feminist Companion to Literature in English* (London: B. T. Batsford, 1990).
19 In *A Letter to the Women of England, on the Injustice of Mental Insubordination* (1799), published under the name of Anne Frances Randall but attributed to Mary Robinson, the author objects to the fact that women are not taught to swim (pp.62–3) and argues that they should be allowed to play ball and take part in 'foot racing' (p.88). Had she the fortune to do so, she would build a university for women (pp.92–3). 'Mrs Bennet Novelist' is included in the list of 'Female Literary Characters' appended to the *Letter*.
20 Blakey, *Minerva Press*, refers to Coleridge's note on his copy of *Conciones ad Populum* that *The Beggar Girl* was 'the best novel me judice since Fielding' and his view in *Table Talk and Omniana* that Scott's comic characters would not bear comparison with Betty Brown.
21 *Monthly Review*, new series, XIV (1794), 74–7. The Bodleian Library copy is annotated, apparently in a contemporary hand, with the initials of the reviewers. In the case of *Ellen, Countess of Castle Howel*, however, the note reads 'Anon. a Lady. Rec^d from D^r B–y'.
22 Rhydderch, 'Dual Nationality, Divided Identity', 12.
23 Judith Lowder Newton, *Women, Power & Subversion: Social Strategies in British Fiction 1778–1860* (New York: Methuen, 1985), p.176, quoting E. J. Hobsbawm, *Industry and Empire* (Baltimore: Penguin Books, 1968), pp.29, 32,

and *The Age of Revolution: 1789–1848* (New York: New American Library, 1962), pp.49, 65.
24 Public Record Office, PROB 11/1136.
25 Fuller, 'Genealogical Medley'.

Notes to Chapter 12

1 Gerald Morgan, 'The First Anglo-Welsh Novel', *Anglo-Welsh Review*, XVII, no.39 (1968), 114–22.
2 [W. J. Rees], 'Memoir of the Rev. Edward Davies', *Cambrian Quarterly Magazine*, III, no.12 (1831), 408–36.
3 Frank R. Lewis, 'Edward Davies, 1756–1831', *Transactions of the Radnorshire Society*, XXXIX (1969), 8–23. Lewis makes extensive use of the Tonn Collection at Cardiff Central Library, which includes many of Davies's surviving manuscripts.
4 Rees, 'Memoir', 410.
5 Ibid.
6 Ibid., 413.
7 Ibid.
8 Meic Stephens (ed.), *The Oxford Companion to the Literature of Wales* (Oxford: Oxford University Press, 1986), p.128.
9 A. L. Owen, *The Famous Druids: A Survey of Three Centuries of English Literature on the Druids* (Oxford: Clarendon Press, 1962), p.216, is merciless:

> In intention, *The Mythology and Rites of the British Druids* offers an exhaustive analysis of poetry which preserves the secrets of the Druids. In so far as Davies's arguments are founded on wrongly dated texts, an approximate equivalent of the task he set himself would be an attempt to prove that the first fifty poems in *The Golden Treasury*, for instance, originally formed part of the Arthurian cycle. With this analogy in mind, it can be appreciated that his mistranslations are only a minor feature of so intricate an assembly of error and fallacy that its author's orchestration, as it were, is itself remarkable.

10 Tonn Ms.3.104, vol.6.
11 The manuscript of *Owen, or, The Fatal Clemency* (Tonn Ms 3.87) has corrections in Graves's hand; both the play and a prose fragment of twelve manuscript pages (referred to as 'The Abortion'), deal with British resistance against the Romans in the reign of Guiderius. The prose tale, written 'in the animated language of my British original', is presumably based on the fourteenth-century manuscript known as the *Brut Tysilio*, now recognized as a version of Geoffrey of Monmouth.
12 Neither Graves nor Davies were published by William Lane's Minerva Press.
13 Lewis, 'Edward Davies', 21, identifies the reference to Anna Seward's *Louisa, a Poetical Novel in Four Epistles* (Lichfield, 1784).
14 Rees, 'Memoir', 417.

15 *Aphtharte, The Genius of Britain. A Poem, Written in the Taste of the Sixteenth Century*, printed by R. Cruttwell (Bath, 1784). On the title-page, Davies is referred to as the Master of the Free Grammar School, Chipping Sodbury.
16 Ibid., p.18.
17 Linda Colley, *Britons: Forging the Nation 1707–1837* (London: Pimlico, 1994), charts the emergence of 'Great Britain' in the eighteenth century.
18 In 'Alexis', a pastoral poem written in May 1774 and printed in *Vacunalia* (1788), Davies laments the departure of a shepherd ('Wallia knew no lovelier swain') for the martial plain ('forc'd to leave his flocks / Without a shepherd on Carneddau's rocks!'). At the age of eighteen, Davies was already opposed to Britain's role in what was to become the American War of Independence:

> And must Britannia's valiant heroes bleed?
> Yes civil discord, thou hast done the deed.
> The Queen of nations who could well deride
> With native force, a threatening world beside,
> Who conquer'd empires on th'Atlantic shore,
> Now stains her honour, in her children's gore. (*Vacunalia*, p.157)

Alexis would willingly strike a blow against his country's foe, but he is being urged to cross the flood ('hateful thought') to shed a brother's blood.

19 Prys Morgan, *A New History of Wales: The Eighteenth Century Renaissance* (Llandybïe: Christopher Davies, 1981), p.39. Morgan devotes a chapter, 'The Discovery of the Past' (pp.67–100), to the recovery of the Welsh literary tradition.
20 William Owen (1759–1835), who became one of Davies's correspondents, is principally remembered for his involvement in the publications of the Gwyneddigion Society and as a lexicographer of the Welsh language. He took his uncle's name (Pughe) when he inherited his estate in 1806. See entry for William Owen in Meic Stephens (ed.), *The Oxford Companion to the Literature of Wales* (Oxford: Oxford University Press, 1986).
21 Edward Williams (1747–1826), usually referred to by his bardic name, Iolo Morganwg, was a stonemason by trade but operated also as a poet in Welsh and English, a copyist, a collector of manuscripts, an antiquarian, a radical in politics, a Unitarian in religion – and a notorious forger. In 1792 he organized the first public meeting of the Druidical society, the Gorsedd Beirdd Ynys Prydain. By the 1890s much of Iolo Morganwg's work, especially that part relating to Druidism, had become suspect in the eyes of scholars such as John Morris-Jones. In *Iolo Morganwg a Chywyddau'r Ychwanegiad* (1926), Griffith John Williams exposed Iolo's contributions to *Barddoniaeth Dafydd ab Gwilym* (1789) as forgeries. See entry for Edward Williams in *The Oxford Companion to the Literature of Wales*.
22 Lewis, 'Edward Davies', locates two copies of Edward Davies's translations of Dafydd ap Gwilym and the prefatory essay addressed to the Gwyneddigion Society. The copy in the National Library of Wales has a note by Davies

under the pseudonym Iorwerth ap Dewi. A second copy, with the pencilled title 'Specimens of an English Metrical Translation of the more ancient Welsh Bards, and of Dafydd ab Gwilym' in W. J. Rees's handwriting, is in the Cardiff Central Library (Tonn Ms.3.99). Quotations in the present essay are from the Cardiff copy.

23 The letter from Davies to Pughe, dated 26 March 1792, is in Cardiff Central Library (Tonn Ms.3.86) and quoted by Lewis, 'Edward Davies', 15.

24 John Walters (1721–97), rector of Llandough near Cowbridge, is remembered for his English–Welsh dictionary (1779–83). See entry in *The Oxford Companion to the Literature of Wales*.

25 *The Myvyrian Archaiology of Wales* (1801–7), which aimed to publish Welsh poetry from manuscript sources – but which also contained many forgeries by Iolo Morganwg – was edited by William Owen Pughe and Owen Jones ('Owain Myfyr').

26 Letter from Iolo Morganwg to the Bath bookseller, William Meyler (Tonn Ms.3.104). Quoted by Lewis, 'Edward Davies', 13–14.

27 *Cambrian Register*, III (1818), 436–68.

28 Morgan, *A New History of Wales*, p.100.

29 Entry for Theophilus Evans in *The Oxford Companion to the Literature of Wales*.

30 In a footnote explaining a reference to 'Cassibe'lan', Davies quotes four lines in Welsh, said to be a stanza in imitation of Lucan: 'I retain it only from memory, having seen it some years ago in the Rev. Mr. Evans's Drych y prif oesoedd' (*Aphtharte*, p.13).

31 *Fifteen Letters, in Explanation of the Essay on the Art of Writing and Origin of Celtic Dialects* (1802) [no page numbers]. Rees, 'Memoir', 410, records that Theophilus Jones dedicated the second volume of his *History of Brecknockshire* (1809) to Edward Davies, 'the associate of his youth, the kind correspondent, and assistant in his literary pursuits, and the sincere friend in mature age'.

32 'In stature he was about the middle height; in early life he was slender, but in advanced age he had become somewhat corpulent. He was so modest and diffident of his abilities, as to be generally reserved and silent in company or among strangers; and as opposition to his sentiments had been the means of exciting him to undertake his literary works, so in order to induce him to speak, recourse was sometimes had by those acquainted with his character, to mention something which they knew to be contrary to his opinion, by which means he was induced to deliver his sentiments. He considered his diffidence to be a great obstacle to his early success in life.' Rees, 'Memoir', 435.

33 *Vacunalia*, pp.21–2.

34 Ibid., pp.51–2.

35 If Davies appears here to be having a joke at the expense of Ossian, he treats the Gaelic poet with great respect elsewhere in his writings. *Vacunalia* includes a 'translation' into English verse (presumably from Macpherson's English prose) of the first book of *Temora*, together with a preface in which he hedges his bets on the authenticity of Ossian. Bound with the copy of *Vacunalia* in Cardiff Central Library is Davies's transcription of the second book, still in manuscript, together with other fragments and a note explaining that when he

carried out the versification, he had worked hastily, intending to correct it later: 'As I have no access at present to the works of Ossian, I transcribed the papers without alteration merely to preserve them to a future opportunity.' According to Lewis, 'Edward Davies', 17, *The Claims of Ossian*, published in 1825, was written about twenty years earlier.

36 *Vacunalia*, pp.47–8.

37 'PROCLAMATION FOR A MEETING OF THE BARDS, *At Midsummer*, 1798' is bound with a volume of letters to Edward Davies (Tonn Ms.3.104, vol.6). In 1797, the sun being in 'ALBAN HEVIN' or the summer solstice, an invitation is given to all who might seek for privilege and graduation in science and bardism to repair to the London meeting upon Primrose-hill, to the Chair of Glamorgan upon Tyle y Gwawl and to the Chair of North Wales at Caerwys, 'where there will not be a NAKED WEAPON AGAINST THEM'. There is more of this, ending with the resounding 'Y GWIR YN ERBYN Y BYD! THE TRUTH, IN OPPOSITION TO THE WORLD!' The note that follows is rather an anticlimax, directing candidates for the prize for the best translation into Welsh of Gray's 'The Bard' to send their productions to Messrs Williams in the Strand, to Mr E. Williams (Iolo himself) at Flimston, or to the Revd Mr Lloyd at Caerwys.

38 Llywelyn ap Gruffudd (Y Llyw Olaf) was killed by English troops in December 1282 at a bridge over the Irfon near Builth. His headless body is said to have been buried at Cwm Hir Abbey.

39 Morgan, *A New History of Wales*, p.80.

40 *Additional Letters of the Morrises*, ed. Hugh Owen (London: Honourable Society of Cymmrodorion, 1947–9), II, p.349.

41 Janet Todd, *The Sign of Angellica: Women, Writing and Fiction (1660–1700)* (London: Virago Press, 1989), p.180. In her chapter on 'The Fantasy of Sensibility', Todd deals mainly with *The History of Lady Julia Mandeville* (1763) by Frances Brooke, *The Histories of Lady Frances S– and Lady Caroline* (1763) by Margaret and Susannah Gunning, and *Coombe Wood* (1783) by Susannah Gunning.

42 Todd, *Sign of Angellica*, p.177.

43 Ibid., p.182.

44 Rees, 'Memoir', 416–17.

Notes to Chapter 13

1 Marguerite Steen, *The Lost One: A Biography of Mary (Perdita) Robinson* (London: Methuen, 1937), p.122. Dorothy George lists the print as 'Florizel and Perdita', no.5767 in the British Library *Catalogue of Personal and Political Satires*, Vol.V, and likewise describes Perdita as wearing 'a high-crowned Welsh hat on the top of a pyramid of hair with its head-dress of lace and ribbons'. Florizel is wearing Roman armour and the insignia of the Prince of Wales. A medallion on the wall of what appears to be the Green Room at

Drury Lane shows a nymph and goatherd, surmounted by a Cupid complete with bow and arrows but wearing yet another high-crowned Welsh hat decorated with a leek.
2   Bristol Record Office.
3   Patricia Meyer Spacks, *Imagining a Self: Autobiography and Novel in Eighteenth-Century England* (Cambridge, Mass.: Harvard University Press, 1976), p.73.
4   *Memoirs of the Late Mrs. Robinson* (London: Cobden-Sanderson, 1930), p.3. All subsequent quotations from the *Memoirs* are from this edition. *Memoirs of the Late Mrs. Robinson, Written by Herself*, ed. M. E. Robinson, was first published in 1801 in four volumes.
5   The world remained hostile even after her death. Shortly after she died, two letters in *The Lady's Monthly Museum*, VI (1801), 259, 382, objected to articles that had recently appeared on Mrs Robinson, one declaring 'we surely want not public panegyrics upon characters which have been lost to decency and shame', the other demanding: 'was not this lady an adulteress?'
6   According to G. T. Clark, *Limbus Patrum Morganiae at Glamorgianae* (1886), Richard Seys had two sons and three daughters: Evan, William, Ann (wife of Lord King), Elizabeth (successively wife of Evan Seys, Lewis Price and James Black) and Margaret (recorded in Burke's *Landed Gentry* as the wife of George Lucas). In her *Memoirs*, Mary Robinson makes much of Lady King and her connections: 'The sister of my great-grandmother, named Anne, married Peter Lord King, who was nephew, in the female line, to the learned and truly illustrious John Locke – a name that has acquired celebrity which admits of no augmented panegyric' (p.3).
7   Jane Kemys was born in 1685, married Sir John Tynte of Halsewell, Somerset, about 1704, and died in Bath in 1747 (GEC, *Complete Baronetage*).
8   Prys Morgan, *Iolo Morganwg* (Cardiff: University of Wales Press, 1975), p.1, records that Iolo's mother, Anne Mathew (or Matthews), who came of an old Coychurch family, was brought up as the proverbial 'poor relation' with her Seys kinsfolk at Boverton. However, according to Ceri W. Lewis, *Iolo Morganwg* (Caernarfon: Gwasg Pantycelyn, 1995), p.19:

> Cafodd Ann Matthew [sic], a oedd yn ferch i Edward Matthews o Dy'nycaeau ym mhlwyf Llangrallo, ei chodi, er pan oedd yn naw mlwydd oed, ym mhlas teulu'r Seisiaid (Seys) yn Nhrebefered, yn ymyl Llan-faes, a chael y math hwnnw o addysg a roddid yn y cyfnod hwnnw i ferch fonheddig – tipyn o lenyddiaeth Saesneg, dysgu canu a gwaith nodwydd, ychydig bach o Ffrangeg, a llai byth o Eidaleg. Yn ôl Iolo, 'she was brought up and educated in a manner that was rather disadvantageous to a woman of no fortune. she had all the qualifications but Wealth that could be required in the Wife of a Peer of the Realm, but it was her lot to marry a mason.'
> [Ann Matthew [sic], daughter of Edward Matthews of Ty'nycaeau in the parish of Llangrallo, was brought up from the age of nine in the mansion of the Seys family in Treberfedd near Llanfaes, and had the kind of education that was given at that period to an upper-class girl – a little English literature, singing and

needlework, a little French and even less Italian. According to Iolo 'she was . . .' (as above)]

9   Somerset Record Office.

10   See M. H. Jones, *The Trevecka Letters* (Caernarfon: Welsh Calvinistic Methodist Church, 1932), pp.48–51, and the entry under 'Thomas Harris' in the *Dictionary of Welsh Biography* (London: Honourable Society of Cymmrodorion, 1940).

11   In a letter to his mother on 17 November 1750, Joseph Harris reported that 'I saw brother Thos and Sister in law very well'. On 12 February 1752/53, Thomas Harris wrote to Howel that 'My Wife Joynes in Love to you & all frinds [sic]'. On 29 March 1754, Howel told Thomas that 'My Wife Joyns in Love to y^r self and Sist$^{r'}$ (Gomer M. Roberts, 'Gleanings from the Trevecka Letters', *Brycheiniog*, III (1957), 130, 131, 133). R. T. Jenkins fails to identify Harris's wife ('Pwy oedd hi, a pha bu farw, ni wyr neb hyd yn hyn') in 'Etifeddion Harrisiaid Trefeca', *Y Traethodydd*, XXIX (1961), 156–62.

12   For a succinct account of the Trefeca community and its subsequent history as a theological college, see Gareth Davies, 'Trevecka (1706–1964)', *Brycheiniog*, XV (1971), 41–56, reprinted as a pamphlet by the Brecknock Society.

13   'He's a very model for our country 'squires. He rides hard, drinks hard . . . 'Twas but at the last meeting he put an exciseman in the stocks, for getting drunk, and swearing. "Damn the fellow," says his worship . . .' (*Angelina*, I, p.49).

14   For the founding of the seminary at Trefeca, see Edwin Welch, *Spiritual Pilgrim: A Reassessment of the Life of the Countess of Huntingdon* (Cardiff: University of Wales Press, 1995).

15   Herbert M. Vaughan, 'A Synopsis of Two Tours made in Wales in 1775 and 1811', *Y Cymmrodor*, XXXVIII (1927), 54–5.

16   Entry under 'Thomas Harris' in the *Dictionary of Welsh Biography*.

17   Maria Elizabeth Robinson's novel, *The Shrine of Bertha* (1794) predates both *Angelina* and *Walsingham*. It was dedicated 'TO THE BEST OF MOTHERS' and included a number of Mary Robinson's poems. Writing from Lausanne, the heroine of *The Shrine of Bertha* celebrates Rousseau ('Often did *fancy* point out the rocks, the woods, the very seats of *St. Preux* and *Julie*' (II, p.35)); writing from Vienna, she claims that the master engaged to teach her German had tutored Charlotte 'so celebrated in the interesting, but dangerous story of the unfortunate WERTER' (II, p.127). In an extraordinary footnote, the author assures her readers that 'This anecdote may be relied on. The gentleman alluded to was the *Authoress's Language-Master*, during her *residence in Germany*, and she gives it from *his authority*' (II, p.128). After editing her mother's *Memoirs* (1801), Maria Elizabeth Robinson brought out an anthology of poetry, *The Wild Wreath* (1804), dedicated to the Duchess of York and illustrated by Mrs B. Tarleton, presumably the wife who replaced Mary Robinson in Banastre Tarleton's affections. She includes a number of her mother's poems, among them 'The Foster-Child'.

18. Thomas Harris's will, National Library of Wales, Tredegar 70/329.
19. See Robert D. Bass, *The Green Dragoon: The Lives of Banastre and Mary Robinson* (London: Alvin Redman, 1957).
20. Coleridge professed great admiration for Mary Robinson as a poet and stoutly declared after her death that 'in *my* eyes, and in *my* belief, [she] was in her latter life – a blameless Woman'. Earl Leslie Griggs, 'Coleridge and Mrs. Mary Robinson', *Modern Language Notes*, XLV (February 1930), 90–5, also records Coleridge's refusal to contribute to a volume of elegies in her memory [presumably M. E. Robinson's edition of her mother's *Memoirs*], his excuse being that as a husband and father, he could not allow his name to be connected with contributors like 'Monk' Lewis and Peter Pindar. He seems, however, to have suffered only a temporary failure of nerve: *The Wild Wreath* includes 'The Mad Monk' alongside poems by M. G. Lewis.
21. In addition to the 'Welsh' poems included in the text of *Walsingham*, Mary Robinson wrote 'Llwhen and Gwyneth. Written in the Year 1782. From Mr. John Williams's prose translation of a lately discovered Welsh Poem, preserved in the Collection of Arthur Price, Esq. It is supposed to have been written by Taliesin, in Ben Batridd, A.D. 534' (*Poetical Works* (1824), pp.93–4).
22. *Angelina* (1796) was printed for the author and sold by Hookham and Carpenter in three volumes. Quotations in this chapter are from this edition.
23. Felicity Nussbaum, 'Heteroclites: The Gender of Character in the Scandalous Memoirs', in Felicity Nussbaum and Laura Brown (eds), *The New Eighteenth Century: Theory, Politics, English Literature* (New York: Methuen, 1987), p.152.
24. 'I was introduced about this time by Merry the poet (to the) most accomplished and delightful woman, the celebrated Mrs. Robinson' ('Autobiographical Fragments and Reflections', in *Collected Novels and Memoirs of William Godwin*, ed. Mark Philp (London: William Pickering, 1992), I, p.51). In his Journal, Godwin noted five meetings with Mary Robinson in February and March 1796 (Kenneth Neill Cameron (ed.), *Shelley and his Circle 1773–1822* (Cambridge, Mass.: Harvard University Press, 1970), I, p.234). Robert Merry (1755–98) lived in Florence from 1784 to 1787 and was a founder-member of the Della Crusca Academy, a group of expatriate English poets. Mrs Piozzi contributed to the *Miscellany* edited by Merry in 1785.
25. Cameron, *Shelley and his Circle*, IV, pp.877–84, identifies Mary Robinson as the likely recipient of a note from Mary Wollstonecraft (bearing the rare signature 'Mary Imlay'), written between 15 April 1796 and 29 March 1797, accepting an invitation to dinner, with Mary Hays as a fellow guest.
26. *The Anti-Jacobin Magazine* (August 1798, February 1800 and April 1800), quoted in Ford K.Brown, *The Life of William Godwin* (London: J. M. Dent, 1926), pp.155–6.
27. *The Anti-Jacobin Magazine* (May 1799), quoted in Brown, *Life of Godwin*, pp.158–9. Eleanor Ty, *Unsex'd Revolutionaries: Five Women Novelists of the 1790s* (Toronto: University of Toronto Press, 1993), focuses on Mary Wollstonecraft, Mary Hays, Helen Maria Williams, Charlotte Smith and Elizabeth Inchbald.

28 Written under the pen-name of Anne Frances Randall and first published as *Thoughts on the Condition of Women, and on the Injustice of Mental Subordination* (1798). A facsimile of the *Letter* is reproduced in Marie Mulvey Roberts and Tamae Mizuta (eds), *The Radicals: Revolutionary Women* (London: Routledge/Thoemmes Press, 1994).

29 Bass, *Green Dragoon*, pp.381, 398.

30 M. Ray Adams, 'Mrs. Mary Robinson: A Study of her Later Career', *Studies in the Literary Backgrounds of English Radicalism* (Lancaster, Pennsylvania: Franklin & Marshall Press, 1947), pp.104–29.

31 Gary Kelly, *The English Jacobin Novel 1780–1805* (Oxford: Clarendon Press, 1976), p.226.

32 Introduction to facsimile reprint of the first edition of *Walsingham*, ed. Peter Garside (London: Routledge/Thoemmes Press, 1992).

33 Kelly, *The English Jacobin Novel*, p.212.

34 Quotations from *Walsingham, or, The Pupil of Nature* in this chapter are taken from the first edition (1797), printed for T. N. Longman in four volumes.

35 Quotations from *Fleetwood* in this chapter are taken from the first edition (1805), printed for Richard Phillips.

36 *The New Oxford Book of Eighteenth Century Verse*, ed. Roger Lonsdale (Oxford: Oxford University Press, 1987), p.571. Parts I and II of *The Minstrel* (1771, 1774) by James Beattie, traced 'the progress of a poetical Genius, born in a rude age, from the first dawning of fancy and reason'. It was reprinted many times.

37 In *The Wild Wreath* (1804), Maria Elizabeth Robinson includes a poem by her mother, 'The Foster-Child. In Imitation of Spenser', written on 22 October 1800, only two months before her death. It is a poem of fifty-five stanzas, divided into two cantos, beginning ''Mid Cambria's hills a lowly cottage stood' and tells the story of a boy of stature low and brow of swarthy hue, left at the cottage by a mysterious lady. It includes the stanzas 'With ebon locks unkempt . . .' already printed in *Walsingham*. 'The Foster-Child' was reprinted in Mary Robinson's *Poems* (1824).

38 When Fleetwood visits the House of Commons, he sees the benches where 'Pym and Hambden [*sic*], and Falkland and Selden, and Cromwel [*sic*] and Vane sat together, to decide, perhaps for ever, on the civil and intellectual liberties of my country.' (I, p.143)

39 Adams, 'Mrs Mary Robinson', p124.

40 *The Analytical Review*, no.27 (January 1798), 80–3, quoted by Garside, in Introduction to *Walsingham*, p.xii.

41 Mary Robinson gave her last performance at Drury Lane as Sir Harry Revel in Lady Craven's comedy, *The Miniature Picture* (*Memoirs*, p.138). A portrait of Robinson as Rosalind in *As You Like It* hangs in the Garrick Club.

42 B. J. Tysdahl, *William Godwin as Novelist* (London: Athlone, 1981), p.120.

43 Kelly, *The English Jacobin Novel*, p.238.

44 Kelly chooses Wordsworth's 'Lines Left Upon a Seat in a Yew-Tree' as a basis for comparison with *Fleetwood* (ibid., pp.240–2). Tysdahl, *Godwin as Novelist*,

pp.117–20, prefers a comparison with 'Tintern Abbey', 'Expostulation and Reply' and 'The Tables Turned', commenting that 'the optimistic belief in the good influence from vernal woods and Welsh mountains in the early Wordsworth is so insistent that Godwin's reaction becomes understandable and refreshing'.

[45] Ibid., p.120.
[46] Brown, *Life of Godwin*, p.222.
[47] Cameron, *Shelley and his Circle*, I, pp.233–5, refers to seven letters written by Mary Robinson to Godwin between 30 May and October 1800.
[48] Brown, *Life of Godwin*, p.192.
[49] Cameron, *Shelley and his Circle*, I, p.233.
[50] Ibid., I, p.235, quoting Godwin's Journal for 1 September 1800.
[51] Ibid., quoting Mary Robinson's letter of 10 October 1800.
[52] *Memoirs*, p.191.
[53] Brown, *Life of Godwin*, p.192. John Wolcot (1738–1819) had practised as a physician and taken holy orders before becoming a writer of satirical verse, using the pen-name Peter Pindar.
[54] Cameron, *Shelley and his Circle*, I, p.235, quoting Godwin's Journal for 31 December 1800.

Appendix

EIGHTEENTH-CENTURY FICTIONS OF WALES

This bibliography of eighteenth-century fictions of Wales (broadly defined as novels or memoirs which include Welsh characters, or scenes with a Welsh setting) does not set out to be exhaustive, but it does list in chronological order all the titles I have accumulated from a variety of sources during my research. In each case I list the earliest edition I have been able to identify, and attribute authorship where this is possible. I have not included reprints of seventeenth-century chapbooks.

[Penelope] Aubin, *The Life of Madam de Beaumount*, printed for E. Bell, J. Darby, A. Bettesworth, F. Fayram, J. Pemberton, J. Hooke, C. Rivington, F. Clay, J. Batley and E. Symon, London, 1721.

[William Rufus Chetwood], *The Voyages, Travels and Adventures, of William Owen Gwin Vaughan, Esq.*, printed for J. Watts, sold by J. Osborn, London, 1736, 2 vols.

James Parry, *The True Anti-Pamela, or, Memoirs of Mr. James Parry, Late Organist of Ross in Herefordshire*, printed for the Author, London, 1741.

[Tobias Smollett], *The Adventures of Roderick Random*, printed for J. Osborn, London, 1748, 2 vols.

The Life and Amours of Owen Tideric Prince of Wales, Otherwise Owen Tudor, printed for William Owen, London, 1751. [A translation of *Tideric Prince de Galles*, Paris, 1677, attributed in the British Library Catalogue to one De Curli. See also an earlier translation, *Tudor, A Prince of Wales*, printed by H.H. for Jonathan Edwin, London, 1678, 2 vols.]

A Genuine Account of the Life and Transactions of Howell ap David Price, Gentleman of Wales . . . Written by Himself, printed by T. Osborne, London, 1752.

Samuel Richardson, *The History of Sir Charles Grandison*, printed for S. Richardson and sold by C. Hitch and L. Hawes, London, 1754, 6 vols.

[Sarah Fielding], *The History of Ophelia*, printed for R. Baldwin, London, 1760, 2 vols.

The Parasite, printed for P. Wilson, J. Exshaw, S. Cotter, H. Saunders, E. Watts, J. Potts and J. Williams, Dublin, 1765, 2 vols.

[Charles Jenner], *Letters from Altamont in the Capital, to his Friends in the Country*, printed for T. Becket and P. A. De Hondt, London, 1767.

[Herbert Lawrence], *The Contemplative Man, Or, The History of Christopher Crab Esq. of North Wales*, printed for J. Whiston, London, 1771, 2 vols.

[Tobias Smollett], *The Expedition of Humphry Clinker*, printed for W. Johnston and B. Collins, London and Salisbury, 1771, 3 vols.

[Richard Graves], *The Spiritual Quixote, or, The Summer's Ramble of Mr Geoffry Wildgoose*, printed for J. Dodsley, London, 1773, 3 vols.

Robert Bage, *Mount Henneth*, printed for T. Lowndes, London, 1782, 2 vols.

The Admirable Travels of Messieurs Thomas Jenkins and David Lowellin, London, 1782.

[William Godwin], *Imogen: A Pastoral Romance . . . From the Ancient British*, printed for William Lane, London, 1784.

Catherine Parry, *Eden Vale*, printed for John Stockdale, London, 1784, 2 vols.

[Anna Maria Bennett], *Anna, or, Memoirs of a Welch Heiress*, printed for William Lane, London, 1785, 4 vols.

[Richard Graves], *Eugenius, or, Anecdotes of the Golden Vale*, printed for J. Dodsley, London, 1785, 2 vols.

H. Cartwright, *Retaliation, or, The History of Sir Edward Oswald and Lady Frances Seymour*, printed for F. Noble, London, 1787.

Powis Castle, or, Anecdotes of an Antient Family, printed for W. Lane, London, 1788, 2 vols.

[– Nicholson], *Catherine, or, The Wood of Llewellyn*, printed for W. Lane, 1788.

Charlotte Smith, *Emmeline, or, The Orphan of the Castle*, printed for T. Cadell, London, 1788, 4 vols.

[Elizabeth Ryves], *The Hermit of Snowden, or, Memoirs of Albert and Lavinia*, printed at the Logographic Press under the direction of the Literary Society, sold by J. Walter, C. Stalkes and W. Richardson, London, 1789.

[James White], *Earl Strongbow, or, The History of Richard de Clare and the beautiful Geralda*, printed for J. Dodsley, London, 1789, 2 vols

The Fair Cambrians, printed for William Lane, London, 1790, 3 vols.

James White, *The Adventures of John of Gaunt, Duke of Lancaster*, printed by J. Crowder for G. G. J. and J. Robinson, London, 1790, 3 vols.

R[ichard[G[raves], *Plexippus, or, The Aspiring Plebeian,* London, 1790, 2 vols.

The Rock of Modrec, or, The Legend of St. Eltram; An Ethical Romance. Translated from an Ancient British Manuscript, Lately Discovered among the Ruins of an Abbey in North Wales, printed for W. Brent, London, 1792, 2 vols.

[Anna Maria] Bennett, *Ellen, Countess of Castle Howel*, printed for W. Lane at the Minerva Press, London, 1794, 4 vols.

[Ann] Howell (formerly Hilditch), *Mortimore Castle. A Cambrian Tale*, printed for William Lane at the Minerva Press, London, 1794.

The Observant Pedestrian, or Traits of the Heart: In a Solitary Tour from Caernarvon to London, printed for William Lane at the Minerva Press, London, 1795, 2 vols.

[Edward Davies], *Elisa Powell, or, Trials of Sensibility*, printed for G. G. and J. Robinson, London, 1795, 2 vols.

Isabella Kelly (also Hedgeland), *The Abbey of St. Asaph*, printed for William Lane at the Minerva Press, London, 1795, 3 vols.

[Frances d'Arblay], *Camilla, or, A Picture of Youth*, printed for T. Payne, T. Cadell Jun. and W. Davies, London, 1796, 5 vols.

[Elizabeth] Gunning, *The Orphans of Snowdon*, printed for Lowndes, London, 1796, 3 vols.

[Susanna Minifie] Gunning, *Delves, A Welch Tale*, printed for Lackington, London, 1796, 2 vols.

[Elizabeth Hervey], *The History of Ned Evans*, G. G. and J. Robinson, London, 1796, 4 vols. [sometimes attributed to Jane West].

[Annabella Plumptre], *Montgomery, or, Scenes in Wales*, printed for William Lane at the Minerva Press, London, 1796, 2 vols.

Mary Robinson, *Angelina*, printed for the author, sold by Hookman and Carpenter, London, 1796, 3 vols.

Regina Maria Roche, *The Children of the Abbey*, printed for W. Lane at the Minerva Press, London, 1796, 4 vols.

[William Beckford], *Azemia: A Descriptive and Sentimental Novel. Interspersed with Pieces of Poetry. By Jacquetta Agnetta Mariana Jenks, of Bellgrove Priory in Wales*, printed by and for Sampson Low, 1797, 2 vols.

[Elizabeth Hervey], *The Church of St. Siffrid*, printed for G. G. and J. Robinson, London, 1797, 4 vols. [sometimes attributed to Jane West].

Harriet and Sophia Lee, *The Canterbury Tales*, printed for G. G. and J. Robinson, London, 1797–1805, 5 vols.

Mary Robinson, *Walsingham, or, The Pupil of Nature*, printed for T. N. Longman, London, 1797, 4 vols.

The Stranger, or, Llewellyn Family. A Cambrian Tale, printed at the Minerva Press for William Lane, London, 1798, 2 vols.

Mary Barker, *A Welsh Story*, printed for Hookham and Carpenter, London, 1798, 3 vols.

Emily Clark, *Ianthé, or, the Flower of Caernarvon*, printed for the Author, sold by Hookham and Carpenter, London, 1798, 2 vols.

[Charles Lucas], *The Castle of Saint Donats, or, The History of Jack Smith*, printed at the Minerva Press for William Lane, London, 1798, 3 vols.

[Adelaide O'Keeffe], *Llewellin*, printed and published by G. Cawthorn, British Library, sold also by Messrs Richardson and J. Wright, London, 1799, 3 vols.

[Mary] Robinson, *The Natural Daughter. With Portraits of the Leadenhead Family*, printed for T. N. Longman and O. Rees, London, 1799, 2 vols.

[William] Williams, *The Journal of Llewellin Penrose, a Seaman*, ed. John Eagles, printed for John Murray and William Blackwood, London and Edinburgh, 1815, 4 vols.

Jane Austen, *Love and Freindship and Other Early Works*, Chatto & Windus, London, 1922.

INDEX

Adams, M. Ray 181, 184
'Address to the Summer' 164
Admirable Travels of Messieurs Thomas Jenkins and David Lowellin, The 26, 33–5, 49
Aeneid, The 170
Agnes de Courci 146
Alfred, King 161
Analytical Review, The 185
Aneirin 170
Angelina 172, 176, 178–81, 185
Anna, or, Memoirs of a Welch Heiress xvi, xx, 130–44, 147, 153, 157
Anne, Queen, wife of King James II 20
Anne, Queen 12, 22, 23, 24
Anti-Jacobin Magazine, The 180
Anti-Pamela, or Feign'd Innocence Detected 50
Aphtharte, the Genius of Britain 159, 161, 166
Arthur, King 94, 161
Arviragus 161
Aubin, Penelope xvii, 11, 12–25, 30, 33, 68, 69, 79, 85
Aubrey, John 117, 119
Austen, Jane xiii, xiv, xv, 72, 142

Barbauld, Anna Laetitia 180
Barclay, Alexander 116
Barddoniaeth Dafydd ab Gwilym 163
Barker, Robert 34
Bartholomew, Lucy 95
Battle of La Hogue, The 38
Beasley, Jerry C. 16
Beattie, James 181, 183
Beggar Girl, The 152
Beggar's Opera, The 58, 63

Bennett, Anna Maria xvi, xx, 130–57
Bennett, Caroline Sophia Pye 131
Bennett, Harriet Pye *see* Esten, Harriet
Bennett, Nancy Pye 131
Bennett, Polly Pye 131
Bennett, Thomas 131
Bennett, Thomas Pye 131
Benyowski, Count de 34
Berchem, Nicolaes 112
'Berghem' *see* Berchem, Nicolaes
Bird, Edward 37, 38
Blair, Hugh 115
Blakey, Dorothy xv
Boaden, James 145
Boadicea 161
Boileau, Nicholas Despreaux 80
Boorde, Andrew 2
Boswell, James 80
Bowles and Carver 102
'Bramble, Tabitha' (pen-name of Mary Robinson) 178
Britannia 165
Britannia Antiqua Illustrata 165
Burney, Fanny 150, 153, 181
Button, Thomas 48
Byron, George Gordon, Lord 41

Caesar, Julius 119, 123
Caleb Williams 127, 147, 181
Cambrian Register 164
Camden, William 165
Captain Singleton 34
Caradog (Caratacus) 161
Carter, Elizabeth 69

Index

Cassibe'lan 161
Celtic Researches 159
Cephalus 63
Chambers's penny tracts 2
Characteristicks of Men, Manners, Opinions and Times 69, 75, 77
Charles I, King 3
Charles XII, King of Sweden 24
Charlotta du Pont 20
Charlotte, Queen 161
Chetwood, William Rufus xvii, 27–31, 54
Churchill, James 65
Churchill, John, 1st Duke of Marlborough 22
Citizen of the World, The 85
Claims of Ossian, The 159
Clarissa 76, 181
Clarke, Dr Samuel 115
Claude Lorrain 179
Clemit, Patricia 117, 129
Coleridge, Samuel Taylor 178
Collier, Revd Dr Arthur 77
Collier, Jane 69, 77
Collins, W. J. T. 56
Columbus, Christopher 48, 170
Columella 113
Comus 115, 121, 127
Confessions, Les 55
Contemplative Man, The 81, 82, 87–8
Cooke, William 115
Cooper, James Fenimore 47
Cromwell, Oliver 166, 183
Crouch, Humfrey 8
Cry, The 68, 69, 77, 78
Cullum, Sir Thomas Gery 177

Dafydd ap Gwilym xx, 163, 164
Damon and Delia 115
Darby, Hester 172, 175
Darby, Nicholas 172
Darby, Polly *see* Robinson, Mary
David Simple, The Adventures of 68, 69, 74
Davies, Edward xv, xix, xx, 158–71
Davies, John 22
Davis, Revd Mr, of Bryngwyn 60
Defoe, Daniel xviii, 18, 34
'Della Crusca' (pen-name of Robert Merry) 180
Dickason, D. H. xvii, 26, 37, 38, 40, 41, 42, 44, 46, 47
Discourse Concerning the Being and Attributes of God 115
Disraeli, Benjamin 84
Distressed Welshman, The 2, 8–9

Doning, Mrs 58
Doning, Winifred 57, 58
Dooley, R. B. 20
Drury, Robert xviii, 27, 34, 49
Drych y Prif Oesoedd 165
Dunciad Variorum, The 13

Eagles, John, xvii, 26, 37, 38, 40, 42, 44, 46
Eagles, Thomas 37, 38, 40
Eagleton, Terry 76
Edwards, Mary 176
'Edwin and Angelina' 127
Elisa Powel xv, xix, xx, 158–71
Elizabeth I, Queen 80
Ellen, Countess of Castle Howel xx, 132, 145–57
Émile 112
England, Martha Winburn 116, 123, 126, 127, 128
Enquiry Concerning Political Justice 181
Esten, Harriet xx, 131, 145, 146, 155
Esten, Lieutenant James 145
Eugenius, or, Anecdotes of the Golden Vale xix, 94, 106–13, 160
Eurydice 30
Evans, Anna Maria *see* Bennett, Anna Maria
Evans, David 130
Evans, Revd Evan (Ieuan Brydydd Hir, Ieuan Fardd) 163, 170
Evans, John 130, 131
Evans, Theophilus 164, 165
Evelina 150

Farley's Bristol Newspaper 57
Farren, Elizabeth 145
Fielding, Henry 30, 50, 68, 69, 98
Fielding, Sarah xiv, xvii, 68–79, 85, 86
First Forty Years, The xv
FitzGerald, Hon. Edward, Knight of the Glinn 27
Fleetwood, General Charles 183
Fleetwood, or, The New Man of Feeling xx, 172, 181–9
Foot, Revd James 123, 127
Freneau, Philip Morin 47
Fuller, J. F. 130
Fyrst Boke of the Introduction of Knowledge, The 2

Garrick, David 178
Garside, Peter 181
Gaunt, Peter 3, 4
Gay, John 58

Index

Gentleman's Magazine 164
Genuine Account of the Life and Transactions of Howell ap David Price, Gentleman, A xvi, 26, 31–3
George I, King 23
George III, King 161
George, Jacob 60
Gilmore, Leigh 50
'Glendour' (Owain Glyndŵr) 165
Gododdin, Y 170
Godwin, Edward 114
Godwin, Revd Edwin 114
Godwin, Revd John 114
Godwin, Mary *see* Wollstonecraft, Mary
Godwin, William xix, xx, 87, 114–29, 147, 172, 180, 181–9
Gold Mine, The 159
Goldsmith, Oliver 85, 127
Gorchestion Beirdd Cymru 163
Governess, or, Little Female Academy, The 69
Graves, Charles Caspar 95
Graves, Morgan 94
Graves, Revd Richard xix, 94–113, 159, 160
Gray, Thomas 117, 169
Greyswood, Ambrose 61
Greyswood, Jane 61, 62
Grub Street Journal, The 13
Guardian, The 159
Gulliver's Travels 37
Gusdorf, Georges xviii, 50, 51, 55, 65
Gweledigaetheu y Bardd Cwsc 22
Gwynn, Captain Charles 40

Hakluyt, Richard 48
Hamilton, Ann Douglass, 146, 155
Hamilton, Douglass, 8th Duke of, xx, 131, 146, 155
Hampden, John 183
Harlequin Happy 63
Harlequin Restored 63
Harris, Howel 67, 98–101, 106, 172, 175
Harris, Joseph 175, 178
Harris, Thomas 175, 176, 177, 178
Hays, Mary 180, 181
Haywood, Eliza 50
Henderson, James xv
Henley, Revd John 13
Henry V 2
Herbert, Charlotte *see* Windsor, Viscountess
Hill, Sir Richard 98
Historie of Cambria, Now Called Wales 165
History of the Druids 118
Holbach, Paul Henri, Baron d' 115, 125, 126

Holdsworth, E. 94
Homer xix
Horace 93
Hughes, Anna Maria 178
Hughes, Samuel 178
Hughes, W. J. xv, xviii, 2
Humphry Clinker, The Expedition of 80, 81, 82, 87–93, 95
Hunter, Captain 38
Hunter, Colonel 146
Huntingdon, Countess of 176
Hyde, Anne *see* Anne, Queen, wife of King James II
'Hymn to the Summer' 164

Iliad, The 170
'Immortality Ode, The' ('Intimations of Mortality from Recollections of Early Childhood') 187
Imogen: A Pastoral Romance from the Ancient British xix, xx, 114–29
Inchbald, Elizabeth 180
Iolo Morganwg xx, 117, 163, 164, 169, 173
Iorwerth ap Dewi *see* Davies, Edward
Irigaray, Luce 19
Italian Letters 115

'Jail, The' 167–9
James II, King 18, 20, 22, 23
Jeffries, Dicky 61
Jeffries, Thomas 62
Jenkins, Geraint H. 82
Jenkins, Philip 82
Jenner, Revd Charles xvii, 81, 85–7
Johnson, Dr Samuel xvi, xvii, 13, 80, 81, 84
Jones, Gwyn xv
Jones, Revd John 177
Jones, John of Llanasa 110
Jones, Revd Malachi 114
Jones, Rice 163
Jones, Dr Samuel 114
Jones, Theophilus 166
Joseph Andrews, The History of the Adventures of 50
Joseph Arkwright's Mill 111
Journal of Llewellin Penrose, a Seaman, The xvii, xviii, 26, 27, 35–48, 49
Jupiter and Juno 63
Juvenal 80

Kahane, Claire 19
Kelly, Gary 181, 186

Kelsall, Malcolm 74
Kemble, Stephen 146
Kemys, Sir Charles 173
Kemys, Jane *see* Tynte, Lady
King, Kathryn R. 139
Knapp, Lewis 90
Kristeva, Julia 19

Lane, William 115, 157, 160
Lawrence, Herbert xvii, 81, 87–8
Lectures on History and General Policy 107
Ledwick, Revd Edward 116–17
Lee and Phillips's booth 63
Lee, Sophia 151
Lejeune, Philippe 50
Letter to the Women of England, A 180
Letters from Altamont 81, 82, 85–7
Lewes, Charles Lee 130, 131, 133
Lewis, Elizabeth *see* Plymouth, Countess of
Lewis, Frank R. 158
Lhuyd, Edward 164
Life and Adventures of Lady Lucy, The 22
Life and Death of Sheffery Morgan, The 2, 9–10
Life and Surprizing Adventures of James Wyatt, The 65, 66
Life of Madam de Beaumount, The 12–25
Llanover, Lady 141
Llywelyn the Last 170
Locke, Don 126, 128
London, a Poem in Imitation of the Third Satire of Juvenal xvi, 80, 81
Loomis, E. xv
Lord, Peter 7, 9
Louis XIV, King 21
Love and Freindship xiii, xiv, 72
'Lycidas' 117
Lyles, Albert M. 98
Lyrical Ballads 87

McBurney, William H. 20, 21
Mackenzie, Henry 186
Madan, Martin 98
Madog ab Owain Gwynedd 48
Malthus, Thomas 96
Man of Feeling, The 186
Mandel, Barrett J. 26, 33, 59
Mansel, Robert 48
Mansfield Park xiv
Marat, Jean-Paul 179, 180
Marken, Jack W. 115, 116
Marshal, James 189
Mary, Queen 22
Matthew, Ann 173

Melville, Herman 47
Memoirs of Charles Lee Lewes 130
Memoirs of the Late Mrs Robinson 172, 173, 175, 177, 180
Merry Masqueraders, The 13
Merry, Robert 180
Metamorphoses 106
Milbank, Alison 19
Millenium Hall, Description of 69
Milton, John 108, 117, 128
Minstrel, The 182, 183
Montagu, Elizabeth 69
Montaigne, Michel Eyquem de 55
Moral Sentiments, The Theory of 75
Moralists: A Philosophical Rhapsody, The 71
More, Hannah 175, 180
Morgan, Elizabeth 94
Morgan, Prys 104, 163, 164, 170
Morgan, Richard 94
Morgan, Thomas 94
Morning Post, The 178
Morris, Lewis 82, 170
Motet's collection of wild beasts 65
Muscipula, sive, Cambro-mua-machia 94
Mythology and Rites of the British Druids, The 159
Myvyrian Archaiology of Wales, The 117, 164

Natural Daughter, The 172, 179–80
Nennius 161
Newton, Samuel 114
Northanger Abbey xiv
Nussbaum, Felicity 180
Nuttall, Geoffrey 98

Old Manor House, The 139
Oldham, John 80
Olney, James 50, 63
Ophelia, The History of xvii, 68–79
Orpheus and Eurydice 63
Ossian xix, 168
Ovid 106, 122
'Owen' 166–7
Owen, A. L. 116, 118
Owen, or, The Fatal Clemency 159, 160

Paine, Thomas 144
Pamela 50, 55
Paradise Lost 170
Parasite, The 81, 82, 83–5
Parry, Harry xviii
Parry, James xv, xviii, xix, 48, 50–67
Pascal, Roy 55
Pearson, Mike Parker xviii, 27

Index 245

Pennant, Thomas 107, 110, 164
Penny Magazine 2
Penny Merriments 2
Penseroso 123
Pepys, Samuel 2
'Perini, Signor' 58
'Perry, Mr' 63
Peter, Tsar 24
Piozzi, Hester Lynch 68, 87, 180
Pleasant and Surprising Adventures 34
Pleasant History of Taffy's Progress to London, The 7–8, 9
Plexippus 94
Plymouth, Countess of 132
Pocock, Nicholas 37, 38
Political Justice, Enquiry Concerning 126, 128
Pollin, Burton R. 116, 117
Polwhele, Revd Richard 180
Powel, David 165
Powell, Elizabeth 59, 61, 62
Powell, Mary 50–67
Powell, Mathew 61
Powell, Elizabeth 59, 61, 62
Pretender, the Old (James Edward) 17, 21, 22
Prévost, Abbé Antoine-François 12
Price, Mr 60
Prichard, T. J. Ll. 158
Pride and Prejudice 142
Priest, Nathaniel 57, 58
Priestley, Joseph 107
Primer, Irwin 116, 117, 119
Principall Navigations, Voiages, and Discoveries of the English Nation 48
Pughe, William Owen 163, 164
Pye, Admiral Sir Thomas 131, 154
Pye, Sam 57

Quevedo Villegas, Francisco de 22

Radcliffe, Ann 19
Rees, W. J. 158, 159, 171
Remarks on Clarissa 77
Rhydderch, Francesca 132, 133, 147, 148, 151, 154
Rich, John 63
Richards, William 5, 123
Richardson, Samuel 13, 50, 54, 77
Richetti, John 13, 30, 32, 33
Rights of Man, The 144
Robinson Crusoe 33
Robinson, Elizabeth 175, 176
Robinson, G. G. and J. 158
Robinson, Maria Elizabeth 177, 179

Robinson, Mary xx, 87, 152, 172–89
Robinson, Thomas 175, 177, 178, 180
Robinson, William 175
Rogers, Mr, of Ross 54
Romaine, William 98
Rosa, Salvator 179
Rousse, Dr 57
Rousseau, Jean-Jacques 46, 47, 55, 112, 116, 187
Rowland, Daniel 98
Rowlands, Henry 117, 164

Salusbury, Sir Thomas 3
Sammes, Aylett 165
Schofield, Mary Anne 13
Scott, Sarah 69
Scott, Sir Walter 30
Sekora, John 89, 90, 93
Selkirk, Alexander 27
Seward, Anna 160
Seys, Ann 173
Seys, Catherine 173, 175
Seys, Elizabeth 173
Seys, Margaret 173
Seys, Richard 173
Shaftesbury, 1st Earl of 69, 70, 71, 72, 75, 77
Shakespeare, William 2
Shamela Andrews, An Apology for the Life of Mrs 50
Shelley, Mary 128
Shenstone, William 95, 113
Shyp of Folys of the Worlde, The 116
Sicilian Romance, A 19
Siddons, Sarah 145
Sketches of History 120
Smallbroke, Dr Richard, Bishop of St David's 56
Smalley, Christopher 110
Smith, Adam 75, 107
Smith, Charlotte 139, 180
Smith, John 115
Smollett, Tobias xvii, 81, 82, 83, 88–93, 178
Snow, Valentine xviii
Some Specimens of Antient Welsh Poetry 163
Spacks, Patricia Meyer 70
'Specimens of an English Metrical Translation of the more ancient Welsh Bards, and of Dafydd ab Gwilym' 163, 164, 167
Spencer, Jane 77
Spiritual Quixote, The xix, 94–105, 106, 113, 160
Spufford, Margaret 5

Stauffer, Donald F. 13, 26, 33, 34
Steele, Sir Richard 56
Stonehenge A Temple Restor'd to the British Druids 118
Stuarts, The 23, 34
Stukeley, William 118, 119
Swarbrick, Mr 58
Swift, Jonathan 56
Swindells, A. 34

Tacitus 120
Tale, A xiv
Tarleton, Colonel Banastre 178
Thompson, Roger 1, 2
Thomson, James 117
Thrale, Hester Lynch *see* Piozzi, Hester Lynch
Todd, Janet 170
Toland, John 115, 116, 118, 119
Tom Jones, The History of 69
Tom Thumb, The Life and Death of, see Tragedy of Tragedies, The
Toplady, Augustus 98
Tour in Wales, A 107
Tour through Wales – in a Letter from a Young Lady, A xiv
Tracy, Clarence 94, 95, 97
Tragedy of Tragedies, The 30, 63
True Anti-Pamela, or, Memoirs of Mr James Parry, The xv, xviii, xix, 48, 50–67
Trumpener, Katie xiv, xix, 148
Twm Shon Catti 158
Tynte, Lady 173
Tysdahl, B. S. 121, 186, 188
Unfortunate Welch-Man, The 9

Vacunalia 159
Van Sant, Ann Jessie 88
Vaughan, Robert 48
Vernon, Admiral Edward 63
Vinicot, Elizabeth 173, 175, 177
Vinicot, Hester *see* Darby, Hester
Vinicot, Jonathan 173
Virgil 69
Vortimer 161
Voyages and Adventures of Captain Robert Boyle, The 30
Voyages, Adventures, and Imminent Escapes of Captain Richard Falconer, The 30
Voyages, Travels and Adventures of William Owen Gwin Vaughan Esq., The 26, 27–31

Walcot, Dr John 189
Wales and the Welsh in English from Shakespeare to Scott xv
Wales, Prince of (later King George IV) 172, 175, 177, 178
Wallography 5, 123
Walsingham xx, 172, 181–8
Walters, Revd John 164
Weaver, Judith 114
Welch Curate, The 102
Welch Doctor, The 4
Welch-Mans Complements, The 4
Welch Mans Inventory, The 7
Welch-Mans Publique and Hearty Sorrow and Recantation, The 4
Welch-Mans Warning Piece, The 4
Welch Traveller, The 2, 8–9
Welsh-Mans Postures, The 3
Wesley, Charles 95, 104
Wesley, John 95, 97, 98, 99, 100, 104, 105, 106
West, Benjamin 26, 37, 38, 41, 44
Whitefield, George 95, 96, 97, 98, 99, 100, 105, 106
Whitfield, Mr *see* Whitefield, George
Whitlock, Charles Edward 146
Whitlock, Elizabeth (née Kemble) 146
Wilkinson, Isaac 134
William III, King 22, 23, 118
Williams, Edward *see* Iolo Morganwg
Williams, Gwyn A. 3, 17, 23, 49, 109
Williams, Helen Maria 180
Williams, William xvii, xviii, 26, 37–48, 49, 54
Williams, William, Pantycelyn 100
Wimble, Captain James 63, 65, 66
Windsor, Viscountess 132
Winter's Tale, The 172
Wollstonecraft, Mary 70, 180, 181
Wonderful Adventures, and Happy Successes of Shon ap Morgan, The 2, 10–11
Wright, Joseph 111
Wyatt, James 65, 66, 67
Wynne, Revd Ellis 22

Xenophon 69

Yearsley, Anna 180
Yorke, Philip 164
Young, Arthur 111